PEOPLE MONEY

The Promise of Regional Currencies

Margrit Kennedy

Bernard Lietaer

John Rogers

Published in this first edition in 2012 by:
Triarchy Press
Station Offices
Axminster
Devon. EX13 5PF
United Kingdom

+44 (0)1297 631456
info@triarchypress.com
www.triarchypress.com

A catalogue record for this book is available from the British Library.

Print ISBN: 978-1-908009-7-60

Contents

Introduction

The global financial crisis that began in 2007 is not the first. Researchers at the International Monetary Fund identified 124 systemic banking crises, 208 currency crises and 63 episodes of sovereign debt defaults between 1970 and 2007.[1] And in the previous 300 years there were 48 major crashes. The causes are systemic and systemic causes require systemic solutions.

In 2003, Margrit Kennedy and Bernard Lietaer discovered that they both wanted to write a book about the possibilities and advantages of creating regional currencies. They were delighted to learn that each of them already had very clear ideas about why the introduction of this type of money would make sense in the near future. Their experiences with local currencies and their knowledge of historical examples were quite different and to bring this broad understanding to the attention of the public it made sense for them to write a book together.

Margrit had already featured alternative money systems in her first book *Inflation and Interest Free Money* in 1991.[2] On her travels in Europe and the Americas, Margrit came across many different efforts to develop new ways of using money, like the Swedish JAK Bank, the Swiss WIR Bank, the Argentinian Credito and numerous Local Exchange Trading Systems, all of which showed that complementary currencies could be of enormous help to the people who used them. Bernard had introduced the term 'complementary currencies' in *The Future of Money* in 1999 and was friends with historians of coinage who had discovered many old coins, dating from the middle ages through to the industrial revolution, that had acted as regional currencies on a large scale across Europe.

Before Margrit and Bernard were able to finish the book, word had spread in Germany about their plans to publish. Initiators from various parts of Germany, who were thinking of implementing regional currencies, began to ask for more information on how to proceed. Neither Margrit nor Bernard knew exactly how to go about it as they had yet to encounter an example of a regional currency that met all their criteria. So, they organised a meeting to discuss the various options. There was a lively exchange of experiences and expectations which inspired everyone to set up the Regionetwork first and two years later the

---

1 IMF Working Paper, 'Systemic Banking Crises: A New Database' by Luc Laeven and Fabian Valencia, (November 2008). Online at www.imf.org/external/pubs/ft/wp/2008/wp08224.pdf

2 Margrit Kennedy, (1991). *Geld ohne Zinsen und Inflation*, (updated new edition 2006).

Regiogeld e.V (see Regional Money Association p.207) to represent regional money systems across Germany.

The resulting book was published in 2004 by Riemann, Munich[3] and became something of a handbook for the first German models. It was later translated into French[4] and Spanish[5]. John Rogers was invited to update and edit the original book for this first English Edition.

Part One: The Case for Regional Currencies contains the essence of the original book. **Part Two: Regional Currencies in Practice** features portraits of local systems around the world, selected from interviews with forty organisers and promoters, and reflects the great variety of current practice. This evidence gives a new impulse and credibility to the concept and helps those who feel compelled to follow in the footsteps of the first initiators to learn from their, often challenging, experiences.

All three authors pay tribute to the courage, ingenuity and perseverance of those local currency pioneers who have shown the way and thank all of the local organisers and support agencies who have given generously of their time to do the interviews. If we have overlooked anyone who should have been included, please contact us and we will include you in the next edition.

A personal thank you from Margrit and Bernard to our life partners, Declan and Jacqui Dunne, who support our work. Declan and Jacqui were, by chance, born in the same hospital in Dublin and their Irish humour and wonderful ability to tell stories continue to inspire us to fill our visions with life and our life with visions. John would like to dedicate the book to the memory of Eluned, who insisted he get started with local currencies, and to Sitara who cheerfully puts up with his obsession.

Up to now, most regional currencies have been initiated by citizens and businesses. Regional and city governments are starting to join them as they search for innovative solutions to the range and scale of problems facing them. We hope that this book will provide enough information and inspiration to local

---

3 Margrit Kennedy, Bernard Lietaer, *Regionalwährungen - Neue Wege zu Nachhaltigem Wohlstand* (2004).

4 French Edition: *Monnaies Régionales: De nouvelles voies vers une prospérité durable* (2008).

5 Spanish Edition: *Monedas Regionales: Nuevos Instrumentos para una Prosperidad Sustentable* (2010).

governments, businesses and citizens to encourage bold new experiments which put regional currencies back on the map for a long time to come.

Please send us your stories about regional currencies for inclusion in future editions of this book to: info@valueforpeople.co.uk

Please register your system in the Online Database of Complementary Currencies Worldwide (http://complementarycurrency.org/ccDatabase/les_public.html) to help researchers compile useful data for the further development of local currencies.

PART ONE
THE CASE FOR REGIONAL CURRENCIES

Chapter 1
Think globally, act regionally

M. Jones
3, My Street
Hometown
Ourshire
United Kingdom
Planet Earth
The Galaxy
The Universe

When we were children we may have tried to imagine our place in the universe by writing an address like the one above. As adults we live our lives at many levels: as citizens, consumers, workers or employers, relating to our families, friends, colleagues, communities, businesses, regions, nations and the wider world.

The case for regional currencies begins with thinking about the appropriate scale for our social and economic exchanges.

Globalisation – a dirty word?

Globalisation is a word that bitterly divides people. The globalisation of values, standards and norms by persuasion, influence or force has happened throughout history. But the kind of globalisation that has taken place in the last three decades is new in terms of its scale, its speed, and its all-encompassing embrace.

Debates about globalisation are often restricted to discussing the globalisation of free trade – to remove regulatory and political barriers to the movement of goods, services and capital across national borders.

The main arguments on the pro side are:

- Efficiency of free markets.

- Access to goods and services worldwide.

- Modernisation of out-of-date structures and habits.

And on the con side:

- The growing gap between the haves and the have-nots.

- Consumerism and exploitation.

- Insensitivity towards local traditions and community, and the loss of cultural identity.

Those who argue for unrestricted globalisation are market fundamentalists; they believe in a mythical 'economic man', who only ever acts in his own best interests. They believe that markets would be perfect if only governments and regulations stayed out of their way.

On the other hand, people who protest about globalisation often find it easier to campaign against it than to make specific, realistic proposals for something better. The slogan of the World Social Forum 'Another World is Possible' reminds us to work on better designs by embracing and working out the details of new possibilities. This all requires hard political and organisational work.

As in all arguments, there is right on both sides. The classical economist John Stuart Mill remarked, 'In all intellectual debates, both sides tend to be correct in what they affirm, and wrong in what they deny'.[1]

The inequities of the market are not a sufficient reason to abandon it. No other system since the beginning of civilisation has demonstrated better potential for the alleviation of poverty, ignorance, disease and pain for many people. We will not cure poverty by destroying a system of wealth-creation, any more than we will cure crime by eliminating law. But these inequities give us sufficient reason to question whether the game being played should be the only one in town.

We are beginning to realise that we need global solutions and strategies in order to combat global problems such as climate change, species extinction and the management of our global commons. Therefore, the real issue is not whether globalisation is good or bad, but whether we can create a win-win globalisation model.

Meeting such a challenge would mean answering these sorts of questions:

- Is there an approach to sustainable global development that would include the majority of humanity in its gains, while respecting different cultural identities?

---

1 'Coleridge', in *Essays on Politics and Culture*, ed. Gertrude Himmelfarb (1963), p. 125.

- What are the strategies that would integrate the human dimensions as well as the narrow economic dimension?

- Are there realistic alternatives available for our future economy that would preserve the benefits of the current type of globalisation while correcting for its negative side effects and blind spots?

A good starting point is a new definition for globalisation to replace the one with which we started this chapter. We would propose this: 'Globalisation is the weaving of a tighter network of exchanges among economies, societies and cultures around the world to improve the life conditions and evolution of consciousness of all people, respecting their diversity as well as the right to life of all beings that share this planet'.

Great strides have been made towards a co-operative kind of economics: three billion people rely on Co-operatives for their food or other necessities and they provide over 100 million jobs around the world, 20% more than multinational enterprises.[2] But there is still a long way to go, as new waves of hard economic globalisation bring a flood of untold millions from the countryside into the cities, particularly in poorer countries.

It is pointless making futile attacks on the current globalisation process, which is vast in its reach. We think a more productive approach is to find a way of revitalising the regions of our world.

Regional development – a global phenomenon

People naturally identify themselves with their local communities, either out of love or necessity. One of the interesting effects of globalisation is that people are valuing their cultures and regions even more. Sometimes this is expressed through regional development and devolution movements that seek to locate more production and consumption at a local scale.

There are detailed debates between economic development specialists over the best approaches for long-term regional growth. More or less protectionism or market incentives? More or less direct intervention and subsidies? More or less decentralisation and political empowerment of the regions?

As part of the policy spectrum, regional currencies can support existing efforts to balance local growth with participation in global markets.

---

2 International Cooperative Alliance, www.ica.coop/coop/statistics.html

Making decisions at the right level

'Subsidiarity' is a simple principle: issues should be dealt with at the lowest possible organisational level. So, international bodies should deal with issues affecting the global commons like climate change and environmental damage; national governments should deal with organising and funding education, healthcare and defence; state, regional and local governments should deal with all other matters that directly affect their area.

This principle is enshrined in the Tenth Amendment to the US Constitution of 1791, which asserts States' rights, and in European Law through the Maastricht Treaty of 1992. It is out of this principle that some of the most successful European initiatives have arisen, including European funding to encourage and support the weaker areas of the Union.

Global problems, regional solutions

In this 21st Century, with the ending of the Industrial Age, and the resulting crisis of meaning, we are already dealing with a range of issues that are unprecedented in their complexity, their universality, and their urgency – from climate change and environmental degradation to systemic unemployment.

Even more predictable are the problems that will arise from a population ageing on an unprecedented scale. Our entire social contract around jobs, retirement and pensions has been based on a population distribution in which many workers are paying for the pensions of a few retirees. In the 1960s, only one out of eleven people in OECD member countries were 65 or older. Today, one in seven of the population has reached 65 and, by 2030, it will be one in four![3] How will the pensions and healthcare costs be taken care of as this grey demographic wave is being played out?

The Bank of International Settlements (BIS) prepared a thorough and highly relevant study entitled 'The Future of Public Debt: Prospects and Implications'.[4] The BIS's baseline scenario assumes that total government revenue and non-age-related spending remain a constant percentage of GDP, and that real interest rates remain unchanged from the historically low levels of the 1998–2007 average. Both these hypotheses should be considered optimistic ones. Nevertheless, in this baseline scenario, by 2020 age-related deficits will increase

---

3 Peter G. Petersen, 'Gray Dawn: The Global Aging Crisis', *Foreign Affairs* (January-February 1999).

4 Stephen G. Cecchetti, Madhusudan S. Mohanty and Fabrizio Zampolli, 'The Future of Public Debt: Prospects and Implications', *BIS Working Papers* (March, 2010).

government debt to 300% of GDP in Japan, 200% in the United Kingdom and 150% in Belgium, France, Ireland, Greece, Italy and the United States. In the longer term, the situation grows even more unmanageable: by 2040 the projected debt/GDP ratios for all these countries range from 300 to 600%. Similarly, the fraction absorbed by interest payments in each of these countries points to the same conclusion: from around 5% today, these numbers will keep rising to above 10% in all cases and climb as high as 27% in the United Kingdom. Some fundamental adjustment will have to be made to prevent these projections becoming reality.

The BIS study states:

> As frightening as it is to consider public debt increasing to more than 100% of GDP, an even greater danger arises from a rapidly ageing population. The related unfunded liabilities are large and growing, and should be a central part of today's long-term fiscal planning. It is essential that governments not be lulled into complacency by the ease with which they have financed their deficits thus far. In the aftermath of the financial crisis, the path of future output is likely to be permanently below where we thought it would be just several years ago. As a result, government revenues will be lower and expenditures higher, making consolidation even more difficult. The recent sharp rise in risk premiums on long-term bonds issued by several industrial countries suggests that markets no longer consider sovereign debt low-risk.[5]

The end of cheap energy – or 'peak oil' – is another mega-trend that challenges both citizens and policy makers to action. The resulting rise in energy costs and transportation will force an overhaul of our entire global economic system, in favour of more autonomous regional development.

Yet, the main institutional tool to deal with all these issues has remained the one inherited from previous centuries: the nation state. Even the global level is addressed institutionally, mainly through the *United Nations*. A number of the decisions that are currently being made at the national level simply don't belong there and will turn out to be ineffective if kept there.

Many social issues such as ecological repair, care of the elderly or child care, youth mentoring and unemployment could be addressed by initiatives taken at the regional level. For instance, it is a lot less disruptive – socially, culturally and economically – to move jobs to where the people already live, rather than obliging masses of people to move to where new jobs are being created.

---

5 *Ibid.*

Stronger regional initiatives do not *replace* national government action where that is appropriate, but they complement and enhance national policies. This idea in itself isn't new, but regional currencies enable regions to *mobilise their own resources to address regional issues* without burdening taxpayers either at the national or regional level. Regional currencies, if developed and supported at the right scale, could re-launch regional economies without incurring deficit spending at either the central or the regional level.

The importance of this policy option becomes clear when we broaden our horizons to understand the nature of our current economic crisis. It is not just another downturn in the business cycle but a deep systemic crisis caused by the rift between a casino economics based on monetary speculation and the social and ecological realities of our time. The only way to bridge this chasm between money and planet, between money and people, is to reinvent money.

One element of this re-imagining is to understand the role of money as an information system representing knowledge about assets and resources. We need to grasp the potential of the tools now available to us in the Information Age to exchange information about underused local resources ignored by the global markets. We can then use the power unleashed by this information to fuel a historical shift from an age of artificial scarcity to one of sustainable abundance. The last time that a shift of such magnitude occurred was when the Industrial Age precipitated the end of the Agrarian Age. Such shifts are not painless: look at what happened to the farmers when the agrarian age was ending, or to the landed gentry that saw their values, power and traditions fade into irrelevancy.

As we begin to reimagine money, we have to face its psychological power over us and how it limits our sense of personal and collective possibility: our 'money blind spot'. Many people agree with the idea that more regional autonomy is a good thing; but it is a different matter to accept that a *necessary condition* for such a strategy is the creation of regional currencies operating in parallel with national currencies.

Chapter 2
Money, the blind spot

Anyone who believes in indefinite growth in anything physical,
on a physically finite planet, is either mad – or an economist.
Kenneth Boulding, economist, systems thinker
and environmental advisor to John F. Kennedy

Money is blind and we are blind about money. It is a physical thing – coins jangle in our pocket and we can buy our daily bread – and rather an abstract thing – digits appear in our bank accounts as wages and disappear again just as quickly to pay electricity bills, mortgages and pensions. It rules our lives. But what is 'it'?

What is money?

Money is one of our greatest inventions. It enables billions of people to do business, feed their families and run their societies every day. It helps us to exchange goods and services, gives us a standard against which to estimate their value and, when it works well, allows us to save for the future. It is both a mechanism for personal use – my salary, my account, my debts, – and a mechanism for collective use – the gross domestic product, the central bank, the national debt.

We need to remove our blindfolds and see money for what it is: a mechanism with effects. Economists talk about money as 'value neutral': national currencies go anywhere and do anything, including much that is illegal. National currencies sell drugs and finance wars; they erect schools, run hospitals and build roads.

Money itself has no conscience, only its users can apply their values to the mechanism. That is why people start ethical investment funds which avoid investing in industries that the investors see as damaging – tobacco, arms, chemicals – or they start social and fair trade enterprises to help people in need or to protect the environment. Same tool, different results.

Money means different things to different people

So, we can remove our blindfolds and use money consciously.

The problem is that we are still using the same mechanism, which has inbuilt strengths and weaknesses. Whether we use pounds, euros, dollars or yen in our transactions, they are all kept scarce, they are created at a profit by private banks, and we are encouraged to hoard through positive interest rates.

What is good about this money? Responsible management of the money supply (referred to as proper or appropriate scarcity of money) is necessary to minimise price inflation; the banking system has centuries of experience in creating and managing money; savings enable future planning and investment; positive interest rates help people to keep savings ahead of inflation and have pensions.

What is wrong with this money? Monetary speculation, which removes the means of exchange from circulation (referred to as artificial scarcity of money), only serves an elite who profit from it, whilst the mass of people suffer from a lack of money to meet their needs and cuts in essential public services. Positive interest rates systematically transfer wealth to the richest 10% of the population, and compound interest creates cancerous exponential growth or cumulative debts in a destructive downward spiral, with disastrous effects on communities and the environment.[1,2]

Shouldn't the money supply be created and managed for the public good? Is it possible to create money that preserves the benefits of national currency whilst offsetting its negative effects? This new kind of money needs to be

1 M. Kennedy, *Interest and Inflation Free Money*, (1995) and *Occupy Money*, (2012).

2 R. Douthwaite, *The Growth Illusion*, (1999).

sufficiently available for trade, well managed, democratically governed (rather than profiting a few) and inflation free. This money needs to act primarily as a medium of exchange rather than a medium for speculation or savings, with special provisions where some savings are desirable (e.g. for old age).

The keys to this alternative are: conscious design desicions for the mechanism; clear, voluntary and enforceable rules for use; engaged, aware users. We will explore how regional currencies manage balancing these aspects a little later on.

What is the cost of money?

If we ask for a bank loan, we want to know 'the cost of money', i.e. how much interest we will have to repay on top of the loan. We can then understand our personal costs. But money does not only have personal costs, it has collective costs.

The global mobility of capital, which has transformed the world into an almost completely interconnected economic space, is not a 'value free' phenomenon. As money races around the planet looking for the best 'return', it causes huge inequalities, unfairness and destruction. The first Club of Rome Report from 1972, which triggered the first sustainability debate, saw the monetary system as a passive accounting mechanism with neither a positive or negative effect on the issue of sustainability.[3] Now, in the new report published in 2012, we can see the systemic effects of monetary decisions much more clearly.[4]

Economic activity creates what economists call positive and negative 'externalities' (or extra effects) created by the activity. The positive kind brings added benefits to people: employment, meaningful work, a sense of community. Negative externalities include environmental pollution and unemployment, with all of its negative side effects, such as physical and mental health problems and community breakdown. Although communities benefit from positive externalities, the costs of negative ones are not 'internalised', i.e. they are not paid for directly by industry itself but 'externalised' onto local communities and environments.

Positive and negative externalities do not always balance each other out. Society tries to offset the worst effects of the negative ones, through state

---

3 Donella H. Meadows, Dennis L. Meadows and J. Randers, *Limits to Growth – the 30-Year Update*, (2004).

4 B.Lietaer, S. Goerner, C. Arnsperger and S. Brunnhuber, *Money & Sustainability,: The Missing Link*, (2012).

health, education and environmental programmes paid for through taxes and organised by government. Local government provides social services directly or commissions the voluntary sector to run social enterprises (businesses set up on a co-operative basis for the benefit of people and the environment) to help people in need – like Bulky Bob's furniture recycling in Liverpool[5] or Greenwich Leisure (now rebranded as Better) [6], which manages 100 public leisure centres across the South East of England. Social businesses can even take on major assets that have failed in the private sector, like Wales's 'Glas Cymru' which provides water utilities to the whole of Wales through Welsh Water.[7] Another approach is to encourage volunteering, which is estimated to be worth over 21.5 billion pounds to the UK economy in 2012.[8]

While it is certainly helpful for government to follow policies that offset the effects of negative externalities, there is a growing awareness that this process is unsatisfactory. It just puts band aids on the problems and is funded by the same mechanism that is creating the problems. The taxpayers resent the tax burden, and at the same time the co-operative economy remains starved of resources.

We all know what financial capital is: ownership of money and other liquid assets. Academics also talk about 'social capital': the richness of our connections with others. We can have lots of money and great networks or lots of money and no friends; we can be really poor and isolated or have wonderful relationships. The more we use our social capital, the more we generate. Trust, commitment, a sense of belonging and reciprocity are universal values at the core of happy societies. Vandalism, crime, lack of information and communication, lack of social networks, people leaving the area, all show degraded social capital and these are often caused by negative externalities, acting like a social pollution, being dumped on communities.

The social (or co-operative or solidarity) economy is made up of organisations that put co-operation, community, diversity and inclusiveness at the centre of their activities whilst operating professionally in the mainstream market. This is a new enterprise model that closes the gap between two apparently incompatible principles: social responsibility and the demands of the market economy. They enhance social capital by harnessing financial capital to meet local needs and

---

5 See www.bulkybobs.co.uk/

6 See www.gll.org/

7 See www.dwrcymru.com/en/Company-Information/Glas-Cymru.aspx

8 See www.3s4.org.uk/drivers/trends-in-volunteering

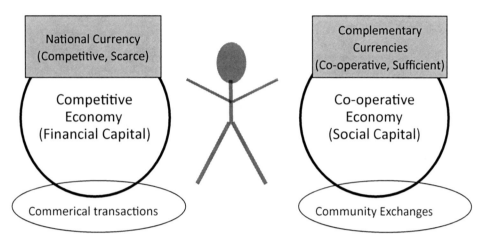

| National Currency (Competitive, Scarce) | | Complementary Currencies (Co-operative, Sufficient) |

Competitive Economy (Financial Capital)

Co-operative Economy (Social Capital)

Commerical transactions

Community Exchanges

Activation of Co-operative and Competitive Economic Circles

create development with a human face to balance the predominant current of globalisation.

Some people think this novel way to solve social problems is just a way of supporting the unemployed. This belief is really a carry-over from single-currency environments – the payment of unemployment benefits intervenes in the market system to transfer resources from the rich to the poor. It is possible that regional currencies could someday replace unemployment benefits systems, or make some of them unnecessary, but they are not a form of welfare themselves: participation is voluntary; they do not require taxes or government subsidies and can become completely self-funding mechanisms to address social problems.

Regional currencies promote innovation, empowerment, increased self-esteem, inclusiveness in the labour market and the local community and present new opportunities for learning and education.

Another cost to society is the artificial scarcity of money, where the medium of exchange itself may be scarce. This absurdity was well expressed by philosopher, Alan Watts, in a 1969 essay 'Wealth versus Money'[9], where he imagined a day in the early 1930s:

> But it was just as if someone had come to work on building a house and, on the morning of the Depression, the boss had said, "Sorry, baby, but we can't build today. No inches."

9   Alan Watts, *Does it Matter? Essays on Man's Relation to Materiality*, (1971).

"Whaddya mean, no inches? We got wood. We got metal. We even got tape measures."

"Yeah, but you don't understand business. We been using too many inches and there's just no more to go around."

Many communities are full of underused resources: individuals with time and talents; businesses with restaurant tables, car hire, printing services, theatre seats; voluntary associations with underused vehicles and rooms; local authorities with underused community and leisure centres. And there is not enough money – not enough inches – to get all those assets moving. Isn't that an absurd waste of human potential?

So communities and organisations around the world have simply solved the problem by creating their own non-competitive, non-scarce currency for one specific purpose: to connect underused assets directly to unmet needs where the market is not interested or money is scarce.

People Money

People using currencies with different rules tell a very different story to the one that is commonly heard about conventional money. Well-managed commercial 'barter' exchanges encourage more co-operative behaviour amongst businesses, like in the Business Exchange in Scotland (p.102); users of the Chiemgauer in Bavaria (p.144) can support their favourite voluntary associations with automatic donations in local currency; neighbours and friends in Dane County Time Bank (p.180) prefer to give 'time credits' for services rather than national currency;[10] participants in the Talente Tauschkreis in Austria (p.126) can earn credits from caring for others now to receive care when they are elderly, because one hour of time will be the same in 20 years time.[11]

These examples of new currencies are amongst thousands of experiments around the world in the last few decades. Most of them work at a very local level, some at the regional level and one or two at a national level. But, who creates them?

Economist Richard Douthwaite describes three types of money.

1. Bank Money – most of the money we are familiar with is created by private banks when they offer loans to individuals and businesses at a profit.

---

10 See also evidence from UK Time Banks in 'The Time of our Lives' by Dr. Gill Seyfang and Karen Smith, http://bit.ly/KbXMbr

11 Zeitvorsorge, http://bit.ly/KHt0ol

2. Government Money – a tiny percentage of money is in the form of notes and coins created by government.

3. People Money – these are currencies created by groups of businesses or groups of citizens.[12]

People Money systems are not national legal tender, which means they may not be used to settle debts in court or to pay national taxes. But that does not make them illegal. They are 'private' currencies issued to circulate amongst a group of people within a certain boundary who agree to their own rules.

Bank and Government Money create pyramids of dependency. People Money encourages the emergence of networks of inter-dependence.

Complementary currencies

People Money is what we call 'complementary' currency. Each currency acts as a complement to the other because each has its own role to play in the regional economy. Complementary currencies act in parallel with national currencies (Bank Money and Government Money), they do not seek to replace it.

There are two main types of complementary currencies: commercial or community oriented currencies.

---

12 R. Douthwaite, *The Ecology of Money*, (1999).

Frequent flyer miles are a well-known commercial application of the complementary currency concept. They started off as a simple marketing gimmick by airlines to encourage loyalty among their clients. Now you can earn them without buying a ticket, just by using a Visa credit card for any purchase. Air miles have become a private, special purpose currency.[13]

The other well-known commercial type is the business-to-business exchange network (also know as 'barter' networks) like RES in Belgium (p.112) or the Business Exchange in Scotland (p.102).

Community oriented currencies are sometimes called community currencies or local currencies and their main goal is to grow community networks and support social or environmental goals. They include local exchange systems and time banks like the Dane County Time Bank (p.180).[14]

The purpose of complementary currencies is to connect unused resources with needs that remain unfulfilled after transactions with conventional money have taken place. The economics of frequent flyer miles illustrates how this process works even in strictly commercial environments. A well-managed frequent flyer miles system obtains something (customer loyalty) at the cost of an unused resource (an airline seat that would otherwise remain empty). We can apply the same idea to a broader operating environment in which the benefits are chosen by the participants themselves in a regional system.

National currencies support industrial growth, trans-regional trade between markets and competition to create wealth. They are interest-rate-driven fiat currencies, created through hierarchical and monopolised organisational structures. Well designed and managed regional currencies, running on different principles (the rules of the game), can fill the gaps left by mainstream money and stabilise the whole system because of their countercyclical action (see WIR system p. 37-38).

Regional currencies

People love their home region: 'I'm a Yorkshireman'; 'I'm a Glasgow girl'; 'Maybe it's because I'm a Londoner'...

---

13 See Appendix 2: The Business Case for Complementary Currencies

14 For a current list of UK Time Banks: http://timebanking.org
   For a current list of Time Banks in the USA: http://timebanks.org
   For a current list of LETS in the UK: http://www.letslinkuk.net

The vision of a world of regions is attractive to many of us as a counterbalance to the power of multinational corporations and international financial markets. The rediscovery of a distinct regional economic identity through a regional currency provides a very real antidote to the negative aspects of globalisation. The present monetary system acts like a pump, siphoning capital from the regions in which it is earned and transferring it to where it will earn the greatest profit.

How can a region conserve its own liquidity? If a new currency serves the region rather than being used to obtain the highest possible yields, it can be designed to stay put, to circulate locally.

We define a region as a geographical area with which people tend to identify themselves. The physical size of a region is less important than the potential density of human interactions and the pride of belonging.

Some local systems print circulating currency; they take great care to design notes or vouchers featuring local landmarks, natural features or historical personalities and create the great sense of identity we see in diverse local currency systems such as Banco Palmas in Brazil (p.24), the Austrian village of Langenegg (p.128), the BerkShares in the USA (p.138) or the Brixton Pound in London (p.122).

A regional currency is a particular form of complementary currency: it is an agreement within the community of a region to accept something other than legal tender as a means of payment. It connects unused resources with unmet needs at the regional level. Some regional currencies start out as small local systems and grow to serve a larger area in response to demand over time, like the Chiemgauer in Germany (p.144) or the Dane County Time Bank in the USA (p.180). Others begin to serve a whole region from the beginning, like the Talente Tauschkreis in Austria (p.126) or the WIR Bank in Switzerland (p.34).

Apart from the WIR Bank, none of the individual systems featured in this book have grown to any significant economic scale but they all play an important role in creating wealth locally and maintaining community.

Policies for regional currencies

Modern money is expected to serve as an exchange medium, a value benchmark or unit of calculation, a value storage medium and a commodity all at the same time. The savings aspect requires an exponential growth factor to pay interest and money now has unlimited mobility through international financial markets. The savings function is in direct conflict with the exchange function and does not support the creation of local jobs.

A regional currency can be designed to emphasise the exchange medium and accounting unit functions and *minimise* the savings function. Its mobility, i.e. its geographic scope of validity, can be reduced to a manageable size and its value as a storage medium must be restricted to being 'merely' stable, without the additional attribute of interest. The essential aims are:

- To create local jobs.

- To stem the drain of purchasing power from the region.

- To open up new avenues to enable local government to fulfil its designated tasks.

Studies have shown that the European Union's regional policies – both top-down and bottom-up – have not prevented the drain of capital, value creation and human resources from regions and that the key factor, the monetary framework, is largely ignored in regional policies.[15] Peripheral regions need (more than others) a financial instrument that is tailored to their specific needs, accommodates public benefit oriented credit mechanisms and entails a reduction in capital mobility.

On this basis, completely new regional economic cycles can develop which promote:

- Economic stimulation instead of stagnation.

- Stabilisation or growth of the population.

---

15 R.Musil, *Geld, Raum und Nachhaltigkeit*, (2000).

- An increase in regional purchasing power and thus an improvement in municipal finances.

- A positive, optimistic identification with the region in the place of disillusionment.

- Improvements to the infrastructure and increased local autonomy instead of the sale of utilities to extra-regional concerns.

- A greater sense, amongst the local population, of having a say in how things are run, of being able to take and exercise responsibility for their destiny and development.

- The preservation and development of employment opportunities and incentives for firms to remain in the region.

Regio is the generic name given to regional currencies in Germany. The term highlights the distinction between the regional currency and a national or international one. The 'godfather' of the Regio is the *mereau* described in Chapter 3. Regio money is designed to be 'worse' than the euro:

- It is not legal tender and businesses are not obliged to accept it – it works on a voluntary basis of mutual agreement.

- It can only be used within a limited geographical area, and maintains its own brand of Regio with its own name and image.

- A charge is levied to convert Regios into euros or into another regional currency.

- It cannot be invested to earn interest.

- Some Regio systems build in a circulation incentive to make the money lose its value.

These deliberate limitations give the Regio a different social and economic space within which to operate. People quickly learn when it is better to use euros and when to use Regios. The Regio is not anti-euro or the euro's usurper: it steps in and stays where the euro leaves. As long as the euro exists, it will remain the main currency of business. The Regio complements it and fills local gaps.

When money is scarce and people are losing their jobs, regional currencies step in and create both jobs and money: for example, Banco Palmas (p.24) has created 1,800 jobs since 1998, with its combined local currency and micro-credit services. But they can also do much more. They can support young people in trouble to give something back to their community and raise their self-esteem, like Dane County Time Bank's youth court (p.180); they can help organic farmers to find new customers for their products like the Bremer Roland (p.193); they can help preserve an old community centre and revive community spirit like the Blaengarw Time Centre in South Wales (p.168).

As an economic tool, regional currencies are much more effective when integrated with other mechanisms: with micro-credit like Banco Palmas (p.24) or BerkShares (p.138); with co-operative and social enterprises like Equal Dollars (p.132); with conventional banking services like WIR Bank (p.34). Every region contains a wide variety of natural partners for a regional currency, such as social economy initiatives like those above, chambers of commerce, voluntary sector umbrella bodies, environmental organisations and Agenda 21 groups.[16]

If the next generation of regional currencies can scale up they will play a more significant socio-economic role. But the impact of genuine regional currencies is much broader than simply the number of people involved or the economic value. The following stories show the different impacts of national and local currencies on local autonomy and cultural sustainability. First a negative example: how regional sustainability was destroyed by the purposeful introduction of a national currency. Secondly, two positive examples show how local currencies strengthen regional sustainability.

A negative example: how to destroy regional sustainability

When Britain colonised Africa in the 19th Century, it was faced with an interesting problem. Many local regions consisted of sustainable communities, who traded amongst themselves within closed circuits and according to their traditions. But what is the point of having a colony if the people there do not need any of your goods? The question was how to break up those centuries-old, perfectly sustainable regional patterns so that there would be a demand for the goods that Britain was eager to export to its colony.

The solution was not to start a big advertising or marketing campaign. It wasn't even to try to prohibit the old exchange patterns or to use coercion to

---

16 See www.un.org/esa/dsd/agenda21

create new ones. It was a lot cheaper, simpler and more elegant than that. The British simply created a new national currency and instituted a very modest 'hut tax' (initially one shilling) that was payable only in the national currency. And within a few years the traditional, sustainable system had shrunk into insignificance.

Why? Every hut – every extended family unit in the country – needed to find a way to earn some of this new currency to pay their 'hut tax'. Only trading outside of the traditional framework in a new national system could help them do that. That was sufficient to break up the sustainable regional patterns.[17]

The lesson should be clear: encouraging local development with a monopolistic national or supranational currency is like treating an alcoholic with a prescription for gin. The colonial administrators knew how to destroy regional sustainability by imposing a national currency; in reverse, our current politicians and civil servants talk a lot about the desirability of more regional autonomy but, because our collective 'money blind spot' is now so universal, they overlook the contradictions between policies pushing for more monetary globalisation and those supporting local development.

Two positive examples of regional currencies

Imperial power gives us a negative example of a dominant currency eliminating diversity.

People Money systems are now emerging to challenge the dominant currency model. Here are two of their stories.

Banco Palmas benefits one poor area of a large rapidly developing country and WIR Bank operates across a small wealthy country: both use the same idea of a dual currency system to support regional identity and economy.

---

17 See http://onlinelibrary.wiley.com/doi/10.1111/1536-7150.00098/abstract

Banco Palmas, Brazil

KEY FEATURES

TYPE: Circulating currency

DATE FOUNDED: Bank founded 1998, currency launched in 2003

REGION SERVED: Conjunto Palmeiras, Brazil

MAIN PURPOSE: Support local economy

BENEFITS: Creates new businesses and hundreds of jobs; makes money go further

PARTICIPANTS: 270 businesses; consumers

CORE MECHANISMS: Local fiat backed by Brazilian Reais; printed circulating currency designed by local artists with full security features; microcredit loans in both national and local currency

NAME OF CURRENCY/STANDARD OF VALUE: One Palmas = One Brazilian Real

TURNOVER: 46,000 Palmas (20,000 euro) in circulation in 2011

GOVERNANCE: Palmas Institute, a non-profit organisation

MANAGEMENT: Six full-time staff

COST RECOVERY: Account fees, transaction fees and grants cover the bank's operating costs; the currency itself carries no extra costs

WEBSITE: Banco Palmas www.bancopalmas.org.br
Palmas Institute Europe: www.banquepalmas.fr

Carlos de Freitas is a French native with Portugese parents who works as an advisor to international organisations. In 2009 he wrote a book about Banco Palmas in Brazil with Joaquim Melo, one of its founders.[18] He now represents the Palmas Institute in Europe. The following profile is based on an interview with him for this book.

'Mummy, do you know you can use Palmas to buy local soap?' The children of Conjunto Palmeiras tell their parents how they can use the local currency. The kids learn about the currency through songs, a fashion week, theatre, photo stories, from the radio and even in their local history class in school.

Banco Palmas is Brazil's great community currency success story: it has created over 1,800 jobs, it is the exclusive source of currency for many people, has sparked imitations in 66 communities around the world's fifth largest country and it has the full support of the Brazilian government and Central Bank. It is

---

18 J. Melo, *Viva Favela: Quand les demunis prennent leur destin en main*, (2009).

the world's best example of a poor community using a local currency to help itself to develop.

Conjunto Palmeiras is a shanty town, an artificial settlement created by removing people from the coast in the 1970s. It has a population of 32,000 and is 22 kilometres from the city of Fortaleza, a city of 2.5 million people in the north east of the country.

The community had to fight a long battle with the authorities to secure access to the most basic amenities. Carlos de Freitas, from the Palmas Institute in Europe, continues the story.

> When they reviewed their achievements in 1997, they saw that they had not created enough permanent jobs in the area and there was no reliable income for desired developments. They heard about micro-credit and other solutions, but there was no infrastructure to introduce such programmes. It was then that they decided to create their own bank to give loans to entrepreneurs.

Banco Palmas launched in January 1998 with a grant of 800 euros from a French organisation. The national television news reported that a slum was launching its own bank – the Bank of the Favelas – and on the second day hundreds of people were queuing for credits. They were told they had to wait: by day two the bank was already bankrupt! The first loans had already been given to five retailers and producers and to twenty families for consumption. In the following months, other international organisations lent money to allow the bank to create more micro-credit loans.

Inspired by the rapid growth of local currencies in Argentina in 2001, Banco Palmas later decided to create its own currency, the Palmas, with redemption into national currency for businesses only. The district Palmeiras takes its name from palm trees and the currency name Palmas suggests palm leaves, the palm that shakes hands and a local expression *bater palmas*, which means to applaud. This local currency only has value in Palmeiras and cannot be spent anywhere else.

Community organiser Joaquim Melo and local businessman Francisco Bezerra both spent two years tirelessly selling the idea to other local businesses: first the larger grocery stores and the gas station, then the smaller businesses – sewing and clothing shops, bakeries etc. As the owner of a large business and head of the retailers' association, Francisco's name gave the project great credibility. He promotes local money to help himself, his business and his community.

Now you see the colourful sign with the green and white palm tree with 'We Accept Palmas' displayed on a third of the local shops. 270 businesses offer a range of discounts (2 to 15% depending on the size of the retailer) to encourage people to buy with the local currency. Each business agrees to the principles of the 'solidarity economy' – meaning mutuality and reciprocity – and promises to help circulate currency. The Palmas keeps on circulating while the Réais (the national currency) leave the district to be spent in the local city of Fortaleza, which used to suck in all local wealth. The efforts of the residents' association and their Banco Palmas have brought the 'most dangerous' area of the city in 2002 to tenth on the list in 2011.

> Once I marked a Palmas banknote in the corner with a pencil. By the end of the day it had returned through my till five times: that means it had passed through five different hands in the community and circulated five times more than the Réais, which usually leaks straight out again as soon as it is spent. Today they talk about us in the economic pages of the newspapers, not just when there's bad news.

Banco Palmas is a unique community bank that is governed and managed entirely by local people, who decide on policy, approve micro-credit loans and manage the local currency.

Carlos de Freitas describes the culture:

> It has a very different feel from banks in richer areas. There are very open spaces where you can talk to another local person in your own language. You can also pay your bills at the bank and every time you go there, you see posters explaining how everything works, the meaning of the whole process, the benefits of Banco Palmas to the community and to each family.

> Staff of the Palmas Institute facilitate weekly meetings at which all subjects are discussed: maybe people think the interest rates are too high or they want to introduce a new project. Meetings always begin and end with the *Bater Palmas Music Band*: the clapping it receives – *bater palmas* – is an expression of both solidarity and joy in the local culture. People are deeply committed because they see the benefits of common objectives. You pay back the community for the benefits you receive with your participation.

The bank shares its premises with the residents association and new employees change jobs every six months to get experience with different tasks. There are six full-time employees with an average age of 25, who get 800 hours of training in management, accounting and retailing. They receive 20% of their wages in local currency. The bank's operating costs are recovered from fees for opening bank accounts, transaction fees and grants. The local currency is fully integrated into the bank and has no fees. All profits from the bank are ploughed back into its operations.

Individuals get local currency in three different ways: they exchange them with national currency (one Palmas = one Real); they receive them in wages; they get micro-credits for local consumption. People getting micro-credits automatically join the community association that runs the bank; other people receiving currency do not have to join anything. The Palmas trademark is owned by the community association.

Community consultants are trained by the bank's youth training programme (Palma Tech) to talk to shop owners and organisations to help them to find ways to earn and spend currency: public bodies and a few companies with offices in the area pay 5 to 20% of employees' salaries in Palmas. People may also pay part of their utility bills in local currency at the bank. This all helps to accelerate the circulation of the local currency; it circulates five times faster than the national currency in the area, creating more economic benefit for more people. There were 46,000 Palmas (20,000 euro) in circulation in 2011. People can pay part of their local taxes in local currency directly through the bank.

Micro-credit combined with a local currency is a powerful tool that encourages more diverse local production and consumption. People start up new businesses and create jobs. Poor families can get loans for consumption, which they pay back with their labour. Being able to convert national into local currency and back again gives businesses the flexibility they need to deal with the traditional market outside the community. The national currency creates wealth, the social currency redistributes it.

One of the regular questions in the early popular assemblies was "Why are we so poor?" and it became clear that wealth did not stay in the community. Every two years, community consultants trained in action research carry out a scientific mapping exercise of local consumption and production patterns based on food, hygiene and cleaning products. Palmeiras residents spent 5.65 million Réais (2.29 million euros) each month in 2011 (1.5 million Réais per month in 2002). Sales from local trade have risen by 30% and the region has become one of the main trade corridors in the outskirts of Fortaleza. In 1997, 80% of the inhabitants' purchases were made outside the community; by 2011, 93% were made in the district. Micro-credit combined with a local currency keeps wealth local, and reduces transport costs, food miles and CO_2 footprints. Local money works to protect the local and global environment.

Because of the bank's success, there is a constant stream of researchers and journalists and the self-esteem of the community has risen with the attention. But this *wunderkind* was nearly strangled at birth. After issuing the first Palmas currency in 2003, local organiser Joaquim Melo was arrested on suspicion of running a money laundering operation in an unregistered bank. The Central Bank started proceedings against him, saying that the bank was issuing false money. The defendants called on expert witnesses, including the Dutch development organisation Stro (p.203), to support their case. Finally, the judge agreed that it was a constitutional right of people to have access to finance and that the Central Bank was doing nothing for the poor areas benefiting from the local currencies. He ruled in favour of Banco Palmas.

What happened next shows the power of dialogue. The Central Bank created a reflection group and invited Joaquim to join in a conversation about how to help poor people. Banco Palmas started the Palmas Institute to share its methodology with other communities and, in 2005, the government's secretary for 'solidarity economy' created a partnership with the Institute to finance dissemination. Support for community development banks issuing new currency is now state policy.

After a local community invites Palmas Institute staff to work with them, it takes at least one year to set up a bank. The main retailers are invited to the first meeting and staff explain the fundamentals with simple tools like a basket with a hole in it to show the leakage of local wealth. Staff facilitate communities to take over responsibility for running their own bank, offering up to eight months training. The recommended starting fund for the launch of micro-credit with local currency is less than 15,000 euros. The whole community is invited to design attractive notes with a significant local name. For instance, the town of Silva Jardim launched the Capivari currency in 2011, featuring the local rodent. The bank had a big launch with music, theatre and speeches from local leaders explaining the process.

Some currencies have wide representation of the whole community, others have narrower representation of businesses and agencies. Some currencies take off very quickly and others require much longer. One area was so keen that there were 70,000 units in circulation after one year, and these were accepted for local taxes and employees' wages. The optimum scale for a community bank is 20 to 50,000 consumers. Above this number the employees do not know people so another community bank is then planted to address the need. By 2011, 66 community banks had been started around Brazil, including in Rio de Janeiro's worst slum Cidade de Deus. The whole community banks' network had a circulation equivalent to 212,000 Réais.

In 2008, Banco Palmas received the Millennium Development Goals Award from the United Nations and the General Secretariat of the Presidency of Brazil. This is one of a long list of national and international prizes the bank has received, all of which make local people very proud. None of this goes to Joaquim Melo's head. He has dedicated himself to life in Conjunto Palmeira since 1984 and believes that this innovative social technology remains well below its potential due to insufficient investment by public authorities involved in the partnership.

Carlos de Freitas explains what remains to be done:

> There is still no proper legal framework for social currencies. You have to fight for acceptance. It is still seen as exotic. People want access to money, to be treated the same as other citizens, although participants understand better now what money is and how to participate in local development. The bank is like a school for both money and community development.

> People have learned that you cannot run an effective local money system in a disorganised community; it needs collective discipline and solidarity. Every step must be owned by the community and you have to sell the benefits to different stakeholders and make sure currency circulates widely to meet the needs of the community.

> We are constantly trying to improve our communication tools to bring the story of money alive and stop it becoming abstracted from people. We use music, theatre, media, anything. People understand the idea better after they hear it a few times in different forms.

> We have to innovate carefully and pay attention to every change in the community such as consumption patterns, goals etc. The first step is always paper money, to embody the identity of the community and create something recognisable. Now we are starting to experiment with mobile phone payments for bills and purchases because cellphone technology is so popular.

Another first for Banco Palmas: the President of the Central Bank apologised for its early negative treatment of Banco Palmas. Support in such high places can work both for and against the embryonic national network of community owned banks. Their future depends on how they use this newly found influence to benefit many more people.

Our second example of an effective regional currency is the WIR Bank in Switzerland. This profile is based on an interview with Hervé Dubois, WIR's Director of Communications.

WIR Bank, Switzerland

KEY FEATURES

TYPE: Business Exchange Network   **DATE FOUNDED:** 1934

REGION SERVED: Switzerland

MAIN PURPOSE: Support local economy

BENEFITS: Mobilises spare business capacity; makes money go further

PARTICIPANTS: 60,000 businesses; consumers

CORE MECHANISMS: Membership based; mutual credit 'currency' created by clearing positive and negative balances between members when they trade; backed by promise to supply local goods and services; all transactions recorded; active brokering of trades; own web based software system – both a trade 'bank' and a marketplace; smart cards and mobile banking; no printed circulating currency

NAME OF CURRENCY/ STANDARD OF VALUE: One WIR franc = one Swiss franc

TURNOVER: 1.627 billion WIR francs in 2010

GOVERNANCE: WIR Co-operative

MANAGEMENT: 205 staff, headquarters in Basel and seven regional centres

COST RECOVERY: Membership and transaction fees

WEBSITE: http://wir.ch

The Bo Katzman Choir is one of Switzerland's most successful touring groups. Since 1987 it has enchanted a million people with its high energy gospel music in sell-out concerts. This remarkable group also strikes up a good tune with a remarkable local currency. It pays for its tour bus, hotel and food with WIR francs, which it earns from ticket sales to other businesses trading in WIR.

The WIR Bank, which began as the WIR Co-operative in 1934, operates the world's most successful non-state currency system. WIR is short for Wirtschaftsring (economic circle) and also means 'we' in German. Hervé Dubois, who studied economics and worked as a journalist for 25 years before joining WIR in 1995 as Director of Communications, takes up the story:

> WIR was created to help people survive the economic depression after the 1929 stock market crash. High unemployment, money hoarding and

protectionism created enormous uncertainty for citizens and business owners. People needed more money in circulation to continue their economic activities. The sixteen founder members were visionaries committed to self-help and co-operative thinking in all areas of life. Although they could not influence the scarcity of national currency, they could create their own interest-free currency. They attracted three thousand participants in the first year of operation.

When I first heard about WIR I was suspicious of the idea. People were saying back then that it was a dinosaur from another age. But after our first talk I realised that this old fashioned exchange ring had the potential to become a modern organisation and I took up the challenge of creating a new image for it. My job was completely new. I gave myself two or three years and I am still here seventeen years later. No two years are the same and I enjoy being a part of this wonderful development that continually throws up new challenges. And nobody calls WIR a dinosaur anymore!

WIR is the only local currency experiment from the 1930s to survive to this day, continuously trading through boom and bust years in the main economy. For local currency activists, it has become something of a beacon of hope and a model to emulate.

Trade between WIR businesses for the year 2010 was equivalent to 1.627 billion Swiss francs (1.083 billion pounds sterling).

Jürg Michel, President of the WIR Bank, summarises the core attractions of WIR in the 2010 Annual Report:

Trust is an invaluable asset, especially for a bank. This trustworthiness is confirmed by both private and business clients in a representative survey. The WIR clearing system as the central anchor in our business model has been based for over seventy-six years on the trust in this currency... The WIR System, oriented towards small and medium enterprises in Switzerland, enables a unique economic network amongst the participants.[19]

At the heart of WIR is the idea of a mutual credit clearing circle: members sell goods and services and receive credits from other members with which they can buy goods and services from different members. The whole trading community acts as a collective of debtors underwriting each other's negative balances, instead of just one business being directly liable to another business. WIR Bank acts as a third party record keeper offering businesses a supplementary means

---

19 Annual Report, (2010): www2.wir.ch/doc/doc_download.cfm?uuid=9AE89DEE5056B8001E3 2C657036142DF&&IRACER_AUTOLINK&&

of payment alongside national currency. This remains its core business to this day.[20]

In 2010, 60,000 businesses, an estimated 16% of all Swiss enterprises, were trading in WIR francs. Members use a sophisticated internal database to search for goods and services of all kinds: from animal feed suppliers to veterinary services, hotels to laundry services, circus acts to clairvoyants. Next to its listing, each business states what percentage of the price it is willing to accept in WIR francs: 30%, 50%, 100% or negotiable.

Any business of any size may open a trading account in WIR. Accounts are of two types: *Teilnehmer mit garantierte Annahme* (TGA) (member guaranteed income) and *Teilnehmer mit Annahme per Vereinbarung* (TVA) (member negotiated income). Members with TGA accounts agree to accept a minimum of 30% in WIR francs on *each* transaction for their first 3,000 francs' worth of trade. Perks of this account include lower transaction fees and adverts in the monthly WIR journal. Members with TVA accounts are free to negotiate the WIR francs part of any price. Businesses are free to choose at any time whether to run a TGA or TVA account.

Each WIR franc equals one Swiss franc. Businesses use WIR francs in five different ways:

- Buying goods, including property.

- Business expenses.

- Capital expenditure (building and renovation work).

- Private expenditure.

- Paying employees (e.g. sales representatives).

For instance, building firms on WIR prefer to employ tradespeople who are also WIR members so they can part-pay wages. This gives those tradespeople on WIR a marketing advantage with WIR building firms.

Several voluntary organisations trade in WIR but membership for individuals was phased out in 1958 because so few took part. Public services are not available and credits cannot be used to pay taxes, which must be paid in Swiss francs. Transactions between members are recorded on cheques, credit cards

---

20 See T. H. Greco and T. Megalli, An Annotated Précis, Review, and Critique of WIR and the Swiss National Economy by Prof. Tobias Studer
http://reinventingmoney.com/documents/StuderbookCritique.pdf

(the only credit card in the country with two currencies) and by internet. Mobile phone payments are on the way. Fees are paid on each transaction. Members negotiate individual debit limits with WIR Bank, based on their trading history and covered by a bank guarantee or credit insurance policy. However, it doesn't admit SMEs in certain categories, such as discounters or department stores that may be damaging to their sector.

Hervé Dubois describes the essence of the WIR trading circle:

> Hotels normally trade in 30% WIR francs and 70% Swiss francs. Off-season they offer 100% WIR deals to customers and use their credits to upgrade equipment or buy marketing and food services. WIR is a complementary tool to national currency that allows businesses more flexibility. It is the jam in the sandwich, it does not try to replace the bread.

Many long-term members also value this business network for its own sake, regardless of trade in WIR francs. Since the first year of operation (1934), members have been organised into 15 regional groups that organise business lunches and social events to promote the idea and help people to get to know each other. WIR is also a great marketing instrument. The network brings people new business leads they might not otherwise have had and these often snowball into much extra business. WIR advises businesses only to earn as many WIR credits as they can safely spend again and offers a complete advisory and budgeting service to members along with regular workshops for newcomers.

Another strong feature of WIR is its local fairs. The 2010 Annual Report describes their effects:

> The WIR Trade Fairs are both a marketplace and a shop window for the WIR clearing circle. Their effects radiate well beyond the borders of each local area. Nowhere else can an outsider experience the WIR clearing circle so directly as here. WIR members from all sectors offer their products and services at these trade fairs, which also heartily welcome the general public.[21]

Around 3–5,000 businesses join or leave WIR each year. There are a variety of reasons why businesses leave, such as business failure, successors who do not want to use WIR, or a lack of trade. Those who stay value it highly. After a two-year record of positive trading, *only* small and medium enterprises (SMEs)

---

21 Management Report, (2010): www2.wir.ch/doc/doc_download.cfm?uuid=9AE89DEE5056B8 001E32C657036142DF&&IRACER_AUTOLINK&&

are then eligible to become *fully registered* members of the co-operative.
WIR normally defines SMEs as businesses with up to 250 employees. Larger
enterprises may open an account and trade with WIR credits but cannot become
members and steer the organisation.

Businesses choosing to become full members invest shares in Swiss francs and
have voting rights and a small yearly dividend on their joining shares. Fully
registered members are designated as 'official members' and all others as 'silent
members'. Silent members actually outnumber official members by two-to-one
across all sectors. This restriction of full voting membership to SMEs keeps
WIR in line with its founding charter's commitment to serve the interests of
SMEs: 'WIR is a self-help organisation made up of trading, manufacturing and
service-providing companies. Its purpose is to encourage participating members
to put their buying power at each other's disposal and keep it circulating within
their ranks, thereby providing members with additional sales volume.'[22]

No group of businesses can take over the governance of the co-operative
because Swiss law only allows members one vote each, whatever the size of
business. This unique governance structure allows SMEs to maintain control
over the organisation whilst allowing for a wider diversity of economic activity.

WIR has also evolved with the times and now offers businesses more services.
Credit is the motor of the economy and businesses need credit in both national
and local currency:

> For the first 60 years, WIR operated solely as a mutual credit exchange ring
> for small and medium enterprises. But in the mid 1990s key advisors and
> clients began to tell us that we needed to diversify to survive. They proposed
> adding traditional bank loans as a second leg to the business. With its old
> banking licence[23], this was relatively easy to add to the portfolio.

In 1998, WIR took the historic step of embracing normal banking business,
alongside its core exchange ring business, and this allowed it to offer a much
more diverse portfolio of financial services, whilst maintaining the unique WIR
franc clearing system at its heart. It changed its name to WIR Bank and remains
a niche player in the banking sector with relatively simple products such as

---

22 P. Beard, 'Alternatives to Globalisation, Co-operative Principle and Complementary
   Currency', (2004): http://reinventingmoney.com/documents/BeardWIR.pdf

23 The Swiss government gave the WIR Co-operative a banking license in 1936 – not because it
   asked for one but because the authorities wanted to keep an eye on its activities. This accident
   of history opened the door to this later development in the 1990s.

pensions and savings. It does not get involved in risky financial products or shares trading.

This dual credit system – WIR Credits (WIR francs) and WIR Loans (Swiss francs) – has many benefits:

- Clients can do exchange ring business and cash money business at the same time (many use WIR as a second bank).

- It provides traditional financial services that are in demand when the main economy is strong and an alternative means of exchange during a recession in the main economy (it can act both pro- and anti-cyclically).

- Clients can combine WIR Credits and WIR Loans – for instance, to build or renovate a house.

Other popular products include Eco Credits for financing local renewable energy power stations.

Low interest rates are charged on loans to cover WIR Bank's administration costs, to maintain a reserve fund and to pay small dividends to members, but the bank does not make excessive profits. Occasionally it raises capital from members through internal share issues that are traded on an internal stock market. WIR's normal banking business had a turnover of 3.799 billion Swiss francs in 2010.

In its long history, WIR has survived many ups and downs and learned some difficult lessons. It is a history of idealism in hard times, rapid growth, tough decisions and innovation. It is a history of ideology adapting to reality. It is a history of a dialogue between two currencies: national legal tender and a complementary exchange medium.

In the early years, WIR issued clearing certificates as one and five franc notes that circulated amongst members. They were only valid for twelve months and gradually lost their value due to a 'demurrage' fee: a circulation incentive designed to keep currency moving and benefitting the economy. The founders based this design feature on the monetary theories of Silvio Gesell, who prescribed a currency without normal interest charges or payments and which slowly 'rotted' in imitation of natural products like grain. WIR francs still operate without earning interest but the demurrage function was phased out in 1948 because members found it too complicated and, in the post-war boom years, people were spending quickly anyway.

Members also voted in 1952 to drop the ideological restriction on earning interest, in order to allow the Co-operative to raise capital in national currency from its own members. This brought much needed capital into the WIR Bank to invest in its own growth.

A co-operative culture of mutual self-help depends on two things: attitudes and rules. Since the beginning there have been a few members who tried to abuse the system but those who break the rules are kicked out and the bank maintains strict monitoring, published in its annual reports, of every kind of risk to its business.

Hervé Dubois describes how WIR has survived so long:

> Sheer tenacity and adaptability over many years and lots of patience. You need a thick skin! Many are coming to us now because of the finance crisis and their mistrust of large commercial banks. They like our culture of co-operative self-help. That means we have to keep on being innovative and develop new products in both currencies.

WIR's stabilisation effect on the Swiss economy

Switzerland's Gross Domestic Product (GDP) for 2010 was estimated at 395 billion euro so WIR's turnover of 1.627 billion Swiss francs was approximately 0.32% of Swiss GDP. At first glance this seems like a drop in the ocean of the national economy: WIR's trading volume is not substantial in comparison to mainstream economic activity. However, a study by Professor James Stodder, an expert on cash-free and direct exchange transactions at the Rensselaer Polytechnic Institute in Troy, New York State, presents statistically significant evidence (with over 98% probability) that WIR's cash-free settlement system plays a role in stabilising the economy.[24]

For over fifty years, the WIR Bank has collected data which shows that the WIR Exchange Ring has an anti-cyclical (stabilising) effect on the economy. In times of economic boom and strong growth, when the risk of overheating the economy is at its greatest, the activities of the Ring were reduced. Times of recession and rather depressed development, on the other hand, coincided with heightened WIR activity: turnover grew faster than the national average.

---

24 http://www.scribd.com/doc/51533781/Stodder-WIR-Study-March-2010

Besides bare statistical results, there are three reasons that explain why WIR is more important than it appears to be on the basis of its trading volume alone:

1. There is a volume leverage effect. Let us assume that someone buys a building worth 1 Million Swiss francs, which they would not have bought for 100% national currency; they pay 20% WIR francs and 80% Swiss francs. The stimulus to the Swiss economy is 1 million in total, not just the 200,000 Wir francs element, so the economic effect of the WIR system is five times greater than its trading volume alone indicates.

2. Timing: WIR is used more when there is a recession, so it helps at a particularly critical time.

3. It is mainly small and medium-sized enterprises (SMEs) who decide whether to use WIR or not, and SMEs provide more than 85% of all jobs in Switzerland.

On reflection, none of this is very surprising: when traders can sell their products without effort, they tend to use the conventional, national money system. When times become more difficult, they are glad to be able to use a cashless system, with its additional possibilities for obtaining credit and finding customers, to help them to increase turnover.

A simple corollary of this effect is that the employment situation also benefits from the anti-cyclical progression. Whenever unemployment figures rose above average, there was increased activity within the WIR Ring, which thus exercised a regulatory effect on the labour market and provided support for the political efforts being undertaken to stabilise the economic conditions.

Professor Stodder drew similar conclusions out of comparative data, provided by the International Reciprocal Trade Association (IRTA) (p.197), about business-to-business exchanges from the USA. The only difference to be noted is that the influence of the Swiss WIR Ring is proportionally greater because it represents a more substantial part of the national economy than the IRTA activities do in the USA.

Professor Tobias Studer, an economist at the University of Basel, reviewed Professor Stodder's findings in an article for *WIR Plus* magazine in October 2000 and concluded:

It is good news for friends and clients of the WIR system of payments, who are sometimes reproached about the destabilising influence the WIR system might have on national monetary policy. It is good to know that, not only are these criticisms without foundation, but that, contrary to those assertions, the WIR system has a positive influence on the national economy. That these conclusions come by way of a disinterested and neutral researcher only serves to increase their value.[25]

It is in the interests of central banks and politicians of all parties to promote complementary currencies rather than treat them as unwelcome competition and troublesome mavericks in an otherwise ordered and unified currency system. The endless struggle for stability waged by the national banks means that they have especially good reasons to welcome complementary systems, as the research report 'The Future of Payment Systems' demonstrates.[26]

What can we learn?

The colonial example shows how a monopoly national currency enforced by a legal tax obligation undermines regional autonomy.

The story of Banco Palmas and the story of WIR Bank teach us that a regional currency is a *necessary but not a sufficient* condition for sustainable and vibrant regional development.

They reveal that a balanced dual currency approach using both national and local currency acts as an interface between the regional and the broader economic systems.

We obviously do not claim that dual currency systems are a panacea to solve all problems – social, cultural or otherwise – but these lessons could be useful to the future of this globalising world. People often complain that globalisation erodes unique local cultures around the world. Banco Palmas shows us how a local currency, designed, managed and governed by local people, fosters pride in local culture and helps to preserve it. And Swiss business people have maintained WIR over many decades to keep their precious culture of small businesses intact.

Next we will discover that regional currency is not such a new idea after all.

---

25 www.americantradesystem.com/WIRPlus_Magazine_Article_Reviewed_Stodder.pdf

26 B. Lietaer, 'The Future of Payment Systems', Unisys Corporation, May (2002).

Chapter 3
An old idea in new clothes

The icons of old are the codings of tomorrow.
And tomorrow holds the promise of recovery of forgotten wisdom.[1]
Jean Houston

The idea of introducing regional currencies to support regional development
may sound like a revolutionary one. In fact, it is an old one that fell out
of fashion a couple of centuries ago. Recent research shows that regional
currencies have a long history of success.[2] They were not abandoned because
they became obsolete or because people gave them up for something better but,
in many cases, because a central authority imposed its own monetary system to
increase its control over a region.

Historical precedents

Local and regional currencies have been in general use in many parts of the
world throughout most of history. In Western Europe, they were used without
interruption for 1,000 years, from roughly 800 AD to around 1800 AD. Recent
studies of medieval and pre-modern financial institutions show that, prior to the
establishment and diffusion of the gold standard, Europe had a well organised
and successful monetary system with a surprising variety of currencies for
different circulation areas.

It was a system based on two very different types of currencies: full-bodied gold
and silver coins, such as French and English royal coinage, and smaller coins
(méreaux) made of lead, tin and copper, which were issued by local aristocrats,
city administrations, bishops or monasteries and mainly used for local
exchanges. Sometimes the same authority, like the independent state of Venice,
would issue both types of currencies.

Luca Fantacci researches historic regional currencies:

> The monetary dogmas of today and yesterday are quite different. Yesterday's
> dogma was that money is supposed to be a unit of account whose value is

---

1   J. Houston, *Life Force: The Psychohistorical Recovery of the Self*, (1993), p. 13.

2   See M. Amato, L. Fantacci and L. Doria, *Complementary Currency Systems in a Historical Perspective*, (2003). The first half of this chapter is strongly inspired by conversations with and, still partially unpublished,documents, from this team.

determined by its intrinsic metal content. Today's dogma is that money is supposed to be universal, without geographical boundaries. Neither one of these dogmas would have made sense during the *Ancien Régime* (before the French Revolution). On the contrary, most local exchanges were facilitated by local currencies whose value was independent of the intrinsic metal content.

The Roman Empire collapsed in the 4th Century AD. Some argue that a key factor was corruption of the coinage over several centuries by greedy emperors. Around 800 AD the emperor Charlemagne re-standardised and centralised the currency system but after this period the system fragmented again. Local lords, bishops and abbeys issued currencies of varying qualities and denominations.

Before the French Revolution, there were two types of objects used for exchange and trade: *méreaux*, and official coinage (*monnaie*). Monetary history usually talks about official coinage and dismisses *méreaux* as coin-like, quasi-money or pseudo-money or it is altogether ignored.

Méreaux looked like tokens and were issued by local authorities or societies for use as a local means of payment. *Méreau* comes from the Latin *merare* meaning 'to distribute'. *Coins* were the official royal currency.

Used as Medium of Exchange

Méreaux — Common Tender

Coins — Legal Tender

In 1265 the king of France specified that only the royal mints had the right to issue coins circulating in the realm, except in the areas where barons had their own emission right, and that only royal coinage would be accepted for the payment of royal taxes. Successive French kings would try to further reduce the baronial exceptions, either by force or by re-purchasing those rights.

In reaction to losing their right to issue new legal tender, local barons gradually increased the use of *méreaux* circulating as common tender. *Méreaux* had existed before that time, some can be traced back to Antiquity, but their widespread use coincides with the increased tightening of the royal coinage monopoly.

In practice the king's exclusive currency emission rights were widely ignored: the city of Arras tried repeatedly to prohibit the circulation of *méreaux* in the 14th Century, and four centuries later the authorities were still issuing edicts to try and stop the practice.

How were *méreaux* used? Cathedrals would incentivise their secular clergy to sing in masses by paying them in *méreaux* redeemable for food, wine and other goods; charitable organisations issued their own *méreaux* redeemable for food and shelter. Over time, the most popular of these *méreaux* would simply end up circulating as common tender in the city.

A more economically significant example is the *méreaux* used for large projects. The workers who made the bells for Chartres cathedral were paid in *méreaux*.[3] One monastic order paid for buildings and other secular activities in *méreaux de salaire*; these were cast in lead with an emblem symbolising the work being done. The monastery was also a supplier of goods, such as food and wine to local inns. Building workers would spend their currency there and the inns would pay the monastery, thus completing a regional circuit. In that same city of Saint-Omer, the town hall also issued its own civilian *méreaux* throughout the 17th Century in payment for the work on its defences. The same process had been used to build the defence system for Lille in 1566 and for Amiens in 1663.[4]

Even the French king himself would issue *méreaux* whenever he could create a closed circuit where he would be the beneficiary: he paid workers who rebuilt the fortress of Montségur after the famous siege of the Cathars in 1244. Later French kings would issue leaden *méreaux* to pay workers in their kitchen, stables, and other royal facilities.[5]

---

3 Bibliothèque de l'École de Chartres, Tome XXXIII (pg 312) quoted by Labrot, p 83.

4 *Ibid.* p 84.

5 *Ibid.* p 82–83.

Good money, bad money?

But did people at the time consider these *méreaux* to be money? The short answer is yes, given the number of them bearing the explicit inscription *moneta*. Another sign that these *méreaux* were taken seriously is that anybody caught counterfeiting them was liable to punishments similar to counterfeiters of official money. These included being boiled to death in oil, cutting off the nose, marking the face with a red iron, and being exposed on the pillory.

What was the relative economic importance of the official tender vs. the common tender? This clearly varied a lot depending on the period, place and people involved. The same object may have initially been issued as a simple token for a specific group of people – and then only gradually accepted in payment by the population at large. Most big money finds from archaeological digs take the form of treasure hoards and high intrinsic value currencies were typically the only ones worth hoarding. The most important collections of *méreaux* have been found when dredging city rivers.[6] *Méreaux* are exhibited less, because they are less beautiful and made from less valuable materials than the official tender. However, the scarcity of finds does not mean that they were rare during their time of use. Common tender probably played a more significant economic role than is generally acknowledged nowadays.

In the 13th Century, Nicholas Oresme had noted that one should distinguish between currencies used for payment and those used for savings. Later, Lord Gresham would reword Oresme's statement into his famous 'law': bad money drives out good. Because the high intrinsic value currencies (pure silver 'good' money) were hoarded, the money that would actually circulate was the other kind (base metal alloy 'bad' money). So we should expect that, on average, one piece of 'bad' money would tend to circulate more actively than official tender and so play a more important economic role in the real life of an ordinary citizen than might be obvious at first glance. In large transactions and in inter-regional commerce, the opposite would be true: the official tender would tend to dominate.

This historical dual currency system is often described as an inefficient system that the international gold standard would later replace. Currencies running in parallel are seen to be inhomogeneous and a hindrance to efficient exchange and price formation.

---

6   The single largest collection of *méreaux* ever found in France was during the dredging of the Seine in Paris during the 19th Century. See A. Forgeais, *Collection de plombs historiés trouvés dans la Seine,* Vol 6, (Paris 1858–1866).

You can also argue the opposite: parallel currencies are a deliberate institutional feature that maintains separate exchange circuits of a different nature (local and long-distance), as well as different monetary functions (the unit of value and the means of payment). Research has shown how the separation of the monetary circuits and functions was a fundamental condition for the maintenance of the general financial equilibrium within the economic and social systems of the *Ancien Régime*.

The monetary system prior to the gold standard was not a faulty and tentative approximation but a viable dual currency system that was economically sound. The political forces that stopped local currencies were more concerned with power than with improvements in overall efficiency or in the economic well-being of the people.

Historical inflation rates

A US Federal Reserve study[7] showed that the average rate of inflation in historical commodity money (gold and silver) was about minus 0.5% per year (yes, that's *minus* 0.5%). This includes periods when there were a number of different currencies circulating, i.e. before the introduction of government sponsored central banks and the development of national currency monopolies. Modern fiat-based monetary systems are assumed to behave well but this study shows that modern money systems have exhibited much higher inflation, on average 6.5% per year *even when cases of hyperinflation (such as the Reichsmark after WWI) are omitted.* (When such cases of hyperinflation are included, the average inflation rate for fiat national currencies is over 18%.)

This situation has only become worse over time. Even the world's formerly most stable national currencies – the German Mark and the Swiss franc – lost about 60% of their value between 1970 and 2000.[8] The US dollar lost 75% and the UK pound close to 90% of their respective values over the same time period.

Michel Dhenin, curator of the Cabinet des Médailles de la Bibliothèque Nationale in Paris, says: 'Some would claim that today pseudo-money has totally replaced real money, and that we have in our purses only quasi money. In fact, there is a lot of truth to such an assertion.'

---

7 A. J. Rolnick and W. E. Weber, 'Inflation and money growth under alternative monetary standards', Working Paper 528, Federal Reserve Bank of Minneapolis Research Department, (1994).

8 Source of data from 1970 to 1990 from Marjorie Deane and Robert Pringle, *The Central Banks* (1995), Table P.1 , p.352–354, completed with the International Labor Office Monthly Bulletin of Statistics.

From gold standard to global currencies

During the 18th Century, Britain led the quest to establish a gold standard in order to make international trade easier. The collapse of the gold standard during the early 20th Century, however, did not interrupt the process of homogenising currency. The Bretton-Woods agreement of 1944 – technically described as a gold/dollar equivalent standard – put the United States firmly in charge of the global monetary scene. When President Nixon unilaterally ended the convertibility of the dollar to gold in 1971, the *de facto* global dollar standard became clear.

There is a constant struggle between the forces of centralisation/monoculture and those of devolution/diversity. Economists John Maynard Keynes, Irving Fisher and Friedrich Hayek all made important proposals to differentiate monetary institutions and functions, but the homogenisation of money has marched inexorably on, not only eliminating the geopolitical boundaries between national currencies, but also obliterating the distinctions between different kinds of economic activities and actors.

Money has evolved into many forms over thousands of years but today we are getting to the point where we use the same kind of money for every kind of economic activity at a local, regional, national and global level: for commercial transactions between private traders; for the redistribution of purchasing power within communities; as a means of exchange; as a reserve; or as a store of value. It is like trying to use a tape measure to weigh something or a weighing scale to estimate length: the result is a confusion of standards and trust.

Local money in the UK

Pat Conaty, a historian of the Co-operative movement, describes the history of local money in the UK during the Industrial Revolution.[9]

> The industrial revolution led to a competition for precious metals. Coins became scarce between the late 1780s and 1820. Paper money issued by country banks in Great Britain developed rapidly to fill this gap and some cities introduced their own coins, like the Lady Godiva half penny in Coventry from 1792. During the Napoleonic wars the metal shortage became worse and the British mint stopped new coinage completely and did not resume production for 20 years until 1816...
>
> In the first half of the 19th Century and as in other industrialising countries, local currency was commonplace in the UK and based upon about a thousand local banks. Each market town had a local commercial bank supported by local people and local traders and each bank produced its own local paper money to support the local economy. The local money was used to promote and support directly the local economy and to link up local businesses and farmers. While the system was not problem-free at all, local money helped promote the economies of market towns and cities and was a source of pride...
>
> Local paper money became widespread but, during the depressions of 1816–19, 1825–31 and 1835–42, there were a number of bank panics. These recurring bank failures and fears about inflation led to the Bank Charter Act of 1844 that removed the production rights of any new issue of local paper money from banks in England and Wales and transferred national currency provision exclusively to the Bank of England.
>
> Prior to this change, the early Co-operative movement experimented to try to develop an interest and debt free co-operative money system based on the Labour theory of value (the then conventional theory of value by economists from Smith to Ricardo)...
>
> During the 1816–19 depression, Robert Owen, a successful industrialist in his own right, set out his vision of Villages of Co-operation and Mutual Unity. A key monetary reform element of this vision was the labour note, an alternative to debt based bank money with an hour as a new standard of value.
>
> Owen worked with Josiah Warren in the USA and Warren developed the first time based currency linked to the exchange of locally produced goods. The Cincinnati Time Store opened in 1827 and operated relatively successfully until 1830 as a retail store with a 4% to 7% mark up on goods priced in the labour involved in production.

---

9 Pat Conaty, private discussion paper, 'Co-operative Money', February 2012.

Owen returned to England in the late 1820s and led the development of the National Equitable Labour Exchanges which were set up and operated from 1832-33 in London and Birmingham. As with the Cincinnati Time Store, Labour money was denominated in hours of work and the labour exchanges operated as warehouses for goods sold in units of time... the warehouses had high development and transaction costs for storage, insurance, staffing etc. and as co-operative businesses they did not prove to be viable. A decade later this early co-operative shop system was succeeded by the consumer co-op model developed by the Rochdale pioneers in 1844. The ingenious quarterly 'divi' system of this model drove the early development of the co-operative movement internationally.

The Guernsey Story[10]

The island of Guernsey lies about 30 miles from the north coast of France and 70 miles from the south coast of England. For centuries it has been part of the United Kingdom.

In the year 1817 it was in dire straits: the roads were impassable in wet weather, there was little trade or employment for the poor and the sea was washing away large tracts of land.

The States of Guernsey government owed the banks £19,137 with an annual interest charge of £2,390. The gross national revenue of the entire island was only £3,000, which left only £610 per annum to run the entire island. Interest paid to the banks consumed 80% of the island's governmental income. It had no money left over to solve its public problems.

A committee of leading citizens decided to finance the building of a public market near the main harbour, Saint Peter Port, so the farmers could sell their products for export more easily. The cost of the new facility would be £6,000. In addition, fixing the dykes would cost an additional £10,000. So how could they do it? Further taxation of the impoverished island was impossible. Borrowing money from the banks would result in even higher interest charges that could never be paid.

The committee made a historic recommendation to remedy the situation:

> The committee recommends that the expense should be met by the issue of State notes of £1 sterling to the value of £6,000... and that these notes will be available not only for the payment of the new market, but also for Torteval Church, roads to construct, and other expenses of the States.

---

10 Based on Olive and Jan Grubiak, *The Guernsey Experiment,* (1969, 1992).

The local banks already had £50,000 of their notes in circulation so there was little to fear from inflation. But, just to be sure, they placed redemption dates on the notes of April 1817, October 1817, and April 1818. The notes were good for payment of taxes and as regular circulating money until the expiration date. Stall holders in the new market hall would pay rental to the local government. However, after the redemption dates, the notes would no longer be legal tender and the state would destroy them.

> In this manner, without increasing the States' debt, it will be possible to finish these works, leaving sufficient money in the Exchequer for other needs.

The citizens realised that these notes worked just as well as bank money and issued additional notes in 1820 and 1821. By 1821, some £10,000 of Guernsey notes were in circulation. No debt, no inflation.

> [It was] the most advantageous method of meeting debts, from the point of view both of the public and the States' finances. Indeed, the public seemed to realise this fact, and, far from being averse to taking the notes, they sought them out eagerly.

In 1824, another £5,000 notes were issued for the markets and £20,000 to erect Elizabeth College and certain other schools in 1826.

> ...it was stated over and over again by eminent men of those times that without the issue of States' notes, important public works, such as roads and buildings, could not possibly have been carried out. Yet by means of the States' issue, not only were these works accomplished, but also the island was not a penny the poorer in interest charges. Indeed, the improvements had stimulated the flow of visitors to the island, and with increased trade, the island enjoyed its newfound prosperity.

Private banks on Guernsey grew concerned at this challenge to their monopoly on currency issuance and began to undermine the effectiveness of the island currency. It never achieved such dramatic effects again.

This historical example shows how a regional government can issue a currency to do essential work, free of interest, debt and inflation, against the promise of future income from taxes and rental. A modern local authority might consider issuing a currency to mobilise and pay workers, reward volunteers or raise new buildings in expectation of return income from local taxes, room and vehicle hire or admission fees to leisure, arts and community centres.

The Wörgl Story[11]

In 1932, in the depths of the Great Depression, the Austrian town of Wörgl issued its own currency. From a population of 4,500, 1,500 were without work and 200 families were penniless. Mayor Michael Unterguggenberger had a long list of necessary projects – repaving the roads, streetlighting, extending water distribution across the whole town and planting trees – but hardly any money to pay for them.

The town council deposited its 40,000 Austrian *schillings* savings in a local savings bank as a guarantee to back the issue of a local stamp scrip currency. These circulating notes needed a stamp attached every month to keep their value. There was a cost associated with the stamp, and no-one wanted to pay a hoarding penalty from holding excessive numbers of notes when the stamp was due. As a result, the notes would be spent as fast as possible, although it was impossible to avoid paying some stamp costs. The 40,000 *schilling* deposit allowed anyone to exchange scrip for 98% of its value in schillings. This offer was rarely taken up though. The money raised from the fees was used to run a soup kitchen that fed 220 families.

Only the railway station and the post office refused to accept the local money. When people ran out of spending ideas, they would pay their taxes early using scrip, resulting in a huge increase in town revenues. Over the 13-month period of the project, the council not only carried out all the intended works projects, but also built new houses, a reservoir, a ski jump, and a bridge. The people also used scrip to replant forests, in anticipation of the future cashflow they would receive from the trees.

People estimated that the local currency circulated 14 times more than the schilling, increasing trade and creating much needed jobs. Wörgl was the only Austrian town to achieve full employment at that time.

---

11 Based on Fritz Schwartz, *Das Experiment von Wörgl*, (2007).

Six neighbouring villages copied the system successfully. The French Prime Minister, Eduoard Dalladier, made a special visit to see the 'miracle of Wörgl'. In January 1933, the project was replicated in the neighbouring city of Kitzbuhel and, in June 1933, Mayor Unterguggenburger addressed a meeting with representatives from 170 different towns and villages. Two hundred Austrian townships expressed an interest in adopting the idea.

At this point, the central bank panicked, and decided to assert its monopoly rights by banning local currencies. The people unsuccessfully sued the bank and later lost in the Austrian Supreme Court. It then became a criminal offence to issue emergency currency.

The town went back to 30% unemployment. In 1934, social unrest exploded across Austria. In 1938, when Hitler annexed Austria, he was welcomed by many people as their economic and political saviour.

Unterguggenberger was opposed to both communism and fascism, championing instead,what he referred to as economic freedom. Therefore, it was deeply ironic that the Wörgl experiment was first branded as craziness by the monetary authorities, then as a communist idea, and some years later as a fascist one.

But the story does not quite end there. In 1933, American economist Irving Fisher was so inspired by the Wörgl story that he published a book called *Stamp Scrip*.[12] It inspired hundreds of businesses and communities across the USA to start their own currencies. Fisher then advised the new President Roosevelt that local currencies could quickly end the Depression. However, the President decided instead for the centralised New Deal solution to unemployment. The local systems were all closed down.[13]

All of these historical examples clearly show local monetary power at work; how underused assets can be mobilised to fulfil unmet needs.

None of the local currencies profiled in this book was started by a local government because there are no examples in the modern era. In all cases they were started by groups of businesses or citizens. Any regional government wanting to introduce its own currency today will have to tread a careful political path to acceptance.

---

12 Irving, Cohrssen and Fisher, *Stamp Scrip,*(1933).

13 Bernard Lietaer, *Future of Money*, (1999).

Regional currencies for regional economies

In 1999, the economist Richard Douthwaite argued:

> If regional currencies had been in operation in Britain in the 1980s, when London boomed while the North of England's economy suffered after the closure of its coal mines and most of its heavy industries, then the North-South gap which developed might have been prevented. The North of England pound could have been allowed to fall in value compared with the London one, saving many of the businesses that were forced to close.[14]

Economist Jane Jacobs also made some powerful arguments for 'city currencies' in her book *Cities and the Wealth of Nations* in 1984.[15]

> Today we take it for granted that the elimination of multitudinous currencies in favour of fewer national or imperial currencies represents economic progress and promotes the stability of economic life. But this conventional belief is at least worth questioning in view of the function that currencies serve as economic feedback controls...
>
> Currencies are powerful carriers of feedback information... and potent triggers of adjustments, but in their own terms... Because currency feedback information is so potent, and because so often the information is not what governments want to hear, nations commonly go to extravagant lengths to try to block off or resist the information... National currencies, then, are potent feedback but impotent at triggering appropriate corrections...
>
> Individual city currencies indeed serve as elegant feedback controls because they trigger specifically appropriate corrections to specific responding mechanisms. This is a built-in design advantage that many cities of the past had which almost none have now. Singapore and Hong Kong, which are oddities today, have their own currencies and so they possess this built-in advantage.

A regional currency is not an end in itself but it could be a very powerful tool for regional planners if designed, managed and governed correctly.

Key lessons

The majority of economic textbooks do not mention any of this history and so most economists consider the very idea of multiple currencies to be a startling, unorthodox, or even dangerous idea!

---

14 R. Douthwaite, *The Ecology of Money*, (1999), p. 64–65.

15 J. Jacobs, *Cities and the Wealth of Nations*, (1984), Chapter 11 'Faulty Feedback to Cities'.

In conclusion:

- The gradual trend towards global monetary homogenisation was predominantly driven by power and centralised control, rather than by motives of economic efficiency or modernisation as people sometimes argue.

- A significant side effect of this trend has been to reduce the degrees of freedom for resolving local and regional problems, and accentuate the concentration of wealth in ever fewer financial centres.

- There is ample historical evidence that well-designed regional currencies can effectively operate in parallel with national or supra-national ones, without creating inflation or other monetary crises.

Chapter 4
Characteristics of regional currencies

Because we have so little experience in designing money systems
to create societies that work for people and nature in nonexploitative ways,
we will need to be creative.[1]
David Korten

Regional currencies can be started and run by a regional authority, a group of businesses or a group of citizens. Although the particular legal and financial issues will be different for each group, the development process will be similar and whoever takes the initiative will, at first, face a lot of choices. This chapter gives an overview of key design criteria.

Each region is different

Some regions seem similar to each other. But on closer observation every region has specific needs, strengths and weaknesses. This truth will become much clearer when you begin to analyse supply chains, underused assets and unmet needs during the design process.

Experience around the world shows that currencies can be introduced in:

Poorer urban areas – Banco Palmas (p.24), Eco-Pesa (p.191), Dane County Time Bank (p.180), Equal Dollars (p.132) and Brixton Pound (p.122);

Richer urban areas – WIR Bank (p.34), Ithaca HOURS (p.150), RES (p.112) and The Business Exchange (p.102);

Poorer rural areas – Argentina (p.161), STRO (p.203) and Blaengarw Time Centre (p.168);

Richer rural areas – Talente Tauschkreis (p.126), Chiemgauer (p.144), BerkShares (p.138).

Some of these currencies serve mixed rural and urban areas too.

Regional currencies work in poorer and richer areas in different ways: people who are cash poor but time rich can convert their skills and service into

---

1 D. Korten, 'Money as a Social Disease'.
   Online at http://livingeconomiesforum.org/1997/money

currency to buy food and other essentials (Equal Dollars); people who are cash rich but time poor can buy local currency backed by national currency to support local economic circuits (Chiemgauer, BerkShares). Inhabitants of rural areas may be more self-sufficient and used to relying on their own resources and initiative, and to producing and consuming regionally. (Banco Palmas and BerkShares both show the importance of balancing loans for local production and consumption.)

Enhanced awareness of environmental issues can stimulate and foster local culture, art and crafts, which in turn makes the region more attractive for tourists. Local people generate opportunities to become aware of and benefit from their own heritage – craft workers can become the beneficiaries of co-operative stores, or farmers can form alliances to develop branded regional marketing strategies for their products. Where the ground has been prepared in this way, the conditions are ideal for the introduction of a regional currency. This is exactly what happened in the region of Bremen when the Roland currency was introduced in 2001 (p.192).

But the majority of the world's population now lives in cities so it is crucial that regional currencies become better established in metropolitan regions that consist of a city and its immediate hinterland. City populations are much more fluid and mobile, which can be a challenge to self-organised systems if key organisers move on and the system then collapses. Successful city currencies sometimes get welcome support from the city authorities and chambers of commerce, as is beginning to happen in Aberdeen, Bristol and London.[2]

Goal: reverse the drainage effect

A problem facing so-called peripheral regions is the tendency for capital to drain towards other regions, which encourages firms and jobs to follow suit, in turn sparking a downward spiral that cannot be stopped using conventional policy instruments.

National currencies do not take regional needs into account. Money as a commodity is expected to provide owners with ever increasing, higher yields and this is only possible over a long period of time in the virtual sphere of money markets, not through investment in peripheral regions. Until the avalanche of a world financial crisis in 2008, money tended to gravitate towards the big financial centres to be passed on to areas promising the highest returns,

2 e.g. Bristol Pound. See online at http://bristolpound.org/

such as the emerging Asian markets. In 2003, the People's Republic of China, Hong Kong and Taiwan alone attracted almost 70% of the total international investment capital. People living in peripheral regions would find that their savings were serving to promote their own unemployment, the outflow of capital and the disappearance of local and national sources of employment.

Money can be retained for reinvestment within a region through a system of incentives and disincentives. Incentives include benefits to businesses, individuals and voluntary associations through locally circulating wealth and fully used assets. Disincentives include penalties to convert regional currency back to national currency and hoarding fees to keep currency moving (WIR Bank p.34; Chiemgauer p.144; Talente Tauschkreis p.126).

A well-designed regional currency can promote any or all of the following aims:

- Selective encouragement of the regional economy.

- Development of a sustainable financial system, providing better protection from the effects of financial speculation.

- Provision of new sources of liquidity, especially for small and medium-sized firms, leading to an expansion of markets for regional products and services.

- The creation of jobs.

- Increased potential for the creation of added value and surplus in the region.

- Closer contacts between producers and consumers, with shorter transport distances and lower energy consumption.

- Outsourcing and co-production of public services to social economy organisations – co-operatives, charities, social enterprises.

- Strengthening of regional identity and self-help attitudes, which can bring about many other beneficial developments.

So, now at least part of our liquidity stays in the region

Key elements of a regional currency

Based on many years of experience in various countries around the world, there are three commonly useful 'building-blocks' for a sustainable regional currency:

1. A *voucher system* or *circulating currency* is used in the same way as conventional cash or current accounts for payment of small, everyday amounts of money. There are various designs: it can be valued at par with national currency (like most systems that issue printed currency, except Time Banks); it can be backed by the promise to supply goods and services (Ithaca HOURS p.150); it can be redeemable for national currency, often for an exchange fee (Chiemgauer p.144, BerkShares p.138, Brixton Pound p.122); it can be redeemable for rewards (Blaengarw Time Centre p.168); it can be issued from an account in an exchange ring (Talente Tauschkreis Vorarlberg p.126).

2. An *exchange ring* allows for the cash-free settlement of bills and the setting up of mutual credit lines between individuals and firms. It works best for small to medium-size enterprises, individuals and voluntary associations. It provides them with improved access to liquid funds or credit. See Talente Tauschkreis Vorarlberg (p.126), WIR Bank (p.34), The Business Exchange (p.102), RES (p.112) and Dane County Time Bank (p.180).

3. A *micro-credit bank* offers low interest or interest-free loans in both local and national currency for production or consumption. See Banco Palmas (p.24), WIR Bank (p.34), BerkShares (p.138) and Chiemgauer (p.144).

1) The voucher system

We all know the gaudy coupons issued by restaurant chains, supermarkets and shopping centres – '10% off this', 'a FREE one of those if you buy one of these', 'Collect loyalty points and get a lovely set of kitchen utensils to go with all the other sets you already own'.

It was a logical leap to create a similar system as a means of payment for specific purposes. Systems that issue circulating vouchers use an ingenious trick: they extend the idea of a customer loyalty scheme by adding the function of a cash-like payment medium, which is valid in a wide range of outlets throughout a whole region.

There are several reasons why this idea has been eagerly put into practice:

- It is a legal way to create a regional medium of exchange that benefits businesses, consumers and voluntary associations.

- Many individuals and groups want to make a contribution towards solving the economic and environmental crises.

- A physical medium of exchange in circulation strengthens regional identity, sparks conversations, gathers stories around it and builds support.

Several leading local currency systems such as Brixton Pound, Chiemgauer and BerkShares use circulating notes or vouchers.

2) The exchange ring

The 'money' in an 'exchange ring' or 'mutual credit' system is produced when two parties exchange goods or services: one party receives a negative balance on their account, the other a positive balance. The positive balance may be spent with other participants.

Theoretically, total negative and positive balances of individual participants always sum to zero across the whole system. In practice, people leave the system with both negative and positive balances and administrators can write these off. Optional credit allowances or time limits for clearing negative balances can be set to maintain the system's viability.

Business exchange (or barter networks) and community-based time banks or local exchange systems are all mutual credit systems and they are all legal. Professional services offered through these currencies are taxable but informal trades are not. Banco Palmas (p.24) and Talente Tauschkreis (p.126) have an added facility where local taxes can be paid in these local currencies.

Both commercial and community exchange rings are popular because people can save their scarce national currency for other purposes and participate in a regional currency by offering their services. Active participants effectively create money. And this money – in contrast to conventional currencies – is always 100% backed by concrete goods or services.

Regional exchange rings have several advantages:

- The regional restriction limits the risks for participants (all members' account balances are published) and for the central clearinghouse, which maintains close contacts with its 'customers' and provides locally relevant advice and information.

- They are large enough to create a professional operation, perhaps as a co-operative or non-profit providing cheaper and more personal services.

- They have the scale to involve the main social and economic players in the region: individuals, small to medium-sized businesses, voluntary associations, local authorities and professional service providers.

An exchange ring opens the way to a special brand of working together. It does not exclude competition but augments it. By co-operating in a circle of exchange, the participating firms and individuals create the facility of interest- free credits for each other. Switzerland's WIR Bank serves 60,000 small and medium enterprises and has provided this facility for 78 years. WIR members can use their positive local currency balance for the purchase of goods and services, to pay operational costs, to finance investments, for private expenditure and also to pay a part of their employees' salaries.

Exchange rings demonstrate mutual reciprocity when:

- Exchanges are given priority over national currency transactions.

- Prices do not exceed those in national currency.

- Customers using both national and local currency are treated equally.

- Contacts between members are fostered and an atmosphere of mutual support is encouraged.

Members co-operate for the common good because it is also in their own interests.

For many users, the exchange ring may, at first, appear to be just a means of getting more business, bridging a turnover slump or obtaining cheap credit without much effort. But the ring automatically forges bonds between participants in a tailored marketplace where they can present their own goods and services, find the right suppliers, and reduce operating costs and bad debts.

3) Micro-credit bank
WIR Bank and Banco Palmas both show the importance of integrating banking services in national currency with those in local currency. Businesses and individuals get loans for both production and consumption. They can pay their bills and conduct their daily business.

The 'best' mechanism? A lively debate!
Local currency designers sometimes get into very heated debates about the ideal mechanism. The problem is that they are often talking at cross-purposes about different goals.

People who promote vouchers or circulating currencies want local people and businesses to see something in circulation in their community: objects, like normal notes and coins, that can change peoples' minds about money. As academic Peter North puts it, they want to create a money with 'moneyness', that gives people the confidence to exchange, measure and store value with it. As we saw in Chapter 2, local money is the historical norm but national currencies have become the dominant reality. Circulating notes with interesting designs that reflect the unique features of a local region can be a great marketing and consciousness-raising tool that persuades people to take part. Backing a regional currency with national currency provides another level of confidence, particularly for new businesses taking part.

So the primary goals of these types of currencies are to create visibility and confidence. And the primary mechanisms they use are circulating notes backed by national currency.

Others promoting mutual credit exchange rings argue that these circulating currencies simply reproduce some of the problems of conventional money: people see money as a 'thing' they need to possess; trades are anonymous – people can use the currency for anything; the local currency only pins national currency down for a short while before people exchange back out and so little new wealth is created or circulated; issuance of the medium of exchange is limited to the amount of national currency available and to those who possess it.

By contrast, mutual credit systems record all transactions between participants in a database, with absolute transparency of record keeping. Everyone can see what is traded and by whom at all times and the medium of exchange (the accounting units) always exactly matches the volume of trade that people wish to undertake with each other, so there can never be a scarcity of 'money' itself.

So the primary goal of a mutual credit exchange ring is to provide a medium of exchange exactly matched to the need for trade. And the primary mechanism it uses is a centralised administration system (often devolved to record-keeping by participants themselves through a website).

Critics of mutual credit systems argue that: the idea of zero sum accounting (all negative and positive balances summing to zero at all times) is harder to sell to high street businesses; not everyone wants to declare every transaction they make to the whole community; the system is abstract because nobody can 'see' the currency in circulation (although a handful of community-based systems also issue cash from a mutual credit account).

Looking at evidence rather than theory, it seems that the world's largest non-national exchange system – WIR Bank in Switzerland – has successfully managed an account-based mutual credit system for 78 years without a circulating currency, as have many other pure business-to-business systems since. Community-based mutual credit systems, like LETS and Time Banks, have tended to remain much smaller and have not attracted many businesses.

Systems that exclusively use a circulating currency, like Brixton Pound, Ithaca HOURS, Chiemgauer, BerkShares etc., are having some impact in terms of consciousness raising, although the economic impact is still small.

Another separate debate concerns the costs of running different systems. Some high profile systems have received a lot of public and private funding to keep them going, with unimpressive numbers of participants or trades for the amount of investment involved. Many small but successful community-led systems have relied on volunteers to keep them going. Each system has to do its own cost/benefit analysis about investment of time and effort in relation to results achieved.

The Talente Tauschkreis Vorarlberg in Austria (p.126) seems to have evolved a convincing hybrid model: from 1996 it established a viable mutual credit exchange ring, which still forms the heart of the system; since 2006 it has added a euro-backed currency and allows exchange of currency between the two mechanisms; the system has no funding or paid staff to run the core operations and, instead, shares the tasks amongst a volunteer 25 person Service Team, who earn local currency for their efforts.

Integration and organisation

No current systems integrate all three elements – voucher, exchange ring and bank: WIR Bank has an exchange ring and a bank but no circulating currency; Banco Palmas and Chiemgauer have a bank and a currency but no exchange ring; Talente Tauschkreis has an exchange ring and vouchers but no bank. Future systems will be more resilient if they can integrate all three elements.

A regional currency needs effective organisation with a central administration responsible for vouchers, accounts and banking services, and independent quality assurance.

The creation of an administration system is discussed in Chapter 6 in Part Two.

All innovations sooner or later face the issue of standards: we agree that all electric plugs are the same size in the same country; we agree for the internet to have open protocols so that all personal computers can talk to each other. Quality marks combined with independent verification, such as with organic and

Fair Trade products, help maintain standards of good practice, transparency and customer acceptance.

The first German regional currencies formed an umbrella association called Regiogeld e.V (Regional Money Association) (p.207) in 2006. This body asks its members to sign up to a voluntary code of standards listed on its website.[3] The International Reciprocal Trade Association recommends business exchanges to follow a similar code.[4]

If Regios are valued on a 1:1 basis with euros, there are obvious advantages: there are no conversion rates and this makes it easier for tax accounting. The only drawback is that Regios are then tied to inflation in euros. Time banks avoid this problem by using the hour as the unit of account. Other systems like Chiemgauer (p.144) that are tied to the euro have a Plan B in the drawer: if the euro got into really serious problems and became untrusted for daily business, they would be able to decouple their currency completely and tie it to the labour hour, kilowatt hour, a basket of local commodities or some other agreed standard.

Criteria applying to a regional currency

A regional currency should ideally:

1. Represent a win-win situation for all participants.

2. Be organised with the aim of mutual social benefit.

3. Be professionally run.

4. Be transparent for its users.

5. Be democratically governed.

6. Be sustainably financed.

7. Contain circulation incentives.

1) Win-win

Win-win means that everyone should be able to perceive a benefit for themselves. It might mean more income, it might mean more opportunities to serve other people or improve local conditions. Individual participants in

---

3   www.regiogeld.de/wertestandards.html

4   www.irta.com/images/ethicsandconductcodefinalapproved9202011.pdf

the Chiemgauer in Bavaria get few immediate economic advantages from participation but they know they are directly benefitting local businesses and voluntary organisations of their choice, which improves the quality of life for themselves in their own community.

2) Mutual social benefit
Commercial business-to-business exchange systems like The Business Exchange (p.102) or RES (p.112) are run at a profit for their organisers but are also mutually beneficial to their members.

Systems like BerkShares (p.138), Chiemgauer (p.144) or Talente Tauschkreis (p.126) are run as non-profit organisations with organisers paid in a mixture of national and local currency.

3) Professionalism
Regional currencies that have endured are run professionally, whether by full-time paid staff or part-time volunteers.

4) Transparency
While national and international currencies lurch from one crisis to another, regional currencies work to a higher standard of transparency. Transparency requires that users have free access to all the information they need for understanding the system and that they have a means of making their own contributions in the form of feedback, criticism and suggestions for improvement. There is much translating work to be done: organisers must make economic jargon intelligible to people with no knowledge of finance through a mixture of skilled storytelling, practical examples and logical arguments. Banco Palmas makes brilliant use of the arts and the media to engage with local people.

5) Democracy
Private commercial systems are governed by their owners. Systems run by citizens or local government require a different approach to governance. Banco Palmas uses weekly meetings to reach consensus and make strategic decisions. Talente Tauschkreis has a 25 people strong Service Team with nine local organisers spread across the region and annual meetings of all members.

6) Sustainable finance
Cost recovery is a critical success factor for local currencies. A regional currency can only be described as sustainable when it has reached a point at

which the costs of running it can be carried by those participating in it. Systems dependent on grants tend to fade away when the grants run out, unless they are very careful to plan for a sustainable future at the outset. Cost recovery can come from joining fees, annual membership fees, transaction fees, rental income, event income, donations, auctions, fundraising, etc.

7) Circulation incentives

The purpose of a currency is to circulate, thereby creating economic and social benefits. There are various ways to encourage circulation:

- The best way is to make the benefits of the currency so attractive that people want to use it for their daily business.

- Regular social events and trade fairs help people to form relationships and trust.

- A circulation incentive (also called hoarding fee or demurrage) makes the currency lose a small part of its value over time – the same effect as inflation but voluntarily chosen.

- Expiry dates for vouchers and notes.

We need to design regional currencies with all of these features to counterbalance the destructive nature of interest on money. Interest constantly shifts wealth from the 'have-nots' to the 'haves' and creates pathological pressure for economic growth through environmental destruction.

The good news is that we now have enough knowledge from worldwide experience to design more viable systems. In Part Two, Chapter 6, we describe some key design processes.

Co-operation with financial institutions

Should a regional currency be supported by local or regional financial institutions? BerkShares in the USA and Chiemgauer in Germany have both flourished with the support of local banks. It is an open question as to whether a regional currency in the UK could form an effective partnership with local branches of large national banks. The Brixton Pound is working with the large London Mutual Credit Union. It tends to be local bankers, rather than branches of big banks, that see the benefits in such an approach.

Regional currency initiatives in Germany, France and Italy actively link the public, private and third sectors, creating strong regional cross-sectoral networks and partnerships. The Italian Banca Etica and the French Groupe Credit Co-opératif decided to support regional currencies by providing the necessary financial guarantees and know-how as part of their commitment to the social economy. Within Europe, there is a tendency towards stricter rules for credit lines and financing by mainstream banks. Third sector and small to medium-size enterprises, which primarily instigate and maintain regional currency circuits and profit from them, feel the negative effects of this development in particular. Mainstream banks do not regard non-profit service providers as being especially attractive, or reliable enough, because of the kind of activities in which they are involved. To meet this demand for capital on the part of the non-profits and smaller companies, solutions in the form of credit unions, mutual guarantee funds and micro-credit organisations are re-emerging. A fully fledged regional currency system with its three components – a cash substitute (vouchers or smart cards), a mutual credit accounting system and a community bank, – presents a number of synergistic advantages. Regional currencies provide capital for new businesses and contribute to the economic and social revitalisation of a region by:

- Providing cheaper loans to regional and local businesses through a backup-fund.

- Providing local capital at a local cost – using either regional currency or the national currency – via mutual credit unions in which regional companies deposit their profits, making them available as credit for others (solidarity principle).

- Providing credit lines in business-to-business barter systems for start-ups.

- Providing fully backed-up financing, in the form of either existing assets or collateral (in case of a barter transaction).

Credit issued in a regional currency is not only cheaper, but it also strengthens the network of regionally active businesses and organisations. Accepting payment in regional credit money is a statement of solidarity towards a newly created business.

Fiscal aspects of regional currencies

Should regional currency transactions be taxed? If they should be taxed, in which currency should the tax be paid? One of the main arguments in favour of not taxing is that if regional currencies help to solve social problems that would otherwise require funding from taxation, its contribution should be included when assessing appropriate taxation levels. If the reduced public expenditure is more than the income that can be raised by taxing the transactions, then all parties involved – including the revenue authorities – would find non-taxation more advantageous. This was one of the arguments used to persuade the US Internal Revenue Service to allow all Time Dollar turnover in Time Banks to go untaxed.

Regional currency used for commercial transactions and professional services are subject to normal taxation. At the moment national tax is payable in national currency on these local currency transactions. If the authorities want to encourage regional currencies, so that their full potential can be realised, the most effective way of doing this would be to accept them in payment of specific taxes. In Talente Tauschkreis (p.126) in Austria it is now possible to pay local taxes in local currency, which is a great stride forward towards wider acceptability and use of the currency.

There are several reasons why support for a regional currency is in the best interests of regional authorities:

- The income generating local taxes produces benefits for public services in the area.

- In this way regional employment opportunities can be maintained or created.

- The positive social and economic effects of the increased value creation in the region allow for savings in public expenditure (unemployment benefits, for instance).

- The stimulating effect on the regional economy leads to a general increase in tax revenue.

If complete freedom from taxation of regional currency transactions appears impractical, unacceptable or unjustified, then there is still room for a *middle way*. For instance, in view of the fact that the taxation of trivial amounts costs more than the revenue realised, it would make sense to refrain from taxing income below a certain limit, e.g. 1000 Regios or its equivalent in euros. This is, indeed, how income arising through use of the French complementary SEL currency is treated by the French tax authorities. Alternatively, businesspeople could be permitted to pay a certain percentage of the taxes due in the regional currency.

Local and regional authorities would be wise to treat a regional currency in their area of influence not as a nuisance or as an exotic but otherwise meaningless phenomenon, but rather as if it were the goose that laid the golden egg – i.e. as something very well worth protecting and fostering.

Regional currency activists and promoters need to cultivate the conviction that their valuable and highly beneficial 'product' requires no apologies or diffident treatment. This will give them the confidence to present the case for a regional currency in a positive, transparent and persuasive manner – especially useful in dealing with politicians and civil servants.

Clearing systems

Before we look in detail at the challenges of creating stand-alone, resilient regional currency systems in Part Two, we need to mention that, once a local system is established, demand often arises for inter-trade with other systems. In our original 2004 book we discussed possibilities for establishing a 'clearing house' function to deal with exchanges between regional currencies. Since that time, new systems have emerged that show how this can be done in practice.

The South African based Community Exchange System (www.ces.org.za) began as a single Local Exchange Trading System (LETS) in 2003 and has since grown into the world's only international clearing system for mutual credit systems, hosting 395 local systems in 43 countries by April 2012.

The za:rt platform (www.zart.org) offers a combined marketplace and clearing system for regional currencies in the German speaking countries of Austria, Germany and Switzerland. Eighteen local systems were registered in April 2012.

German and Austrian exchange rings have also developed their own clearing platform: Ressourcen-Tauschring (RTR). (www.tauschen-ohne-geld.de/ressourcen-tauschring-rtr)

Other more visionary approaches aiming to enable future global trading between multiple types of system include:
Meta-Currency Project – http://metacurrency.org;
Open Money – http://p2pfoundation.net/Open_Money;
Ripple – http://ripple-project.org

PART TWO
REGIONAL CURRENCIES IN PRACTICE

Part Two examines the practice of regional currencies.

5. A global community of practice
A sketch of regional currencies around the world.

6. How to implement a regional currency
The key elements of effective design processes.

7. The people and their systems – portraits of regional currencies
Some of the world's leading regional currencies, based on interviews with organisers.

8. Research, develop, support – the role of agencies
Many local currency systems received a helping hand from support agencies. Interviews with the leaders of these key organisations to reveal what challenges they face.

9. Learning from practice – the power of regional currencies
Highlighting the power of local currencies to support and create positive change.

10. Future Positive
The most promising trends and some recommendations for action.

Chapter 5
A global community of practice

We should not have to dodge and compensate for an inadequate financial system by devising ... supplementary exchange mediums. We should not have to go scurrying around printing tokens, calculating and administering a secondary exchange network at considerable personal effort.
Michael Rowbotham, *Grip of Death* [1]

People running local currencies have been scurrying around for decades trying to make up for the deficits of Bank Money: working thousands of unpaid hours; running meetings, events and trainings; networking, arguing, persuading, lobbying; resolving conflicts; maintaining databases; printing up cheques, notes and directories; laughing, crying, screaming.

Many individuals have burned themselves out trying. It is hard work. It is frustrating. It takes years of sustained effort to forge a system that lasts. But, when you take part in it and see it working – people helping themselves by using their skills and assets to meet others' needs, people growing through service, people achieving their goals and solving their problems together – it all feels very worthwhile.

In the above quotation, UK monetary reformer Michael Rowbotham is arguing for centralised reform of our broken national monetary systems; he thinks we should not have to run around making our own money. He, and many others, want to see Government Money issued debt-free, instead of Bank Money being lent at interest. But even if their campaign finally achieves its aims, we will still need People Money because, in a complex modern society, no government and its committees can calculate how much money each individual or community needs for their local exchanges with others. People Money creates a ready medium of exchange right where people need it: in their own community. It is of the people, by the people, for the people.

Of course, it is outrageous that ordinary citizens have to stand up and start their own money systems because the dominant money system is rigged against them. And yet people grow through the challenges. People engage in a learning process that the great Brazilian educator Paulo Freire once described

---

1   M. Rowbotham, *The Grip of Death*, (1998).

as 'conscientisation': their consciousness is raised through organising or participating in their own solutions. No government or corporation is going to do it for them; they are learning by doing. It is the story of a global community of practice, a vast learning community.

People Money is also coming of age. In its early years, the local currency movement came up against the natural boundaries of place, resources, social and economic realities and it played around with various strategies. As a teenager it tested how far it could break the rules and push the boundaries: it tried out wacky hairstyles, strange outfits and weird behaviours. It has learned a lot and is now poised to become part of the mainstream of adult life.

Learning from doing

Here are some of the lessons being learned around the world:

> It gets people thinking. Money is not a subject that people enjoy talking about because it is the place where dreams and reality collide. The realists say forget your dreams, the dreamers say reality is at fault; can we learn to measure the relationship between the two? Our currency is a credible rather than an incredible mechanism for a finance system.
>
> *Alex Walker, Eko, Findhorn, Scotland*

> Some people get frustrated with the new system and just ignore it. Others just glow about it because they have given and received so much help and it has transformed their personal lives.
>
> *Tim Jenkin, Community Exchange System, South Africa*

> People have learned the power of community action using local barter as a tool.
>
> *Will Ruddick, ECO-Pesa, Kenya*

> More people understand the problem of compound interest. People understand the relationship between economy and ecology better. You can have a big educational effect with a relatively small circulation of currency, and this may be the most important effect of a local currency.
>
> *Peter Krause-Keusemann, Coinstatt, Germany*

Is it a movement?

In Chapter 3, we saw that regional currency is actually a very old idea and that the increasing centralisation of money by central banks and governments put a stop to most local money issuance. The only exception is the Swiss WIR Bank (p.34), which has traded continuously since 1934.

Since the advent of personal computing power in the 1970s, local currencies have had a new lease of life. *Business exchange networks* have supported businesses to use their spare capacity in 'mutual credit' clearing circles, effectively turning unused inventory into currency for trade with other businesses. Many of these exchanges are beginning to include consumers. What began as an unregulated movement in the USA is now a global industry. The International Reciprocal Trade Association (IRTA) (p.197), one of the industry's leading trade bodies, estimates that over 400,000 companies worldwide use trade exchanges to share their excess business capacities and underperforming assets to earn an estimated $12 billion dollars in previously lost and wasted revenues.[2]

Local Exchange Trading Systems (LETS) (called *Tauschring* in Germany and *SEL* in France) and *Time Banks* have supported communities to mobilise their underused assets since the early 1980s. Estimates vary widely as to how many active systems there are or how much turnover they have.

Regio currencies have taken off in Germany since the first system, the Bremer Roland, launched in 2001. The German Regional Money Association (p.207) keeps up-to-date figures of active systems.

Transition currencies are at the core of the Transition Movement. The launch of the Totnes Pound in 2006 inspired other small towns, like Lewes and Stroud, to create their own currencies. The Brixton Pound (p.122) is the first local currency backed by national currency to be launched in an urban setting in the UK.

Business-to-business exchanges inhabit a very different world from Time Banks or LETS, which are also different from Transition currencies, but all of them follow the same impulse: to re-energise local communities and/or economies using a local medium of exchange. Each model has the potential to start small in one locality and grow to serve a whole region.

---

2 http://www.irta.com/

People Money is a great idea that works – when it is organised properly. For newcomers to local and regional currencies, the variety of practice can be a daunting jungle, with many competing theories and dogmas about the 'right' way to do things: e.g. mutual credit or backed by national currency; record all trades in a database or use printed circulating currency only; circulation incentive (demurrage) or not.

Like all movements for social change, not everyone agrees about everything but they are moving in similar directions: business exchange systems are reaching out to include citizens and local government, community-based systems are becoming more professional in their management, and many are experimenting with internet and mobile technology. You will find representatives from all types of local currency systems taking part in the same internet discussions.[3]

Why do people start them?

There are a variety of reasons why people start the process of creating a regional currency. These might include:

- Wanting to test their theories about alternative forms of money.

- Wanting to improve life in their community.

- Wanting access to help from others.

- Wanting to prepare a lifeboat for their community in case of financial tsunamis.

- A vision of a more compassionate, convivial world.

My best bet for the future is in a society that works. My personal good is only possible within the framework of the common good.
Tim Reeves, Regional Economic Communities, Munich, Germany

We were intrigued by the idea of making good use of peoples' time and skills.
Hayden McGrail, Wairarapa LETS, New Zealand

The money system is like someone swinging a knife around and injuring people. The status quo does not relieve our worst problems, it is always Band Aid on the wounds, it never gets to the source.
Phil Stevens, LOAVES Project, Ashurst, New Zealand

---

3   e.g. CC Collective Skype Conference: http://www.lietaer.com/2010/09/the-cc-open-collective/

I was inspired by the phrase 'We have what we need if we use what we have' from the Time Banking movement. Since the earthquake I've noticed that the biggest hindrance to moving forwards is in our heads. Since then people can see that we need each other, that the systems we have are not working. There is far more 'we' thinking.

Margaret Jefferies, Project Lyttleton, New Zealand

It was an Elton John song that started it: 'To survive you need a meal ticket, To stay alive you need a meal ticket'.

Alex Walker, Eko, Findhorn, Scotland

We wanted to convert donor funding into something that would stay longer to benefit the target community.

Will Ruddick, ECO-Pesa, Kenya

We wanted to create a currency to bring people and nature together.

Peter Krause-Keusemann, Coinstatt, Germany

I heard about it on the radio. I thought 'That's it!'

Frank Jansky, Urstromtaler, Germany

Where are they?

A map showing where the emerging regional currencies are in one country – Germany – is available at: www.regiogeld.de/initiativen.html

This map shows all types of local currency around the world: http://complementarycurrency.org/ccDatabase/maps/worldmap.php

Africa

For thousands of years native Africans supported themselves through gift economies and reciprocal exchanges. Europeans introduced national currencies in the 19th Century in order to increase their control of local economies and the effect was to destroy local self-reliance. Now, in the early 21st Century, experiments with local currencies are underway to counter the dependency on national currencies: Eco-Pesa in Kenya (p.191) and the Community Exchange System in South Africa (p.174).

America (Central & South)

Central and South America have a strong tradition of 'solidarity economy' – mutual self-help rather than charitable assistance or paternal control – based on old native traditions. Many local and regional currencies have emerged from this movement and we feature portraits of puntoTRANSACCIONES in El Salvador (p.117), Banco Palmas in Brazil (p.24) and various systems in Argentina.

America (North)

Native Americans created interdependence through trade and used currencies like wampum beads and tobacco for hundreds of years. Colonial scrip currency helped the early European settlers reduce their dependency on Britain before the American Revolution, but this was regulated after US Independence and the creation of a Central Bank. Local 'emergency' currencies were issued in 1932/33 but were all outlawed by President Roosevelt (p.51).

Business exchange networks – like Community Connect Trade (p.107) – have developed since the 1960s and Time Banks – like Dane County Time Bank (p.180) – since the 1980s. Other models include Ithaca HOURS (p.150), Equal Dollars (p.132) and BerkShares (p.138).

Canada is home to the original Local Exchange Trading System (LETS) and Community Way (p.186), Calgary and Toronto Dollars, and Salt Spring Island Dollars – a currency for tourists.

Asia

Asia is a term introduced by Europeans to describe everywhere east of Istanbul! With 60% of the world's population, this continent includes the completely diverse cultures of Japan, India, China, Malaysia, Korea, Burma, Thailand, Vietnam and Sri Lanka.

Japan experienced a boom of experiments in local currencies between 1999 and 2003 but there are now very few working systems.[4]

China's centralised political system has made such local experiments impossible, although the old communist system of 'work points' that flourished from the 1950s to the 1970s was effectively a local currency system for rewarding local labour:

> The system of work points gave enormous flexibility for making use of labour power in a whole range of productive activities over and above that required seasonally for agriculture. People got their work points, and

---

4   M. Hirota, 'What have Complementary Currencies in Japan really achieved?', *International Journal of Community Currencies Research.*
See online at www.ijccr.net/IJCCR/2011_%2815%29_files/05%20Hirota.pdf

therefore their share of their co-operative's output and income at the end of the year, whatever activity they were engaged in. Such activities included building new infrastructure, schools, health centres, and the establishment of various village industries, such as equipment manufacture and repair, fertiliser production, and other value-added and diversification activities. The system enabled some really gigantic projects, such as the construction of the Red Flag Canal in Linxian (now Linzhou township).[5]

India has had a handful of local currencies, including a new experiment linking pedal power to SunMoney (p.191).

South Korea experimented with local currencies in the wake of its 1998 financial crisis, including the high profile Hanbat LETS.

Cambodian Buddhist monks started some small scale LETS.[6]

Australasia

Like other native cultures, the Aboriginals of Australia and the Maori of New Zealand have long-established traditions of mutual help that form a background to modern experiments with local currencies.

In Australia the most popular form of currency is the Local Exchange Trading System (LETS)[7], introduced in the late 1980s. The school based Maia Maia Project (p.190) helps people to reduce CO_2 emissions.

New Zealand has LETS, Time Banks and new initiatives backed by national currency: such as Wairarapa LETS, Lyttleton Time Bank and LOAVES Project.

Europe

Europe's rural communities also preserve kinship and favours networks which are an unconscious model for modern local currencies.

Austria: Talente Tauschkreis, Vorarlberg (p.126) and a national network of exchange rings.

Belgium: RES (p.112), Torekes and many LETS.

---

5 J. Jones, 'On the System of Work Points that Operated in China between the mid-1950s and late-1970s, (unpublished paper).

6 www.catuddisa-sangha.org/english_outline.html

7 Australian LETS site http://www.lets.org.au/

England: LETS, Time Banks, and Transition Town currencies (Totnes, Lewes, Brixton (p.122), Kidderminster, Bristol).

France: 400 SEL (exchange rings) and 9 regional SOL currencies, e.g. SOL Violette (p.150).

Germany: National network of exchange rings; Regiogeld (regional currencies) such as Bremen, Chiemgauer (p.144) and Sterntaler.

Greece: local exchange rings emerging since the euro crisis.

Scotland: The Business Exchange (p.102).

Wales: Blaengarw Time Centre (p.168).

Chapter 6
How to implement a regional currency

In theory, there is no difference between theory and practice;
in practice, there is.
Yogi Berra, baseball coach

Local currency is one of those great ideas that many people fall in love with. But what happens when the honeymoon with the idea is over and the real work begins? What makes the difference between a short outing and an expedition to the mountains?

Over recent decades, thousands of communities around the world have tried to launch local currencies. Some of them, like BerkShares (p.138), Banco Palmas (p.24) or Chiemgauer (p.144), have received a lot of media attention because the whole idea of a local currency in a mono-currency world intrigues people and these pioneers in their covered wagons have staked out new territory. Some systems travel a long way then slow down because of a change of driver, like Ithaca HOURS (p.150). Others putter along with small numbers of participants, sometimes for many years. Many other systems crash before they have left the garage. Local currency remains a radical idea to most people and if the first attempt fails it may take a long time to gather support for a re-launch.

Learning from a currency that failed

A group of citizens in the prosperous city of Stuttgart, Germany, started developing a regional currency called the Rössle in 2007 (www.roessle-regional.de). By the beginning of 2011, they had 53 businesses, 263 consumers and 13 voluntary associations registered. But the everyday reality was that only a few members actively used the currency. Some people remained members because they supported the idea in principle but never traded. After many efforts by the organisers to get new members, they finally gave up their attempt to establish a regional currency at the end of 2011. One of the core group explained what she thinks happened:

> The Rössle Project suffers from four illnesses: first, the core group is burned out and greatly reduced and we have definitely also made mistakes; secondly, we haven't reached a critical mass of users; thirdly, the awareness that a local currency is something good has not yet arisen in this rich city; finally, distances between users in the city are too great – in other words the participating businesses are too spread out from each other, which drives transaction costs up.

None of these 'illnesses' is unique to this group but they are, along with cost recovery, governance and management issues, typical of the many systems that fail.

However, by analysing successful examples and failed initiatives, we now understand the key development processes and internal dynamics necessary to create viable systems that last.

Whether you are a local government authority, a group of businesses or citizens exploring the idea, similar principles apply. Introducing a new currency to a region is always a development process within a community. In all new currency systems, the company or group of citizens starting it needs to sell their idea. Business barter systems use techniques of marketing and persuasion to engage businesses to participate within that community of users. A local authority or group of ordinary people has a different selling task: to persuade other members of their community that a regional currency will enhance social and economic life for a broad range of people.

This process of developing a community of interest should always come first and remain first throughout the design process.

The currency mechanism serves the goals of the users and not the other way round:

community development + currency design = sustainable system

Development process

There are many different ways to develop and introduce a local currency. We offer the following simplified process as a starting point for your own ideas. There are five key phases, arranged into the mnemonic ORDER.[1]

O = Ownership: initiate the process; form a steering group; gather allies; form working groups; agree goals.

R = Research: find out about all the design features available and critically evaluate the pros and cons of each option.

D = Design: choose design options that fit your goals.

E = Engage: launch and run the currency and find out from experience what works (often different from theory!).

R = Review: evaluate everything regularly, redesign or tweak.

---

1 The ORDER process was developed by John Rogers for consulting and training purposes: www.valueforpeople.co.uk

The Ownership phase begins a process of community development that will engage people with the idea.

The Research phase is when specialist working groups critically evaluate all the existing design options for a local currency.

In the Design phase the key group owning the process makes design choices that fit the stated goals and appoint people to key positions ready for launch and engagement with the public.

The Engage and Review phases test all systems agreed in the Design process.

The Ownership phase should always start the process to ensure a sound basis for the other phases. Once the core groups, the allies, the vision and the goals have been agreed, the other phases begin to be addressed – but none of the phases are self-contained and separate, and they should continually feed and influence each other. Ownership lasts as long as the system lasts, Research will continue during the Design and Engage phases in order to feed into the Review phase, which may begin a new cycle of Ownership, Research, Design and Engage.

Many local currency groups get so caught up in the process of Design that they skip Ownership and even Research. One person might impose their ideal design on others, with little knowledge and without inspiring people with a clear vision or agreeing any overall goals. This is a big mistake and a common cause of failure. We need more methodology and less ideology.

ORDER PROCESS

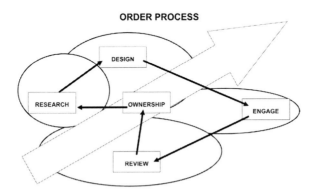

This design cycle - Ownership – Research – Design – Engage – Review – is an upward spiral. The more we learn from practice, the more it feeds back into theory and new design possibilities, which steers new practice and so on.

Complex system

A currency is a complex human-created system, like a school, an airport or a symphony orchestra. It is not as predictable in its behaviour as a bridge or a computer, which have mechanisms that are engineered to perform in certain ways under controlled conditions. Currencies involve connections, relationships and dynamics between human and mechanical elements: the users, managers and mechanism.

We may understand the necessary complexities and relationships around a local currency better by using an analogy to visualise its various interacting elements – the dynamics of running a bus company.

Get on board

Starting a regional currency is like creating a bus service.

The regional currency bus promises to transport people to where they want to go – away from their problems and towards their goals. Each passenger gets on the bus at a different stop and has a different destination, but they do not travel alone because the bus is full of other people with the same intention. It is a collective journey.

So, who builds and maintains the bus, runs the bus company, prints the timetables and tickets, hires the drivers and provides a good service to the passengers?

Models of ownership – who can start it and how long does it take?

The person or group initiating the Ownership phase invites others to join them in building the bus. They may simply be visionary entrepreneurs who inspire people to get on board with the idea and then leave, or they may still be running the bus company decades later.

In a sense it does not matter whether a regional currency is started by businesses, individuals or local government. Local authorities will have more legal hurdles to jump, businesses will need to integrate dual accounting into their daily practice and citizens will need to develop co-operative forms of working with good strategies for conflict resolution. The main challenges will be similar:

- Cost recovery to sustain the system.
- Effective management.
- Sound governance.

Some initiatives develop too fast, others develop too slow: some get carried away by this amazing idea and build a bus without any real planning that soon crashes; others spend years exploring every possible bus design and never launch because they lose the energy and enthusiasm that they started with. In some situations it may be better to start experimenting with real people sooner to get feedback on what works; in others it may be better to take much longer to get the details of the design right and enough people on board to make it work. A typical timescale for going from Ownership through Research and Design to Engage is two to three years. But, there are exceptions: BerkShares (p.138) took 25 years from its first experiments with micro-loans to the launch of a currency!

The Ownership phase is about finding out who is for or against the idea, what problems a currency might help solve without causing new ones, and what goals it might achieve. In this phase you gather allies, identify potential opposition and look for support.

The Amoeba Game.[2,3] was developed by Alan Atkisson to teach people how innovations get introduced into society. It is a great way to see which characters in your community accept, embrace, promote or block change. We have adapted it to help groups understand the process of introducing a new currency.[4]

Strengthening regional identity and prosperity is an evolutionary process and introducing a regional currency can be a key catalyst. Part of the new regional identity will include a sense of 'emancipation' from old views and convictions along with future oriented dialogue.

Local and global change keeps accelerating. Everyone in the working groups involved in the development process of a regional currency goes through a steep learning curve. Our deep-rooted beliefs, values and feelings around money are challenged; the ideas may be so new that we need time to process these new understandings. This can be the most difficult phase of the development process, when people air their economic dogmas and ideologies or try to push these onto others. A well-known model describes the key stages of group dynamics: Forming, Storming, Norming and Performing. Facilitators of the development process need to work carefully to allow for these dynamics to play out, without unproductive conflict. There are many group techniques[5] that can

---

2 Amoeba Game, www.context.org/ICLIB/IC28/AtKisson.htm

3 Innovation Diffusion Theory, http://en.wikipedia.org/wiki/Innovation_diffusion

4 The Currency Game, www.valueforpeople.co.uk/currencygame

5 Participation methods, www.peopleandparticipation.net/display/Methods/browse+methods

be used to support the process, including Future Conference, Scenario Planning, Simulation Games, Open Space, World Café, Art of Hosting.[6]

If enthusiasm starts to wane – and economics and currency design can become a very dry and dull subject – add some juice! Use your imagination! Tell stories, play games, explore the adventure playground of metaphor. You can have great fun inventing new ways of describing a currency: 'it is like... blood circulating around the body of our community... an immune system against attack... a sheltered garden to grow endangered plants...'

Group dynamics

Researching the routes and destinations – the key economic and social players

A 'currency' is a key element in the system called economy. During the research phase, it is very important to agree on what we are talking about when we focus on regional economy. The following questions need in-depth research and detailed answers:

- What makes up the regional economy?

- Who are the key players?

- What kind of economic relationships do they have with each other?

- What are their supply chains?

- What underused assets are there?

- What unmet needs are there?

---

6 Art of Hosting, www.artofhosting.org/home/

So, an effective research process begins with thinking about the regional economy as a dynamic system in which key social and economic actors are at work, rather than first focusing on the currency mechanism itself. Who are these 'players' and how will they use a currency? And which design will be flexible enough to meet their needs without losing touch with the principles on which it is founded?

There are a variety of models that can meet the needs of a regional economy but in different ways. The simplest local currency systems involve business-to-business exchanges, e.g. The Business Exchange (p.102), or individuals exchanging favours with each other, e.g. Dane County Time Bank (p.180). Some of the strongest local currencies have successfully involved businesses, individuals and voluntary associations, e.g. BerkShares (p.138), Chiemgauer (p.144). The most advanced systems also bring in a fourth player – local government, e.g. Banco Palmas (p.24) or Talente Tauschkreis (p.126) and people can now pay local taxes in local currency.

These 'players' can help us to develop a simple design language for talking about the users of local currencies, so that we can better understand how the currency might be used in practice. We divide them into two categories: individuals and groups.

A = Individuals: citizens, employees and consumers.

Groups are of three main types:

B = Businesses; **C = Voluntary Associations**; **D = Government Bodies**.

There is, potentially, a broad range of dynamics between these four 'players' in the local economy. Each player can do exchanges with a player of a similar type: A to A, B to B, C to C, D to D. Or they can trade with a player of another type: A to B, A to C, A to D, etc.

Take one example: B to C, business to voluntary association exchange. Businesses make donations to voluntary groups of their choice, say a sports club or a charity. C to B is a different exchange dynamic: voluntary associations spend local currency in participating businesses. (For a good example of this dynamic see the Chiemgauer p.144).

There are also hybrid players, for example, individuals running businesses as sole traders or voluntary associations running businesses as social enterprises. The purpose of simplifying the players is to see the main types at work and how they interact with each other. We have developed a game to help designers and participants in local currencies to explore these dynamics.[7]

Designing the bus – choosing the currency mechanism

A healthy community development process is essential to develop ownership of the system that emerges but, in itself, it will not produce a viable currency system.

Many people want to set up a local currency so quickly that they grab the first design they see. They look at a smart Greyhound bus over there and say 'We can really go places, we want one of those!' when in fact what they need is a minibus for ferrying a few people around the neighbourhood. Or they look at an old clapped-out bus that is really expensive on fuel and cannot be retrofitted to drive long distances efficiently.

Research and Design should naturally flow from the Ownership process. A core steering group appoints specialist working groups to evaluate the different models of local currency and the range of design features available to arrive at a working design.

In Chapter 4 we described three common elements of local currencies that have produced robust systems: circulating notes, the exchange ring and the micro-credit bank.

You need to research each of these elements in turn and find out what challenges of management and governance each one brings up in practice.

" A clear case of blood vessel deflation... only a circulation incentive can help."

---

7 Exchange PLUS, http://valueforpeople.co.uk/exchangegame

There are many decisions to be made when you design your local currency:

- **How will currency be *issued*?**
  - * *Mutual credit* – issued by each person when they trade, every transaction recorded on software.
  - * *'Local-backed fiat'* – issued by some local body (business, community association, co-operative, local government) as circulating currency backed by goods, services, rewards or national currency.[8]
- **How will it *circulate*?**
  - * Do we need a broker to set up trades and manage currency 'hotspots' and 'coldspots' to keep it moving?
  - * Do we need a circulation incentive (demurrage)?
- **How will it *retire*?**
  - * Is it a mutual credit mechanism with currency issued and retired in zero sum balance?
  - * Is it a local backed fiat mechanism exchangeable for national currency or rewards?
  - * Is it a printed circulating currency with expiry dates?

Creating a bus company – formalising ownership and governance

Many passengers just want a bus that turns up on time and takes them where they want to be. They do not care who runs it. Others really take an interest in how the bus company is managed, what the drivers are like, what routes the buses travel and whether they are safe.

Somebody has to take strategic decisions about the local currency to ensure its long-term development. This requires appropriate structures and processes. Ideally, the correct form of governance should emerge naturally from the Ownership and Research phases.

Business-to-business exchange networks are often run as privately owned businesses so the governance is in the hands of the owners, although some are developing more co-operative structures with shared governance.

---

8 We use the term 'local backed fiat' as a catch-all to include all non mutual credit systems with circulating currencies. They are all 'fiat' systems in that the currency is issued by some kind of local 'authority' that guarantees the validity of the currency and in many cases backs the currency, e.g. Ithaca HOURS issues currency against future purchasing power of local goods and services; Blaengarw Time Centre issues time credits for community service exchangeable for various 'rewards'; Brixton Pound, BerkShares and Chiemgauer issue currency that businesses may exchange back into national currency.

Most citizen led systems also use a variety of non-profit mechanisms, depending on the laws of their country: co-operatives, incorporated associations, charities, community interest companies and social enterprises. Large non-profits like Resources for Human Development in Philadelphia (p.132) simply integrate the currency into their existing governance and management structures, which brings many advantages, such as reducing duplication and waste.

Whatever particular legal form is chosen, the human dynamics of governance will be like those in the Ownership phase and need to be well facilitated using similar tools. One tool that co-operatives have found very useful for gaining insight into such processes is the Viable Systems Model, which views a human organisation from a systems point of view.[9]

Hiring the drivers and servicing the passengers – management of the currency

Even when they are not run *as* businesses, local currencies need to be run *like* businesses: efficiently, professionally, responsibly.

They need to hire good managers, who balance maintenance of the mechanism with maintenance of relationships and networks. The managers may be full-time, part-time, paid in national and/or local currency – the point is that they give good service at all times.

The ideal system is one in which the users of the currency do as much of their own administration as possible.

Here are some of the key tasks for managers, depending on the system design:

- Community development.
- Recruiting new participants.
- Brokering trades.
- Membership services.
- Maintaining databases.
- Designing and printing notes or vouchers.
- Local currency accounts.
- National currency accounts.
- PR.
- Marketing.

---

9   Viable Systems Model, www.esrad.org.uk/resources/vsmg_3/screen.php?page=home

- Social event organising.
- Training for participants.
- Monitoring & evaluation.

In Chapter 7 we will learn about the habits of the planners, designers and organisers of local currencies and interview people running 14 successful currencies.

Keeping the bus on the road – recovering costs

Many systems crash because they do not recover their own *start-up costs* and *running costs*. A sound cost recovery model can evolve during the development phases, but who funds the development phase? Developing a new currency takes time and many people, driven by high ideals, have put in large numbers of hours to create new systems. This depends on peoples' goodwill and ability to work in their 'free time', which is not always reliable. Whoever starts the development process will need to gather allies and look for all kinds of support: rooms to meet in, finance for travel expenses and phone bills, etc.

A common solution that gives the currency a strong base to work from is to integrate it into an existing organisation where financing is already in place. Equal Dollars in Philadelphia (p.132) was integrated into a well-established human services organisation, and Blaengarw Time Centre (p.168) was started by the pre-existing Creation Development Trust. Regional authorities could do the same or commission a local voluntary organisation to manage it.

Another solution is to find private start-up capital, which can shorten the development process, but may create inappropriate pressure for the system itself to 'make money' to pay back the loan.

Strong financial support at the start has several advantages:

- It makes it easier to reach critical mass and a broad market more quickly.

- High profile support of important voluntary organisations, businesses and local authorities inspires more confidence than a currency issued by a small group of enthusiasts and accepted in only a few shops at first.

- Project initiators can expect to receive recognition of their work in the form of 'normal' payment more quickly. This may give volunteers reassurance to continue their work.

What if the currency fails as soon as the start-up capital runs out? Walther Smets's entire sales team at RES in Belgium walked out after a week and his backer panicked. Walther had to hit the streets and talk to hundreds of businesses personally to salvage his great idea and turn it into a success. This is why the Research and Design phases are so critical – to play out different scenarios and anticipate potential problems.

Once the bus is on the road, running costs become the critical factor. The ideal is to reduce central costs to an absolute minimum. Members administering their own accounts via the internet helps to speed up this process. Wise organisers do not depend on one source for income; they create a mix of revenue from membership and transaction fees, grants, advertising, income from events, donations, sponsorship and sales.

Telling people about the service – marketing

It is no use designing a great bus service if nobody knows about it. Some systems are lucky; they get great media coverage and do not have to spend on marketing. Systems like BerkShares (p.138) or Brixton Pound (p.122) that print attractive notes have an advantage because well designed notes in themselves attract attention from the public and the media. Other groups, especially those with no circulating currency, have to find ways to reach their target groups through existing local and online networks, collaborating with public and voluntary sector bodies, using time limited vouchers, taster evenings, training days, social events, talks and whatever radio, TV or newspaper coverage they can attract. Local newspaper stories are a particularly good way of reaching new people with the idea.

Summary of Development phases

By the end of the Development phase you should expect to have:

- Currency mechanism.

- Cost recovery model.

- Management structure and key job descriptions.

- Appropriate governance model.

- Marketing strategy: a suitable name and the beginnings of a corporate identity.

- Training needs assessment and plans to recruit 'multipliers' who will publicise and explain the concept throughout the region.

- Map of local resources and needs (see below – When to launch?).

- Map of other projects in the regional and social economy, which are complementary to the regional currency and could work together.

- Project presentation portfolio for decision makers and multipliers.

When to launch?

One of the important lessons is about timing the introduction of a regional currency. Many systems launch with a few people and struggle for years to attract enough participants. It can be a lot of hard work for little return. Some newer systems are learning from this and delaying launch until they reach a critical mass of participants. What is the right number? It is not wise to be prescriptive about this because local circumstances vary so much but our experience of new currencies shows that there is a better chance of success if you have, say, 100 businesses, 500 individuals and 50 voluntary organisations signed up to give the system a chance to hit the ground running at launch. The early adopters will then sell the idea to others.

The key principle is that there should be variety: a good mix of businesses, consumers and voluntary associations; a range of goods and services in different categories; a variety of locations handy for people to get to.

An exciting possibility emerging from new technology is 'crowd-mapping': you invite individuals and groups to sign up and ask them to list their offers (underused assets and resources) and their needs; they all appear on a map on a website so that potential participants can see the variety literally growing before their eyes during the development phases. This all helps build momentum towards reaching an agreed critical mass ready for launch. After launch you can consolidate and expand on this base. Good use of the press and media with some good stories can all enhance take-up at the start.

Remember to review

It is the aim of a regional currency, however small in relation to national currencies, to bring about lasting social and economic changes locally. The success of the currency must be judged on its ability to meet this challenge.

Monitoring and review processes need to be built in from the start, not as an after-thought. They serve two audiences: internally – the participants themselves; externally – the general public, non-participants and decision makers.

Web technology makes it very easy to perform surveys and accumulate metrics of different kinds. The steering group will need to decide what it wants to measure. The quantity of exchanges, amount of transactions and annual turnover are typical measures. But you may also want to know more about the quality of transactions or the general culture – Are people happy? How many social events are happening? Is there more music, art, crafts, theatre and storytelling going on? Are citizens protecting and enhancing their local environment?

Inviting formal research by universities also helps build the case for regional currencies in the minds of policy makers and officials.

Ways in which the system itself can be developed, as time and resources allow, include the introduction of electronic payment and accounting systems, the establishment of a regional micro-credit fund and on-going professionalisation of the administration. Regional financial management services, networking with local financial institutions and the establishment of clearing houses for communication with other regional currencies can follow. On the other hand, if it is possible to engage the support of a well-respected local financial service provider right from the start, this could inspire confidence in the viability of the currency.

Now it is time to meet the organisers.

Chapter 7
The people and their money –
portraits of regional currencies

Who starts them?

In the last chapter, we saw the importance of design, governance and management. We discovered that people are as important as mechanisms in creating a system that lasts.

Richard Logie in Scotland, Annette Riggs and Amy Kirschner in the USA and Walther Smets in Belgium are all business people who see the advantages of a local currency to small and medium enterprises; Stephanie Rearick in the USA and Margaret Jefferies in New Zealand are community organisers who intuitively grasp the power of Time Banking to weave community networks and keep the fabric of society intact; Peter Krause-Keusemann in Germany, Alex Walker in Scotland and Will Ruddick in Kenya are 'Greens' who grasp the power of local money to motivate people to protect and enhance their local environment; Paul Glover in the USA and Tim Jenkin in South Africa are seasoned political activists who realise that local money is a primary tool for social and economic justice.

These business owners, community activists and campaigners are all practical radicals who have learned to play the long game of system change through the patient work of organising, networking, persuading, learning from mistakes and improving. From completely diverse starting points, these utopian realists are converging on similar solutions that embrace sound systems and procedures and the most appropriate technology to do the job.

The many habits of highly effective local money organisers

What is the difference between local organisers who succeed in creating sustainable systems over many years and those who lose momentum after the initial enthusiasm and idealism have worn off?

Although the portraits featured later in this chapter are based on interviews with individual leaders, all effective local currencies depend on organising teams with a good mix of skills.

The common habits practised by individual organisers and leadership teams are:

They articulate values
Advertisers never sell us products these days, they sell us values wrapped up in goods and services: 'Just do it'; 'The power to be your best'; 'Because I'm worth it'.

Local currency organisers know that people are motivated by values. Edgar Cahn, inventor of Time Banking, used four core values that continue to inspire the global movement:

- We treat people as assets.

- We value all contributions to community as real work.

- We practise both give and take or reciprocity.

- We grow our social networks.

The regional currency movement in Germany inspires its members with messages about loyalty to their region, buying locally and creating 'money with legs' that circulates faster and brings more benefits.

They commit themselves to change
Some organisers have remained involved in their local system for twenty years; they are willing to go through all the ups and downs because they are committed to social and economic change.

They focus on goals
A local currency is never an end in itself; it is a means to grow the local economy or weave community networks.

Effective organisers support local people to identify their everyday needs and to reach personal and collective goals; they create a currency system to realise them. They review the goals in the light of experience and redesign the system, if necessary.

They share the work
Many people have burned themselves out by trying to run a local currency system alone. It doesn't work. Even full-time networkers, like Paul Glover, gather others around them to share the load. In the Talente Tauschkreis Vorarlberg in Austria, which has been operational since 1996, a volunteer 25-person service team shares the tasks of running the system.

They sell benefits

No business sells features or philosophy, they sell values and benefits.

They channel abundance

The primary purpose of a local currency is to connect underused resources to unmet needs – those resources and needs that the money economy ignores.

Local organisers take three steps to identify the resources and get them moving:

1. Analyse where the resources are:

personal skills – professional skills, hobbies and general help or favours
community resources – underused halls, vehicles, rooms, photocopiers
business assets – underused inventory, 'low' times, services
local authority assets – underused leisure centres, theatres.

2. Advertise the resources:

People fill out questionnaires describing the goods and services they can offer and agree to the information being advertised in printed and online directories.

3. Broker the resources:

Many systems offer an extra brokering service to connect resources and needs because it helps people to overcome their initial fears, get to know people and get trading.

They make maps

Expressing values, goals, benefits and assets are all types of map making. These activities help people to orientate both *internally* (Why are we doing this? What's the purpose?) and *externally* (Where are we going? How do we get there?).

Physical maps can be very valuable: the most clicked page on the German Regiogeld website is the map showing where all the regional currencies are.

Online mapping tools are now making it possible to view real time data about local systems around the world and it will soon be possible to include data about resources and needs and begin to connect them much more powerfully.

They network

Networks are the blood vessels of social and professional life. Successful networking is the ability to tap into existing networks, create new ones and keep them alive.

They integrate into existing structures

It is tough running a local currency as a stand-alone operation. It takes people, time and money. If there are existing structures in the community it makes sense to integrate a local currency into them. This brings many benefits both to the host organisation and to the currency itself:

- Governance and management of the currency are integrated into the host structure, saving costs.

- The host has a new mechanism for generating involvement in social and economic activities and rewarding volunteers.

- They can conduct their marketing jointly.

The only danger might be association of the currency with one particular organisation rather than as a generic mechanism for the whole community but this depends on local circumstances and scale.

They keep a balance

There are many balances to be kept in running a local currency:

- Personal balance between life and work: many currency organisers are deeply committed to what they do and need to look after themselves too.

- Balance between maintaining the community and maintaining the mechanism: you have to develop co-operative structures and processes to maintain the community and develop good monitoring systems to maintain the mechanism.

- Ideally, a local currency serves all sectors of the community: it is good to ensure that individuals, businesses, voluntary organisations and government agencies can all meet on the common playing field of the currency.

They flow with emergence

Nobody has all the answers on day one. New possibilities emerge with new members, new ideas, new funding sources, and new technology.

They innovate carefully

Innovation for its own sake is just fashion; it soon passes. Careful innovation means evaluating the costs and benefits of any proposed change and selling it to the potential users. The unceasing pace of technological change means that organisers have to keep themselves informed about new possibilities and judge which innovations might help them to improve service, reduce administration and make life easier for everyone.

Established systems learn from their mistakes and to practise patience and persistence for the long haul. They manage the growth of the system by choosing next steps carefully, making sure they have the capacity to handle enquiries and new membership applications and service existing members.

They challenge people to grow

Participation in a local currency teaches you to take responsibility for your transactions with others on every level: socially, emotionally and technically. Organisers help participants to grow by encouraging them both to give and to receive and make opportunities for them to do so. They also encourage people to do as much of their own administration as possible and not to become dependent on central organisers.

They simplify what can be simplified

Albert Einstein advised us to 'keep things as simple as possible and no simpler'. Organisers aim to simplify the system's design, administration and management, user interfaces, explanations and messages about the currency.

They work with limits

Organisers work within the limits of geography, participation levels and the currency mechanism they have designed or inherited. They keep currency moving as much as possible within these limits.

They model best practice

Organisers show people how to use the currency by trading in it! They model the values the currency embodies by engaging in reciprocity and local exchange.

They implement common standards

Some 'brands' of local currency are more advanced as a result of decades of trial and error. Time Banks subscribe to the common set of values promoted by Time Banks UK and Time Banks USA; Regio systems in Germany sign up to the quality criteria set out by the national Regiogeld Association; business exchange networks can voluntarily subscribe to the common standards laid out by the International Reciprocal Trade Association.

They use appropriate technology
Every locality or region is different. Some places have distinct geographical features or strong historical traditions that inspire people to create circulating notes with great designs that build local loyalty and are collectable by tourists. Others embrace the latest electronic technology of swipe cards and mobile payment systems. Some use both. The point is to analyse local conditions carefully and use the most appropriate technology for the groups of users.

They manage internal relationships
Many systems fall apart through internal conflicts – e.g. personality clashes, different values and organisational styles. Organisers manage internal relationships through transparent decision making and communications.

They manage external relationships
A regional currency is, potentially, an important element of local life. Organisers keep good public relations with the business, voluntary and public sectors, and with the press and media.

A simplified typology of regional currencies

Several people have attempted to produce a comprehensive classification of non-national currencies.[1,2] It is notoriously difficult to produce a satisfactory system that includes all known cases in one schema.

For the purpose of the following portraits, we introduce four simplified categories to show the *main purpose* and the *core mechanism* used by different types of system.

Most systems start out with a *main purpose*: to *support the local economy* or to *grow community*. Many achieve both whilst remaining focused on their primary aim.

Supporting local economy includes stimulating both established and new local businesses through business-to-business and business-to-consumer exchanges in local currency.

1   e.g. J. Blanc, 'Classifying "CCs": Community, complementary and local currencies' types and generations' in *International Journal of Community Currencies Research.* Online at
    http://www.ijccr.net/IJCCR/2011_%2815%29_files/02%20Blanc.pdf

2   e.g. J. A. Martignoni, 'New Approach to a Typology of Complementary Currencies'. Online at
    http://www.ijccr.net/IJCCR/2012_%2816%29_files/IJCCR%202012%20Martignoni.pdf

Growing community means using a local currency to stimulate neighbour-to-neighbour exchanges, form new community groups and encourage people to volunteer for activities that benefit the whole community.

Most systems begin with a *core mechanism*: either *mutual credit* – where each trader issues credit to others when they trade in a mutual credit clearing circle; or *local backed fiat* – where a local 'authority' issues the currency and backs or guarantees its value with goods and services, rewards, future energy consumption or national currency (for an exchange fee).

The following symbols show the combination of purpose and mechanism with examples of different systems that demonstrate these characteristics. Squares support economy, circles grow community. Empty squares and circles use the mutual credit mechanism, filled shapes use local backed fiat.

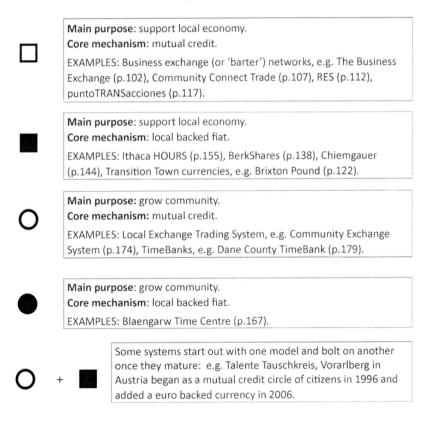

Main purpose: support local economy.
Core mechanism: mutual credit.

EXAMPLES: Business exchange (or 'barter') networks, e.g. The Business Exchange (p.102), Community Connect Trade (p.107), RES (p.112), puntoTRANSacciones (p.117).

Main purpose: support local economy.
Core mechanism: local backed fiat.

EXAMPLES: Ithaca HOURS (p.155), BerkShares (p.138), Chiemgauer (p.144), Transition Town currencies, e.g. Brixton Pound (p.122).

Main purpose: grow community.
Core mechanism: mutual credit.

EXAMPLES: Local Exchange Trading System, e.g. Community Exchange System (p.174), TimeBanks, e.g. Dane County TimeBank (p.179).

Main purpose: grow community.
Core mechanism: local backed fiat.

EXAMPLES: Blaengarw Time Centre (p.167).

O + ■ Some systems start out with one model and bolt on another once they mature: e.g. Talente Tauschkreis, Vorarlberg in Austria began as a mutual credit circle of citizens in 1996 and added a euro backed currency in 2006.

Interviews with local organisers

The next section features portraits of leading systems from around the world, based on interviews with organisers and ordered under the following broad headings:

- *Currencies that support local economy*

  Business exchange systems
  Examples of primarily business-to-business, expanding to business-to-consumer.

  Other local economic models
  A range of other economic-focused models.

- *Currencies that grow community*

  Time Banks
  Local neighbour-to-neighbour exchanges based on the hour standard.

  Time Centres
  Local citizen-to-community exchanges based on the hour standard.

- *Sectoral currencies*

- *Other regional models*

Currencies that support local economy – Business Exchange Systems

Like the WIR Bank we met in Chapter 2, business exchange systems (also called business barter networks) create a platform for businesses to turn their spare capacity into currency for trade with other businesses and to move towards 100% capacity. Some of them are beginning to involve consumers in their economic circuits.

All business exchange systems use the mutual credit clearing mechanism.

The primary focus of this type of system is to foster economic exchanges. Secondary effects may include the growth of community.

We meet the organisers of four of these exchanges:

☐ **The Business Exchange, Scotland**

☐ **Community Connect Trade, USA**

☐ **RES, Belgium**

☐ **puntoTRANSacciones, El Salvador**

Key:

☐ **Main Purpose:** to support local economy.
   Core Mechanism: mutual credit.

The Business Exchange, Scotland

Based on an interview with Richard Logie.

KEY FEATURES

TYPE: Business Exchange Network   **DATE FOUNDED:** 1995

REGION SERVED: Aberdeen and Scotland

MAIN PURPOSE: Support local economy

BENEFITS: Mobilises spare business capacity; makes money go further

PARTICIPANTS: 200 businesses; consumers

CORE MECHANISMS: Membership based; mutual credit 'currency' created by clearing positive and negative balances between members when they trade; backed by promise to supply local goods and services; all transactions recorded; active brokering of trades; own GETS web based software system - both a trade 'bank' and a marketplace; smart cards and mobile banking; trade in IRTA's 'Universal Currency' with 100 other exchanges worldwide; no printed circulating currency

CURRENCY NAME/STANDARD OF VALUE: One Trade Credit = one UK Pound

TURNOVER: NOT DECLARED

GOVERNANCE: Limited Liability Company moving towards Mutual Society

MANAGEMENT: Two owner-managers plus sales team

COST RECOVERY: Membership and transaction fees

WEBSITE: http://www.tbex.com/

Aberdeen is known as the Oil Capital of Europe. Ever since oil and gas reserves were discovered under the North Sea in the mid 20th Century, it has been a boomtown. The energy industry supports half a million jobs in the local economy. One night in July 1988, the Piper Alpha oil rig exploded, killing 167 men. It is remembered as one of the worst offshore oil disasters and Aberdeen was deeply affected by the tragedy.

Richard Logie, founder of The Business Exchange, remembers the effect on the local community:

> After the first shock, people started asking questions. How could this happen? What went wrong? They wanted answers. A government enquiry identified many monitoring and management failures leading to the disaster and new international standards were put in place to try and prevent future incidents.

While the oil industry was being regulated, the financial industry was being progressively deregulated. All over Britain, century old mutual building societies were being privatised and sold off. Companies were maximising profit through outsourcing and asset stripping – owning nothing, leasing everything. Richard could not understand why the financial system was selling everything off. It all seemed such a waste.

Then he heard about business barter exchanges. Businesses have always directly exchanged services for services but an organised system allows third party 'bartering'. Most businesses are operating at less than 100% of their potential business capacity. The barter exchange seemed to offer a sensible alternative to the waste of 'turbo capitalism' by connecting underused assets and business capacity with unmet needs.

So, Richard and his partner Linda started The Business Exchange in 1995. People told them it was easy money, they would soon become millionaires and spend the rest of their lives on the beach!

They discovered that barter exchanges had a reputation as an unregulated industry. People were setting up exchanges, raiding the till to meet their own needs and then disappearing. One person set up seven systems in a row. Things were so bad they feared that legislators would close the industry down.

Business exchanges are mutual credit clearing circles. That means that the currency – 'trade credits' – is issued by traders when they trade. So, when an exchange begins, some businesses go into debit and others go into credit immediately. This requires a lot of trust that people will not default on their debts.

Richard and Linda made mistakes and learned through hard experience how to win the trust of their members:

> We knew nothing about business. I thought it was just about making deals. In the beginning we were grateful that anyone joined because they helped our business grow. One company ran up lots of debits in the exchange, went out of business, set up a new company the next day and wanted to rejoin the exchange. We took it personally. We learned to protect our currency.

Another key lesson was to attract larger, well established businesses into the network and to encourage them to buy spare capacity from others first. This strategy creates confidence in the circulating trade credits.

All businesses joining The Business Exchange must fill out a credit line agreement, put up security to join the network and establish a positive trading history of selling before they are issued credit lines. Since implementing these procedures the exchange has only had two defaulters. It has also set up a bad debt reserve, funded through a 1% fee on all transactions.

The exchange puts a magnifying glass over the business culture:

> At the time we started, it was dog eat dog, members were ripping each other off but we eventually filtered them out. Everyone realises how important local reputation is; once you are a member of an exchange, you are in it together.

Richard relates his experience of growing up in a small village in the Highlands of Scotland:

> Technically we were poor, but we always had stuff. My dad was a Jack of all trades, he was always doing jobs for other people and I learned that if I did favours for others, I got things. I did all kinds of jobs – servicing cars, cutting logs, anything. Sometimes you winged it but you knew that you were valuable to the community. I bartered at school all the time, always trading up. The most important things were reputation and trust. I'm a talker, a salesman but I still have to back it up with quality service if I want to work for someone again.

While Richard is out selling, Linda makes sure that the backup systems work – this is a common division of labour in the business exchange industry. When they started The Business Exchange, Richard was working in the financial sector and Linda in the oil industry. Their own experiences with business barter confirmed to them the importance of common quality standards: the ISO 9002 international standard for quality assurance in production, installation and servicing would later form the basis of their 450 page manual for running a business exchange.

A barter exchange acts as both broker and bank. Each member pays an annual fee in national currency that gives them an account for debiting and crediting purchases and sales with other members. The common unit of account, the 'trade credit', ensures a common standard of value and overcomes the uncertainties of direct barter. It is an attractive option for businesses wishing to maximise their existing investments, keep their operating costs down and find new customers.

It is also a great social club. People make long-term friendships and become more locally responsible because they see that ethical business is a web of relationships and obligations. The Business Exchange flourished, attracting over 200 business members from all over Scotland.

They made a good living but Richard was not happy. He realised that the impact of local exchange systems on the economy and society was still marginal, with a high failure rate. They seemed to promise so much but deliver so little for the effort involved. They were not game-changing. He wanted more:

> When we started out, we thought we were creating a barter company. Now I realise we were in the currency creation game. And that is a serious business. If you create a currency that people rely on to do their business, you had better treat it seriously and teach others to respect it too. I love going to local markets, wherever I am in the world. You don't get a deal if you are nasty to people, only if you are charming. Every transaction is a relationship. Currencies are relationship systems.

> In a mutual credit clearing circle every trader is potentially an issuer of currency and so we should know who you are, how long you have been in the community, what is the quality of your work and your reputation. Local currency is the ultimate two-way loyalty programme.

> Local currency users need to be brand loyalists: to use it regularly and recommend it to others. 99% of our new members are referrals from existing members. The first member of our exchange in 1995, the owner of a local 5 star hotel, is still totally loyal. In a recent meeting with the chief executive of Aberdeen City Council he said, 'I wouldn't even buy a teaspoon without looking at the Exchange first.' In business, cash flow is king and the Exchange had a major effect on his cash flow because he could buy essential services with trade credits and put his available cash to better uses.

Running a barter exchange also teaches you a lot about local economics:

> I never studied economics but, as the years went on, I realised that we were running a small economy. Instead of the mythical trickle-down economics in which the poor are supposed to benefit from the economic activities of the rich, we are creating trickle-up economics by creating our own wealth together. There are two types of people in the economy: predators and producers. We aim to encourage more local producers. And the key to supporting producers is brokering: you aim to help them reach as near to 100% business capacity as possible by matching their underused capacity with the needs of others. Running an exchange means you can do things no other business can do. You ask what people have got and what they need and bring them together to improve everyone's cash flow.

But if so many local exchange systems fail, what can you do about it? Were there any inspiring models to learn from?

Look at Europe. It had two World Wars and then said enough! So it created the European Union to ensure better relations between the countries of Europe. Or look at the credit card industry in America in the late 1960s. It was in chaos. Then along came VISA, a voluntary agreement between credit card companies to create a common platform worldwide. Our own experiences with the exchange are now part of our DNA and we realised it's about agreeing to common standards and using the best technology available.

Richard believes strongly that the de-mutualisation he witnessed in the 1980s was a bad thing and that we can return to mutualism by creating peer-to-peer financial systems with good governance. So they created the Global Exchange Trading System (GETS), which is both a philosophy and a system. GETS is based on the same principles as the European Union and VISA. It creates standards through agreement to a common set of rules. Over 30 exchanges worldwide are using the GETS combination of software, systems and procedures, governance and anti-corruption features and it is capable of running all sizes of exchange, from a local community-based system to a very large business-to-business system:

When you are running the bank, it is always a temptation to give yourself credit. Transparency is essential. No transactions can be deleted from the software, a full audit trail is guaranteed. We only ever spend what we earn.

What keeps Richard motivated?

My father died in 2008 and it got me thinking about legacy. What will our grandchildren say about this generation? That they left us drowning in financial and environmental debts? Or will they say that we realised our errors and created systems that helped them to survive and thrive?

Up to now The Business Exchange has only facilitated business-to-business exchanges but with GETS we now have the potential to create a real regional currency that can be used by consumers and employees as well. Eventually we hope to include voluntary organisations and local government as participating traders too.

Another critical future step is that we will give up ownership of The Business Exchange. We hope it will become a mutual society, jointly owned between local businesses. It will have an ownership structure based on the VISA model of Participants, Associates and Principals.

Maybe Richard and Linda will finally retire to the beach like they were promised all those years ago.

COMMUNITY CONNECT TRADE ASSOCIATION, USA

Based on an interview with Annette Riggs.

KEY FEATURES

TYPE: Business Exchange Network   **DATE FOUNDED:** 2008

REGION SERVED: Denver/Boulder area of Colorado, USA

MAIN PURPOSE: Support local economy

BENEFITS: Mobilises spare business capacity; makes money go further

PARTICIPANTS: 400 businesses; consumers; voluntary organisations

CORE MECHANISMS: Membership based; mutual credit 'currency' created by clearing positive and negative balances between members when they trade; backed by promise to supply local goods and services; all transactions recorded; active brokering of trades; web based software system - both a trade 'bank' and a marketplace; smart cards and mobile banking; trade in IRTA's 'Universal Currency' with 100 other exchanges worldwide; no printed circulating currency.

NAME OF CURRENCY/ STANDARD OF VALUE: One Trade Credit = one US Dollar

TURNOVER: NOT DECLARED

GOVERNANCE: Limited Liability Company moving towards Co-operative

MANAGEMENT: Manager plus sales team

COST RECOVERY: Membership and transaction fees

WEBSITE: www.communityconnecttrade.com

Annette Riggs is a veteran of the Modern Trade and Barter Industry. She got her first job as a trade broker at the age of 20 and learned quickly through hands-on experience.

There are four main types of business barter systems:

- *Retail trade exchange* – localised business-to-business systems offering their own currency to participants, often networked for 'inter-exchange' commerce.

- *Corporate barter companies*.

- *Media and niche trading* – often 'direct barter'.

- *Counter-trade* – country-to-country.

Annette gained experience in all types of systems over a 25-year period, both as a broker and an international consultant. She now heads up the Community Connect Trade Association serving the Denver/Boulder area of Colorado, USA.

When Annette started work as a trade broker, business-to-business trade exchanges were part of an unregulated, underground economy and, largely because they had no cash revenue to cover operations, many had created inflation in their own currency by running up deficits to cover their own expenses. All fees were paid in 'trade credits' so the operators commonly 'cash converted' goods out of their systems to raise cash needed to operate. Over time this created large deficits and the inevitable inflated currencies. There were many unhappy members and a lot of frustration over opportunities (or the lack of them) to spend and get value from their earned trade credits.

Annette later worked for a very different type of exchange, run by an ex banking executive, that had tight credit lines, no deficits and cash fees to cover operations:

> Very early on, I had these two opposite experiences: too much money supply over here produces inflation and discredits the currency; too little over here means people do not have enough medium of exchange to trade. It was my first real lesson in economics.

In the early 1980s, the US Internal Revenue Service (IRS) began to examine business exchanges. Industry insiders became concerned that they would be made illegal and at this time the International Reciprocal Trade Association (IRTA) lobbied the IRS to legalise the industry with a requirement only to report income. Many thought it would put trade exchanges out of business; they thought businesses would not participate if they had to report the income. The result was the opposite: the quality of businesses taking part was significantly raised because it legitimised the industry. It was no longer part of an 'underground' economy with the associated risks.

Around the time of the new tax reporting requirements passed by Congress as part of the *Tax Equity and Fiscal Responsibility Act of 1982 (TEFRA)*, a start-up business called ITEX began converting existing exchanges and guaranteed to transfer 'trade credits' earned in those systems. Annette was the first regional manager in San Diego, CA and began a steep learning curve:

> I thought the ITEX guarantee was a solution for businesses that were going to be left with trade credits that had no value due to the number of exchanges that were failing and could not meet the new requirements that Tefra established. I spent the first six months converting businesses from Barter Systems to ITEX so that they could receive value from their Barter Systems trade credits. Some gave up and took a loss. Many converted. It was very labour intensive and I eventually became concerned that ITEX was not standing by its promise to 'back with goods' the trade credits it was bringing

in from all the exchanges they were converting over (which was all debt). After a couple of years I moved on – ITEX still exists today but I was ready to learn more and moved into media and corporate barter.

She worked with Corporate Barter Companies and helped large companies to sell their spare capacity and/or inventory. Selling unsold inventory for 'trade credits' can be considerably preferable to liquidation at a huge loss.

By 1993, many large companies were putting trade credits on the books as assets just to look better to shareholders and increase their stock value. The Securities Exchange Commission then made a ruling that companies could only book credits they had spent (EITF 93-11); this was the opposite position to that of the IRS who wanted to know what had been earned. The result was greater transparency rather than 'smoke and mirrors', forcing them to prove the actual value of the trade credits by spending them.

Over the following years, Annette gained valuable experience by working with colleagues who were experts in international countertrade. She continued to be a consultant in retail and corporate barter systems.

By the late 1990s, she was looking to work with systems more in line with her personal and spiritual values and that could have a more positive effect on the world. She took a break from the industry and met with leaders of the complementary currency movement like Thomas Greco and Bernard Lietaer, who have challenged the Trade Industry to broaden its view of what it is and the effect it could have on the world economy.

In 1998, the dot-com boom hit California and Annette gained her first experience with venture capitalists. She was a founder and the first President of Barter.com. The business model combined the best of retail and corporate barter with an added layer designed to address social and local benefits that had not been considered before.

The venture capital companies had other ideas though. Often, they put in their own people (in some cases, young MBAs with no experience) and invested all of their resources into building web based technology and very little on the much needed marketing effort to build public awareness of the value of the exchange process:

> All of these dot-com barter companies failed. Many of them changed the business model to 'roll up' existing trade exchanges in order to show faster growth so they could reach their real goal of going public and getting a big payday. The industry has never recovered the peak it reached in the 90s.

> Some of the best independent exchanges were bought out and when the dot-com failed, exchanges that had been serving their communities for decades were lost. The massive amount of money that was invested did not bear fruit at that time.

There was much anxiety about survival and the money issue leading up to the year 2000 and the so-called Y2K problem (the fear that the date change had the potential to cause widespread chaos in computer systems). Out of many conversations, Annette gained a different awareness of the potential of local and private currencies to create substantial value on a social level:

> This cross-fertilisation was very creative for me. I was involved with the first Business Alliance for Living Local Economies (BALLE) conferences and the early stages of the 'buy local' movement. I started a non-profit called Current Innovations and worked as a consultant to local groups wanting to start community currencies. I shared what worked for businesses with activists and very passionate individuals but discovered a great disconnect between those who didn't understand the needs of businesses and the few businesses who were taking part in a local system out of goodwill rather than identifiable benefits for their business. In the local groups, there was not enough leadership with the right experience. After investing a great deal of time and effort, I felt like we weren't accomplishing enough and decided that a non-profit is not the best structure to use to make things happen for local currencies. They need to be self-sufficient in a short enough time period to avoid failure.

She was determined to overcome this disconnect between citizens and businesses and to create a business-to-business exchange integrated with the local community.

In 2008, she started the Community Connect Trade Association (CCTA) that now has 400 businesses serving the Denver/Boulder area of Colorado. Participants are encouraged to think of themselves as members rather than customers. The currency is made as simple as possible to use: 'trade credit' transactions can be recorded online or sent to the trade 'bank' accounting system via QR codes from smartphones or other readers. Businesses will also be able to use their trade credits as 'rebate points' for cash customers, extending the currency for use by citizens of the community. Loyalty points, rewards and rebates are generally non taxable; services to the community or charitable donations are tax deductible. CCTA aims to build a local currency without citizens having to understand the inner workings of it. They are just getting measurable and clear value from their daily transactions.

CCTA's goal for 2012 is to increase the membership substantially and roll out more community initiatives.

CCTA recognises that adoption is the biggest challenge and good governance and agreements are very important.

CCTA is becoming a big enough player in the local scene to deliver hundreds of businesses to an event; voluntary organisations currently get donations from member businesses and they could be big players as consumers in the future; local government involvement will happen when the system grows bigger; more collaboration with banks and credit unions will also help firmly embed the exchange in the local economy.

CCTA has a web based software system that acts as both a trade 'bank' and a marketplace. Members can also trade in IRTA's 'Universal Currency' with 100 other exchanges worldwide. Annette believes you should identify the *right* software system to match your needs. The 'best' technology doesn't make you successful.

CCTA operates as a Limited Liability Company; all members will have the option to become shareholders. In the future, CCTA hopes to evolve into a Co-operative to facilitate more collective decision making. It funds itself from dollar transaction fees.

Annette remains interested in all forms of innovation in private currencies and continues to consult on projects. She also serves on the global board of the International Reciprocal Trade Association (IRTA, p.197), drawing on her long experience in the industry to help develop guidelines and recommendations on various subjects such as ethics, deficit management, standards and governance.

How does Annette see the future?

> We have seen more interest in these systems in the last few years than ever before, because of the state of the world economy. There is a growing awareness, with many more people getting engaged to learn the fundamentals of what money is, how it's issued, taxation and banking systems in general.

> The level of innovation today is so vast, I believe that this sector will look completely different ten years from now. With peer-to-peer systems and currencies targeted for specific purposes evolving so quickly – economies in general may be turned in totally new directions.

RES, Belgium

Based on an interview with Walther Smets.

KEY FEATURES

TYPE: Business Exchange Network   **DATE FOUNDED:**1995

REGION SERVED: Belgium

MAIN PURPOSE: Support local economy

BENEFITS: Mobilises spare business capacity; makes money go further

PARTICIPANTS: 5,000 businesses; 100,000 consumers; voluntary organisations

CORE MECHANISMS: Membership based; mutual credit 'currency' created by clearing positive and negative balances between members when they trade; backed by promise to supply local goods and services; all transactions recorded; active brokering of trades; web based software system - both a trade 'bank' and a marketplace; RES cards with pin numbers, phone and mobile banking; no printed circulating currency

NAME OF CURRENCY/ STANDARD OF VALUE: One RES = one Euro

TURNOVER: 2011 trade volume: 35 million Euro equivalent; working budget: 3.5 million Euro.

GOVERNANCE: Co-operative Company with A, B and C shareholders

MANAGEMENT: 21 full-time staff

COST RECOVERY: Membership and transaction fees

WEBSITE: http://res.be

Very few of the 5,000 businesses and 100,000 consumers using Belgium's most successful regional currency system know the meaning of the word RES, but they certainly experience its benefits every day.

Walther Smets is a serial entrepreneur with business in his blood. He started RES almost by accident:

> I was a local businessman in Leuven, the main university city near Brussels. For 15 years I ran several successful local restaurants, all of which I sold for a profit. Then I decided to go into the designer furniture business. It was a big mistake and I lost all the money that I had made before. I had lots of visitors but no buyers. It was more like a museum than a shop. Everything was too expensive.

> One day a guy came into the large 2000 square metre showroom. He wanted to buy big combinations but not pay in money. He was the son of a famous editor and offered me media space in return for furniture. I took the offer. It was not enough to save the business but it sowed the seed of an idea in me, which gave me my later success.

I lost my house, had debts and three small children to feed. I took a year to think about what to do with the rest of my life.

It was 1995, the beginning of the internet in Belgium.

It should have been easy for me to open a restaurant but I wanted to do something else. Then I saw a report on TV about a saleswoman in the Amazon selling Avon products all on barter. No money. It reminded me of my own experience in the furniture shop. I woke my wife up in the middle of the night and said all our problems are solved! I saw it clearly before me. I would create a system without money and make a living. We would use the internet to connect people.

So I created a system whose main goal was to protect small businesses and help them to do transactions without the banks, without money. That is still the goal today. Avoid the banks.

I was completely convinced and wanted to do it professionally. I had very good lawyers who researched this new currency idea. They gave me great advice and told me to create a co-operative company in which all the merchants are shareholders. There are two main reasons: if you create a currency you need to make sure it only circulates in a closed circuit amongst shareholders to avoid legal problems; the co-operative lets you sign up participants easily, it is the only form of company that allows that.

When the project was ready on paper, I visited a wealthy friend and asked for a loan to the value of 250,000 euro.

Half of the loan financed an office, documentation and software. The other half was invested in a sales team of 20 people to sign up merchants.

The first disaster happened almost immediately. The sales team all quit after a week. They hadn't signed up one business. The investor started to panic. I was sitting in my office all alone with a big debt and a system. My wife and others said I was completely crazy but a voice inside me said it would work. I was convinced I was right because the idea is so simple. I just needed to persuade the market.

I started to play the missionary. I would convince people one by one. Leuven is a small university city of 40,000 people and I know a lot of people. I put pressure on small retail businesses of all kinds: florists, barbers, food retailers, etc. I persuaded 300 businesses to sign up in the first year.

The name RES emerged in a brainstorming session with a consultant after rejecting 150 other names.

He said 'Res'. I said 'That's it!' I just knew it was right. RES means 'business' or 'interest' in Latin. Res Publica means 'public interest'. It became our brand.

> At this stage I was still not aware of other systems in the world. Then I
> began to search the internet and found the term 'barter system'. Ah, so
> I am not alone! I am not crazy! I've found my family! I was pulling out
> information day and night. I started travelling to Australia, Canada, wherever
> people were running barter systems. I was hungry to learn. I discovered the
> WIR Bank in Switzerland and the US barter industry.

Armed with this new knowledge, Walther started to adjust his system and build
in business rules that had worked elsewhere. He calls this the first development
phase. The second phase was between 1997 and 2001. He studied currency
functionality, financial systems and Bernard Lietaer's *Future of Money*. He
made a conscious decision to run a local currency rather than a barter system
because he did not agree with the philosophy of the barter industry. He stuck
to his original idea: a co-operative company to benefit small businesses, not a
system to help big chains.

RES has always focused on recruiting upmarket businesses that respected the
rules and were trustworthy. They check each business thoroughly before it is
admitted.

> For instance, we only sign up restaurants that are already successful or
> stable. We don't want people just to offer a spare table at the back: we are
> not selling leftovers but premium steak!

The basic model for RES is the WIR Bank's business-to-business system. They
also added a business-to-consumer loyalty system and consumer-to-consumer
transactions in 2003. The consumer saves RES points to buy at a discount inside
the network. They have 5,000 businesses and 100,000 consumers, 80% in the
Flemish speaking areas, 20% in the French speaking region.

One RES = one euro. This is vital to create confidence and ease of pricing.
Although it ties RES to inflation in the national currency, people don't worry
about this inflation yet. It is always possible to float free from the euro if the
circumstances are right.

RES has gone through several brand variations: it began simply as 'RES', then
'RES Barter System', then 'RES the complementary currency' and its new
brand for 2012 is 'RES. More Money!'.

RES is structured as a co-operative company with three types of share:
main founding shares, 100% owned by Walther Smets; each participating
merchant buys a B share, worth 1 euro, for legal registration on the system;

B shareholders are eligible to buy C shares costing 2,500 euros each, with a maximum of 10 shares per member.

This was another lesson learned from the WIR Bank. B shareholders become much more active members when they can also buy shares and invest in the development of the company. So far 120 C shareholders have raised 350,000 euro working capital. They elect members to the RES Advisory Board who bring great ideas to the table. This system allows RES to raise capital inside its own system and C shareholders also get commercial advantages such as a Gold Card with flexible credit lines.

RES takes its legal status seriously and uses it to bolster its credibility with the public. They have fought several court cases against businesses with persistent negative balances that did not trade positively. They wanted to build up a series of test cases and have won every case.

A few years ago the Belgium Bank Commission started asking questions because RES was calling itself a currency. The Commission decided it could not make a ruling because RES was not trading in euros and passed the case to the Ministry of Finance, which deals with tax controls. There were long negotiations with lawyers and the Ministry. In 2007, the state officially accepted RES as a complementary currency in Belgium with detailed agreements about how to do the accounts and internal controls. It cost RES 450,000 euros to get this agreement but they calculate it will be worth far more than that in the future.

But there was more to come:

> In 2009 we got an unbelievable breakthrough. I sponsor a popular TV quiz show watched by many people. As a prize I gave a prepaid RES card with 2,000 euro value. Two lawyers from the Bank Commission who both had RES loyalty cards were watching the show. The next day they called me for a meeting and I went with my own lawyers expecting the worst. But sometimes things happen in a normal way without a fight!

> The Bank Commission gave us a light bank authorisation with limits. This means we are allowed to sell RES currency to consumers for cash. We give them 10% to motivate them to buy into our network. We have payment cards and online banking so we are technically like a bank. We are obliged to publish our figures so third parties have access. We have nothing to hide.

RES has 21 full-time staff – with offices around Belgium. Its goal is to recruit 20,000 merchants and 250,000 users by 2017.

The RES Business model:

- Free signup for consumers who receive a RES loyalty card with 2.5 Res euro per year administration fee.

- Individuals can only buy RES with euros but then trade with other consumers or businesses using RES cards with pin numbers, phone and mobile banking.

- Free signup for merchants, who pay 6% commission on transactions, decreasing to 3.5% after 10,000 RES of sales.

- Guarantee fund for debt provision.

- Annual external audit published in yearly reports to create transparency and confidence.

What is the key message of RES?

The finance crisis has focused people on problems in the money system and potential alternatives. People want transparency and flexibility. Our most important word is CONFIDENCE. We persuade people to test the system by taking small steps and building up trust.

We have a push and pull strategy to engage people. So we pull them in with free membership and good deals then gently push them to use the currency as much as possible.

Up to now our user base has been mainly customers of upmarket businesses. Now we are experimenting with prepaid cards to allow us to reach a broader market.

Some people consider us as too commercial. They say we don't help ordinary people. But my message is that without a healthy small business sector we do not have a healthy community. I believe the main reason I lost my furniture business was because the banks took advantage of my failure to make a lot of money. They did not support me to create a healthy business.

But sometimes the prophet is without honour in his own country.

I get invited all over Europe to collaborate and present but not in Belgium. My main driver for the last 15 years has been to prove that I am not crazy. At least my wife is now convinced!

puntoTRANSacciones, El Salvador
Based on an interview with Koen de Beer.

KEY FEATURES

TYPE: Business Exchange Network   **DATE FOUNDED:** 2008

REGION SERVED: Mainly San Salvador

MAIN PURPOSE: Support local economy

BENEFITS: Mobilises spare business capacity; makes money go further

PARTICIPANTS: 300 businesses; consumers; voluntary organisations

CORE MECHANISMS: Membership based; mutual credit 'currency' created by clearing positive and negative balances between members when they trade; backed by promise to supply local goods and services; all transactions recorded; active brokering of trades; Stro's Cyclos software system - both a trade 'bank' and a marketplace; smart cards and mobile banking; no printed circulating currency

NAME OF CURRENCY/ STANDARD OF VALUE: One Point = one US Dollar

TURNOVER: Not declared

GOVERNANCE: Registered shareholder company of the non-profit Fusai Foundation

MANAGEMENT: 12 staff

COST RECOVERY: 70% membership and transaction fees plus 30% shareholder capital

WEBSITE: http://www.puntotransacciones.com

---

puntoTRANSacciones is an exchange network promoting transactions between member businesses and consumers in El Salvador. The small ads on the homepage advertise everything from pizza and espresso to cosmetics, motor services and orthopaedic surgery.

Koen de Beer is a Belgian who lost interest in economics because it was all about numbers rather than people. After a Masters degree in international development he became an expert in microfinance. When the Fusai Foundation and Stro (p.203) offered him a job to set up puntoTRANSacciones, he leapt at the chance to do something creative with local currency.

> Businesses had invested heavily in expanding their capacity. Then came the global economic crisis and these businesses lost a lot of trade. The network has helped its 300 business members to convert their unused capacity into profit and preserve jobs. Members can optimise their production capacity, access low-cost financing, and exchange goods and services. We make small business more sustainable in El Salvador.

Koen gave himself three months to see how it would work out. He is still managing the project four years later.

> You learn how long it takes to get things going. Traditional micro-enterprise development projects operate at a small scale. We were more ambitious. We wanted to create larger business circuits involving many small enterprises so that trade currency could circulate for a longer time through the network and businesses could earn more. It took us three years to sign up 300 enterprises in the capital city in a long educational process.

> It's not about the currency, it's about people and relationships, it's about changing business culture, getting people to eat in a local pizza restaurant rather than a chain.

> You have to coach individual businesses in how to give good service through the network. We try to create a club atmosphere for members, we invest in meetings and free lunches to build partnerships and alliances amongst small businesses. You have to get people trading quickly so they get into new habits.

> There are three distinct groups: first, the businesses that were in trouble are grateful for a loan and support, and use the network a lot; others see it as a game – it is not core to their business but it does not harm them and they get to know new people; then there is a group who hardly use it. You need strategies for each group, you have to invest time in convincing people – it's not about spending money on nice publicity campaigns. We stop advertising businesses that do not regularly trade within the exchange.

Restaurants get credit immediately because people like to eat. Network managers are much more careful about issuing credit to beauty shops and new businesses until they are established. On the other hand, some businesses are very conservative and only see the scheme as a savings account so are not willing to run negative balances.

Businesses and consumers may also buy Points for dollars at a 15% bonus. The network uses the incoming cash to buy computers and other products outside the network and sell to members at a small profit. Members who sell a lot can also get cash credits and they can pay off their loan with Points. All of this activity creates a dynamic trading network.

Some NGOs, mostly those working with children, are active trading members and get donations in Points, but managers are cautious about direct government involvement because of the potential for instability when the party in power changes.

Membership and transaction fees cover 70% of the network's running costs, including 12 staff. The other 30% of costs is covered by shareholder capital.

puntoTRANSacciones is a registered company with shareholders; the Fusai Foundation – a local non-profit to support socio-economic development in El Salvador – owns 50% of the shares. It elects a new board every 2 years.

The network is now well established amongst businesses and consumers.

> It has changed the minds of many people; they say I did not believe you could do business without cash but now I sell more. They like the transparency too; people with family accounts can see how members of their family spend credits. They are proud of it; they want us to have more publicity in the media.
>
> We have saved a few businesses based on our promise and now we want to reach 500 businesses and help more customers. We have to be proactive and identify what the network needs: more restaurants, more printing services, etc.
>
> In the near future we aim at partnerships with important local financial institutions to connect their clients with the small businesses associated with the network through an exchange of points.
>
> Embracing technology without leaving behind people who are established in their habits has to be carefully managed.
>
> We are introducing SMS payments, not for the sake of it, but because phonecalls to clients confirming transactions are expensive for us. The present system is easy for them so we have to introduce the technology slowly so people grow to accept it.

Stro (p.203) – the Dutch research and development agency – has played a critical role with financial and technological support, particularly with its Cyclos software.

Koen de Beer challenges himself and others to grow through the job and makes great use of the network himself.

> It's a difficult job and I have sometimes suffered but I never thought about quitting. Inspiring stories keep me motivated. I believe in people. We all grow through our experiences. When we started, I could not go on holiday – it would have fallen apart without me. Now I can go away for a week and people get on with it. Before this job, I did not know this country well. Now we spend more time with family because I have extra income to spend on travel or restaurants.

> Local currency has so many parts I like. It's not only about currency but about changing people's attitudes. So much can be improved but we do not do it; business can be done much more productively; we can value people rather than numbers. I have a vision of an abundant society. That's why I am still here after four years. I want to look back at the end of my life and say I did something differently.

Currencies that support local economy – other local economic models

Apart from business-to-business systems, other models support local economic development in different ways:

- Encouraging consumers to use high street businesses or village shops to keep the local economy alive: Brixton Pound; Talente Tauschkreis Vorarlberg; BerkShares; Chiemgauer; SOL Violette; Ithaca HOURS.

- Enabling a large non-profit organisation to integrate a currency to enhance its normal operations: Equal Dollars.

As with business exchange systems, the primary focus of these systems is to foster economic exchanges. Secondary effects may include the growth of community.

■ **Brixton Pound, England**

■ + O **Talente Tauschkreis Vorarlberg, Austria**

■ **Equal Dollars, USA**

■ **BerkShares, USA**

■ **Chiemgauer, Germany**

■ **SOL Violette, France**

■ **Ithaca HOURS, USA**

Argentine Stories

Key:

■ **Main purpose:** support local economy. **Core mechanism:** local backed fiat.

O **Main purpose:** grow community. **Core mechanism:** mutual credit.

BRIXTON POUND, ENGLAND

Based on an interview with Josh Ryan-Collins.

KEY FEATURES

TYPE: Circulating currency   **DATE FOUNDED:** 2009

REGION SERVED: Brixton, London, England

MAIN PURPOSE: Support local economy

BENEFITS: Mobilises spare business capacity; revitalises high street businesses; makes money go further

PARTICIPANTS: 200 businesses; consumers

CORE MECHANISMS: Local fiat backed by UK pounds; printed circulating currency designed by local artists with full security features; banking services with London Mutual Credit Union

NAME OF CURRENCY/ STANDARD OF VALUE: One Brixton Pound = One UK Pound

TURNOVER: 30,000 Brixton Pounds in circulation

GOVERNANCE: Brixton Pound Community Interest Company, a non-profit organisation

MANAGEMENT: Four part-time staff

COST RECOVERY: Sponsorship; funding

WEBSITE: http://brixtonpound.org

"We're changing Brixton from being infamous to being famous", beams Blacker Dread, owner of a popular independent record shop, who stars in the promotional video for the Brixton Pound (B£) in London.

It has taken the area a long time to throw off the violent image created by the riots of 1981. Now there is a new confidence, thanks to a circulating currency showing pictures of 'heroes' with a connection to Brixton, such as James Lovelock, Vincent van Gogh, David Bowie, Len Garrison (founder of the Black Cultural Archives), Violet Szabo (WWII spy), and Luol Deng (internationally famous basketball player).

'Money that sticks to Brixton': this promotional message for B£s has convinced 200 small businesses and local consumers to put 30,000 B£s into circulation. Notes are purchased 1:1 with sterling and there is no expiry date on the second edition. They are not legal tender and no business is obliged to accept them. There are no exchange or circulation fees. People are encouraged to ask for their change in B£s. A recent survey showed increased pride in the area and more awareness about shopping with independent local businesses.

Business sponsorship helps fund management of the currency. Independent businesses that are normally invisible off the high street get free marketing that helps them become more vibrant.

Brixton is a large village of 60,000 people at the heart of a great city. Its population is a lively multi-cultural mix with a good sprinkling of politically active 'bohemians' who want to challenge 'the system'. In 2008, a group of local people, allied with the emerging Transition Towns movement, decided to investigate the possibility of a local currency. Then the finance crisis gave their efforts a new urgency: businesses were closing and rents were rising rapidly. Brixton Pound is a classic case of concerned citizens impatient to find concrete solutions to global problems that play out at the local level: scarce money; peak oil; environmental degradation. They intuitively grasped that local money was a smart solution and they acted quickly to test the idea.

> We were keen to experiment and see what happens when you introduce a sterling backed local currency to a city borough – nobody had tried it before. Overall, we were surprised it worked so well.

Josh Ryan-Collins is senior researcher at the New Economics Foundation (nef) in London and a co-founder of the Brixton Pound. He studied sociology and economics, possibly a perfect combination for a local currency designer. Work at nef made him realise that money is not the neutral, value-free medium taught in economics. He saw the systemic effects of the money mechanism in social and environmental problems and wanted to try a money system with a different design.

> A group of us got inspired by the launch of the Lewes Pound in September 2008. Their currency looked fantastic and there was tremendous energy in the hall. We came home inspired and discussed different local currency models. We thought that a sterling backed currency would be more attractive to high street businesses.

The international media coverage at the launch of the Brixton Pound in September 2009 was estimated by the local council to be worth £100,000 in free advertising to the borough. The town centre director glowed: 'This is the best thing to happen to Brixton since the lighting up of Electric Avenue in 1880!'

Because they were in a hurry, both the community development and currency design processes were not as thorough as they might have been:

> On reflection, we could have spent more time talking to businesses and the
> local council before launch; we could have thought more about the model –
> it is not the optimal design. But the sterling backing does attract businesses
> and we are learning a lot from experience. It is a development process.
> People accept Brixton Pounds instead of money as normal for local trade
> now and that in turn opens up opportunities for more radical approaches like
> electronic payments.

The pilot e-currency was launched in September 2011 with 35 participating
businesses. Customers receive 11 B£s for every £10 they pay into an online
account: 10% extra spending power. They may 'Pay by Text' in any business
that accepts B£s: either party can send a text message with a PIN code to
confirm the transaction. They pay a 10% fee if they wish to change back to
sterling.

But the future usefulness of the currency is about more than advanced
technology:

> It should be more than a marketing stunt for businesses. We need to convince
> them of wider benefits to themselves and the community. We need to create
> more demand for the currency so that it really competes with money and
> helps keep wealth in the area. Ultimately, people should be able to pay their
> business rates and council tax with it.

Supply chains are key:

> We mapped the supply chains of local businesses a year after launch and
> discovered that lots of businesses source stuff from outside Brixton. We
> need to do more work on creating viable exchange circuits for them. One
> wholesaler thought the whole thing was a waste of time, with additional
> costs, but changed his mind after customer demand increased.

Voluntary organisations could also play a bigger role:

> Voluntary groups buy B£s at discount to cover expenses but we need more
> connection between businesses and voluntary organisations. One idea is an
> employment creation scheme placing people in small businesses.

Local authorities like Lambeth, which includes Brixton, are facing up to 30%
cuts in public services. This climate makes it even more difficult than usual
for them to innovate, but the Brixton Pound has the full support of the chief
executive and has been given grant-funding from the council as part of its
'Co-operative Council' policy approach. One option both Brixton Pound and
Lambeth council are considering is to extend the scheme across the whole
of Lambeth, which has land with local food production possibilities and a

population of 250,000 people. Brixton Pound is also keen to co-produce public services with citizens and it may be possible to reach a more sustainable scale for the local currency by partnering with Lambeth Council. The Council is also examining ways in which it might be able to accept the currency for local business taxes.

Brixton Pound is governed as a community interest company (CIC) with seven directors and run by a team of four paid employees, who work part-time to support the project. The funding has come from grants and business sponsorship. Brixton Pound CIC recently moved its sterling reserves out of a high street bank and into London Mutual Credit Union, which it sees as a key partner for the future. The Credit Union, which recently opened a branch in central Brixton, is co-operatively owned and makes low cost, ethical loans to local people on low incomes. These individuals often struggle to get bank accounts with the mainstream banks or pay exorbitant rates to Pay-Day-Loan operators.

As part of a continuing drive to professionalise and upscale, Brixton Pound has entered a partnership with the Dutch development agency QOIN (p.205), who have adapted the Open Source Cyclos software developed by Stro (p.203) and branded it as Community Currency 2.0 to run the mobile payments system.

Like many local currencies, Brixton Pound also faces paradoxes. Although it is primarily designed to help smaller independent businesses, its success may well have contributed to Brixton's trendy image and helped attract new national chain stores to the area. But the Brixton Pound CIC will continue to focus its efforts on strengthening local businesses and working with key stakeholders such as Lambeth Council and London Mutual Credit Union.

B£s have got past the gimmick stage and are now firmly part of local life:

> Once people get it, they love talking about their currency. They understand they can challenge the status quo and be proud of Brixton's independent spirit.

TALENTE TAUSCHKREIS VORARLBERG, AUSTRIA
Based on an interview with Gernot Jochum-Müller
with contributions from Rolf Schilling.

KEY FEATURES

TYPE: Exchange ring plus circulating currency   **DATE FOUNDED:** 1996

REGION SERVED: Vorarlberg, Austria

MAIN PURPOSE: Support local economy and grow community

BENEFITS: Revitalises village economies; makes money go further

PARTICIPANTS: 758 members, including organisations and companies

CORE MECHANISMS: Membership based; mutual credit 'currency' created by clearing positive and negative balances between members when they trade; backed by promise to supply local goods and services; all transactions recorded; active brokering of trades; Stro's Cyclos software system – both a trade 'bank' and a marketplace; additional printed circulating currency backed by Euros

NAME OF CURRENCY/STANDARD OF VALUE:
Exchange ring: 10 Talents = 1 Euro   **Circulating currency:** 1 Taler = 1 Euro

TURNOVER: 293,000 Talente in 2011

GOVERNANCE: Talente Tauschkreis Association and Talente Co-operative

MANAGEMENT: 25 person service team

COST RECOVERY: Membership and exchange fees

WEBSITE: www.talentiert.at

Vorarlberg has a reputation for being different. Bounded on three sides by other countries – Liechtenstein, Switzerland and Germany – it is the only region that claims to be both independent and a part of the Austrian state. In the early 20th Century, ordinary soldiers could choose their own officers. Now local people can choose their own currency for trade, known as Talente or the Z(w)EITgeld. Zweitgeld means the 'second money' and ZEIT means time, because people base their services on an hourly rate calculated in Talente.

In June 2011, Talente Tauschkreis Vorarlberg (Talent Exchange Circle) celebrated 15 years of continuous trading. At its core is a mutual credit system with a euro-backed currency as an additional option. A total of 758 members traded 293,000 Talentes in 2011, an average of 3,850 Talente per participant.

Gernot Jochum-Müller advises companies and non-profits and he uses this knowledge to guide the development of the Tauschkreis, one of Europe's most mature local currencies:

> People start local currencies for many different reasons: some people want to support products from the region; some want a better quality of life with more time to do the things they love; others want to support alternative economic forms or interest-free currencies. And many also want to find a community, to meet new people or make new friends. Really there is something for everyone in the idea. Which means a big opportunity and a big risk: a risk because it speaks to everyone but cannot really fulfil everyone's expectations; the opportunity is that a greater diversity of people have the chance to meet and complement each others' strengths. It is like an eco-social jigsaw with pieces of many different colours and shapes.
>
> We set ourselves a clear goal to sign up 30 members by the end of the first year. When we got 95 participants, we were greatly encouraged to continue our experiment. Since then we have always tried to strike a balance between attracting individuals and businesses into our circle. At the start we regularly had financial problems. One member of our first group financed the software we used to record exchanges and another gave us a large interest-free loan to get us through the first few years. We later paid it back.

After its early teething troubles, Talente Tauschkreis has evolved into a mature organisation, with an Association founded in 1996 as the basic legal structure. The members elect a new board and a 25-strong Service Team every couple of years. Nine local organisers lead the work in different parts of the Vorarlberg region. Each member of the team has a clearly defined role but also lots of freedom and encouragement to do what they like doing and they are given full responsibility over the way they choose to carry out their job. New team members get training and a copy of the organisational handbook describing all key tasks. The whole team meets up once every six weeks and spends a whole day together once a year. Members of the Service Team work 50% as volunteers and 50% for Talente. No-one is paid in euros and because there is no pressure to chase money to pay salaries they have had the freedom to let the system grow slowly, from 95 members in 1997 to the current 758, including organisations and companies.

> Many groups break up because of personality conflicts. We have learned from experience how important it is to go through conflicts rather than avoid them and to have good reflection time and good will on all sides. Many people starting local exchange systems come with a great deal of idealism: they want to work from the principle of consensus and avoid traditional hierarchical forms. This is very positive but at the same time it's not always

appropriate to involve everyone in every decision. Most ordinary members already find it a challenge to master an alternative kind of money system and only have enough energy to trade with each other and make new friendships. Only a few people are interested in the details of organising. We need to fit our organisational forms to the people not the other way round: any structure is only a means to an end and never an end in itself.

Offers and Wants are advertised on the website, in a monthly newsletter and a twice-yearly directory. There are lots of handicrafts, food products and tools on offer. Typically for an exchange ring, there are also many adverts for psychological and esoteric services but there are not so many exchanges in those categories. The recommended minimum hourly rate is 100 Talente per hour (=10 euro). Members then negotiate a price around this rate.

The most important thing is trust. If I buy a service someone is advertising, I ask first whether they have a good reputation in the exchange circle.

Membership fees are paid in euros and Talente to cover all costs. Members with no time to exchange may pay in euros only to support the system. Participants are legally obliged to pay tax on professional services offered in Talente but not informal exchanges.

The circle also acts as a small business incubator. A children's clothes designer held a fashion show amongst members and now has her own collection using locally produced materials. This is a very important symbol for a region that was home to Austria's largest textile producing company up until the 1970s.

In 2007, members were so impressed with the growth of Regio systems like the Chiemgauer (p. 144), that they decided to add euro-backed currency to bind purchasing power into the region. This began the second major phase of development which required a stronger legal structure, so they began the Talente Genossenschaft (Co-operative). The Co-operative is responsible for the administration of four circulating currencies: the Langenegger Talente serves one village; the Kloster Taler serves one valley; the Walser Thaler serves a national park; the VTaler can be used anywhere in the Vorarlberg region.

The village of Langenegg won the European prize for village renewal in 2010. One of the reasons cited for the prize was the Langenegger Talente, which has been in circulation since 2008. It encourages the 1,100 inhabitants to take collective responsibility for the newly renovated shop by spending local currency there. An estimated 80% of the villagers come into direct contact with Talente through friends and family, even if they do not use the currency themselves.

> If one of your main goals is to help people consume locally produced goods, then you must attract local businesses to use the currency: the butcher, the baker and the candlestickmaker! When I can buy my daily bread for say, 30% in local currency and 70% euros, then the whole thing becomes much more attractive to many more people. And it must be easy to use.

To encourage use of the currency in local shops, consumers must first buy Talente *Vouchers* at the rate of 1 euro = 10 Talente. They can spend them in all participating businesses and members of the exchange ring. Participants can redeem them back either into euros at a 15% loss of value (these euros help fund the administration and donations to voluntary organisations) or into Talente as electronic credits to spend in the exchange ring. The accounts of the Co-op record received euros as an asset and emitted Talents as a minus sum. The euro-backed currency acts as a great entry point for many into the exchange ring as they build up their trust in the whole system. Paper money makes daily trade much easier but is costly to run. Organisers decided against using a circulation incentive (demurrage) on the circulating currency as they thought it too complicated for people to understand for daily trade.

The Co-op also serves as a platform for members to develop new ideas based on social and environmental goals: a car sharing project; a renewable energy project; a project for people to save 'caring credits' for use when they are old. Young people aged 15 to 20 have started the 'Tuasch Tuscha' exchange ring with its own website. Members also maintain an active support project assisting a local currency system in Ecuador.

After 15 years, the Talente Tauschkreis acts like a rhizome spread throughout the region, sprouting up new forms in different areas according to need. Some projects take off quickly when the conditions are right, others take much debate before coming to fruition: one proposed new circulating currency has still not taken root because too many businesses objected to the exchange fee for converting Talente back into euro. The accumulated reputation and knowledge of the exchange ring make it easier to guide new developments.

Members of the Service Team have worked hard to provide both a professional service to members and a great image in the form of a website, flyers, posters and vouchers.[3]

---

3 www.talentiert.at

> We are always testing and improving our systems, we have to give as good
> a service as a bank otherwise people will not believe in the idea of a local
> currency. We have done very little marketing because we wanted first to
> develop ourselves. But now we have members who want to improve our
> public image because they see we have reached a professional stage.

Participants should experience real tangible benefits but the true achievements
of the system are not always easy to measure.

> The prime measure of the success of an exchange ring is the exchange of
> goods and services using a local currency. But we have other goals, which
> are just as important, like neighbours helping each other, or promoting
> organic and fair trade. It's not so easy to measure these effects even though
> they are central to what we are doing. Most participants say the social side is
> more important to them than economic benefit. Some also value the different
> feel of this form of economy. It brings people together who might not
> otherwise have met. People make new friends and business relationships and
> for new people to the region it provides an instant network. In the exchange
> ring the big question is not 'Where do you come from?' but 'What do you
> offer?' or 'What can you do?'. And we constantly see how much joy people
> get from discovering creativity, skills and potential they never knew they
> had.

And there is a paradox.

> Many people get to know each other through the exchange system, record
> a few trades and then just help each other. That's a success for them and a
> success for us because we have helped grow community. But for the system
> it creates sluggishness when trade drops off and then we need to recruit new
> members, which requires more effort.

Gernot Jochum-Müller has collected some more 'paradoxes of local currencies'
over the years.

> Many assumptions that we make about local currencies are not right.
> Practice teaches us the best. People say that exchange rings work in the
> countryside but not in the town, but we see the opposite. We also assumed
> that people who come to public trading events would trade more but our top
> traders do most trades in private. People coming to public meetings come
> more for the social side. Another paradox I've noticed since the finance
> crisis – when you would expect people to rely on the system more – some
> members have left us saying they must earn euros, they have no more time
> for our 'play money'.

Success attracts attention and Gernot was approached by a local political party
to stand for election, but he prizes the political neutrality of their local currency.
This does not mean they are not politically active. In fact, in 2010, their local
authority authorised the payment of a portion of local taxes in local money – a

first in Europe. Payment of local taxes sends out an important signal to the public that the system is fully legal and that participation brings real benefits.

So, what remains to be done?

> We still need legal clarification. Laws are formed around centralised money systems with no room for other forms. You have to be careful when you introduce innovations to make sure they integrate with existing systems.

> We need to keep ahead of technology like mobile phone payments and carefully introduce them when time and resources allow.

> We are not reaching the Turkish immigrant population and we need to do more outreach.

Members keep on learning together the true purpose of a community economy. One unemployed man who got deeply involved cried, "Hey, we can make our own money, we have no interest to pay!"

And every year they have a Gift Day: everyone brings something to give away and everyone goes home laden with gifts – no currency involved and smiling faces all round.

EQUAL DOLLARS, USA

Based on an interview with Bob Fishman and Deneene Brockington.

KEY FEATURES

TYPE: Circulating currency   **DATE FOUNDED:** 1995

REGION SERVED: Philadelphia, USA

MAIN PURPOSE: Support local economy

BENEFITS: Allows large non-profit to act as bank to create loans, part-pay salaries and support internal economic circuits; makes money go further

PARTICIPANTS: Consumers

CORE MECHANISMS: Local fiat backed by US Dollars; printed circulating currency designed by local artists with full security features

NAME OF CURRENCY/ STANDARD OF VALUE: One Equal Dollar = $US 0.80

TURNOVER: Not declared

GOVERNANCE: Resources for Human Development, a Common Good Corporation

MANAGEMENT: One full-time manager plus 3 staff

COST RECOVERY: Sponsorship; funding

WEBSITE: http://www.equaldollars.org/   or   http://rhd.org

Aleja Rivera could not believe her luck: two lobster tails for 7 Equal Dollars! She had never bought lobster before because it is so expensive. She felt rich. The weekly food market run by Resources for Human Development (RHD) in Philadelphia, USA, is a popular programme. A large food wholesaler donates surplus food, which is sold in family-pack bags for Federal Dollars and Equal Dollars.

RHD is a large 'common good' corporation started in 1970 with a grant of 50,000 dollars to provide outpatient mental health services. It now has over 160 programmes worth 210 million dollars employing 4,000 people across 14 states.

Bob Fishman grew up in Brooklyn, New York and got angry about poverty early in his life. He took a Master's Degree at Columbia University on a quest to find out how society works and what role organisations play in the process of change. Years later he published a book about money and power, outlining a vision of a new organisation: *The Common Good Corporation, The Experiment has Worked*.

When we started RHD, I agreed with the board that we could do anything anywhere that was legal, starting in the non-profit realm. This gave us great room to experiment: we created a range of businesses with social goals, helping people on low incomes to get access to prescription drugs, food and jobs. We believe that the underused assets in the community are immense; the culture of RHD is built around taking care of people, who no one else wants to bother with, and empowering communities that are the most disenfranchised.

But there was something missing. Equal Dollars was the fruit of Bob Fishman's continuing reflections on money and its role in society.

I knew that the federal dollar simply creates skewed systems that keep people poor, but why? I read Silvio Gesell's *Natural Economic Order*[4] and understood for the first time how one kind of money designed for the investment of capital cannot meet social needs. Money is a powerful tool that defines the society we live in. Therefore, I realised we had to develop a second type of non-interest bearing money and began to experiment with its use.

The money problem bugged me. Centralised fiat money destroys community. It makes us deal with human beings like we deal with dented cans – we throw them away when we can't make profit from them. Would a different kind of currency make any difference to the poor? I realised we needed a currency that employs the unemployed, – people the market does not want right now. We need a currency that is a tool that fits in where federal dollars cannot.

So, in 1995, we started our experiment: we issued our first primitive notes, loosely tied in value to federal dollars but not backed by them. We wanted to create a currency to reward community caring. We decided to invest resources in the currency as a sub-unit of our corporation doing non-profit work through a local medium of exchange. And it has added great value to our other programmes.

Bob became a role model for the currency by requesting that some of his salary be paid in local currency. Others followed suit.

We demonstrated you can create a currency and issue it into pay cheques. We put 40,000 Equal Dollars into circulation this way.

The currency had its ups and downs over the years. RHD hired various people to run it, both full-time and part-time, and much was learned about how to

---

4   S. Gesell, *The natural economic order: a plan to secure an uninterrupted exchange of the products of labor, free from bureaucratic interference, usury and exploitation*, (1929).

manage the basic systems. But the turning point came in 2008 when they hired Deneene Brockington.

> She has a big engaging smile and great interpersonal skills: when she talks, people listen.

Deneene worked in theatre administration for 15 years, learning all about budgeting, financing, and programme development. When she got invited to interview for RHD, she knew nothing about currencies.

> They were all talking about community currencies and I had no idea what they were talking about! Bob suggested I read Thomas Greco's books. After reading *Money and Debt*[5] I became so mad about the money system I wanted to scream: "It's a fraud! The whole system needs to collapse! Why don't people know what's wrong? Why do some people not want you to know?"

> When I started at Equal Dollars I inherited a lot of history. We had 1,600 members offering lots of services, special trading events and a good general awareness of the currency. But the problem was that nobody was meeting their everyday needs like food, clothing, shelter, healthcare, etc. My main focus was to get members to spend 10 Equal Dollars a week so it became part of their daily economy. The pharmacy accepts up to 5 Equal Dollars per prescription, which makes a big difference to someone needing to get several prescriptions filled every month.

Eventually these little steps began to add up and brought in all kinds of retailers. A start-up bakery got an interest-free dollar loan on condition that it would also accept Equal Dollars in the till. This example inspires Bob Fishman to make an analogy.

> A two currency system is like baking a cake: you can't bake only with flour, you need sugar and flour. The balance between sugar and flour changes with each deal – you need both for the mix.

Once Deneene Brockington grasped the potential of Equal Dollars, she became a very creative evangelist.

> We had to do two things: we needed everyone to stop thinking of Equal Dollars as 'play money' and, secondly, the employees of RHD themselves had to become ambassadors for the currency, so that people in the community started taking it seriously. We gave bonuses in Equal Dollars to over 300 employees working in the corporate office and we gave people real notes that looked good. I got inspired by a visit to BerkShares (p.138), redesigned our notes and ordered 72,000 units.

---

5 T. Greco, *Money and Debt: A Solution to the Global Crisis*, (1990).

Once this new money is in people's hands it becomes more real to them and you have to back it with real value. It was then that we stumbled on a model to do that. RHD spends close to half a million dollars a year with US Food Service (the second largest food distributor in America). They asked us if we could use some surplus bananas. Sure we can. We ended up getting six pallets of every kind of vegetable, fruit and herb – all food that was going to landfill. We packaged it up nicely and started a weekly market. Suddenly Equal Dollars have value: I can put food on my table.

When we need help with projects we offer an Equal Dollars gratuity of 25 units to volunteers who give up to 4 hours of service and 50 units to those who give 4–8 hours of service in a given day. Volunteers also get first choice at the market. We intentionally set prices low – most items are $1 + 1ED – particularly when we can source other cheap second-hand goods. We have been operating the market for over two years and it is very popular.

Equal Dollars is not designed to patronise the poor: it is a tool they can use to help themselves.

Certain types of charity create dependency. It is a disservice to continuously give something to a person of lesser means and for that person not to have a way to participate in the exchange. We had an ex offender, here in Philadelphia, who wanted to give something back to the community. Is it better to keep on punishing him or reward him for giving service and support him to build a future?

We need to think differently about the market: people want to work for their community and that work should be rewarded. Currency is a reward that can be used to feed your family. We give new members Equal Dollars to get them spending when they join: 50 units to individuals; 150 to small businesses. Once people have shown their worth, then they can get an interest-free Equal Dollars loan.

When you present this idea to the community, they connect with you; they know you are not talking down to them.

Being such a large organisation puts RHD in a powerful position: part of it can act as banker to another part. In 2010, Equal Dollars loaned 25,000 units over five years, interest-free, to RHD itself. The loan was created by the Equal Dollars bank to help RHD pay bonuses to its 300+ employees at headquarters; they spend their currency at the RHD market which goes back to RHD to service the loan. RHD also charges rent in Equal Dollars to organisations using office space at headquarters, who in turn get their suppliers to pay them in the currency. Virtuous economic circles are created. This is a modern version of the loan by Guernsey's government to its island community in 1817 (p.48). Bob Fishman understands clearly the power they hold.

> We discovered that non-profits had the power to issue currency but local government cannot under US law. We keep state government people aware of our activities; they understand what we are trying to do. During the early years, we got a 200,000 dollar economic community block grant to support our work.

> We see ourselves as educators to communities and governments about the need for a second currency. People are angry about the costs of a fiat money system with interest and we decided to show that there is an alternative that works. We have a working model that creates abundance and prosperity rather than poverty and scarcity.

> The next step with local government is to say, 'We'll start lending you millions of dollars if you take it in taxes. You already contract with us for millions of dollars, you can start paying us with Equal Dollars and let citizens pay their local taxes with the currency'; they will have to accept it.

In 2011, RHD made a deliberate economic decision to increase the flow of currency: they reduced the value of Equal Dollars to 80 cents on the dollar and adjusted all outstanding loans and balances.

> We are constantly learning how to play this game of local currency to benefit the users. We want others to copy and improve what we do and we will support them to do it. Here's a tool, you define how you use it. We offer a grant to the first state or local government officials who want to study it and implement an interest-free currency.

Equal Dollars is run by four staff, who solicit ideas from participants through conversations and surveys. Deneene Brockington wants to help people to earn more local dollars so Equal Dollars is expanding to include more businesses in a business-to-business exchange, using the GETS software developed by Richard Logie's team (p.102). They are adapting the software to include individual accounts. Increased activity brings internal challenges. Staff in the finance department are monitoring trade volume for tax and audit requirements.

And there are always interesting new developments: Amish farmers, an hour and a half away from Philadelphia, have recently joined because they need oatmeal and brown sugar in exchange for their farm produce: another great symbol for a dual currency. Someone else started a kite making class, payable in local currency.

Bob and Deneene know they have created a winner out of trial and error.

> We work more by experience than theory, by playing with the model. You don't know until you try, you learn from mistakes. We are modelling the currency for ourselves and for others. People are constantly stimulated by our system: they say, 'now we understand why you introduced a local currency'.

> When a community feels disenfranchised, we want them to understand WHY the system is stacked against them. Our members do not have to endure a means test: they are now a part of the 'have' society instead of a throwaway society.

> We see the amazing impact of the food market: a truckload of 10 pallets arrives full of goodies; we never know what is going to be on the truck and then we panic and wonder how to get this stuff out but we always do!

> We create our own bank with our own rules. This is not money to make money, but to honour the 'human' in human beings.

BERKSHARES, USA

Based on an interview with Susan Witt.

KEY FEATURES

TYPE: Circulating currency   **DATE FOUNDED:** 2006

REGION SERVED: Berkshires, Massachusetts, USA

MAIN PURPOSE: Support local economy

BENEFITS: Mobilises spare business capacity; revitalises high street businesses; makes money go further

PARTICIPANTS: 400 businesses; consumers

CORE MECHANISMS: Local fiat backed by dollars; printed circulating currency designed by local artists with full security features; full banking services at 13 branches of five locally owned banks

NAME OF CURRENCY/STANDARD OF VALUE: One BerkShare = $US 0.95

TURNOVER: 3.5 million BerkShares issued since 2006

GOVERNANCE: BerkShares Inc., a non-profit organisation

MANAGEMENT: One full-time manager

COST RECOVERY: Sponsorship; funding

WEBSITE: www.berkshares.org

BerkShares is one of America's most high profile local currencies, inspiring global media interest since its launch in 2006. It has issued 3.5 million BerkShares into circulation, serving 400 businesses in the Berkshires region of Massachusetts, USA.

Susan Witt is education director of the New Economics Institute and founder of BerkShares. She credits her strong connection with the landscape, its culture, and its people as the inspiration for her work in local economics. Her goal with BerkShares is to create a kind of 'conscious money' – money used with full consciousness of its effects.

> Currently we do not know what our money is doing tonight. It may be earning a three percent return, but that abstraction does not tell us if it is financing an organic farm in our region or a distant chemical factory using child labor. At its core, the economic life is no more than that place where human labor, organised by human ingenuity, transforms the natural world into products for use by others. That process can be life affirming, or can be degrading to those involved and to the planet itself. Our task, it seems to me, is to ensure it is life affirming at every level.

Susan began her first experiments with local economic development in the early 1980s when she and her partner, Bob Swann, launched the SHARE programme.

> To most people the primary purpose of money is to enable the process of consumption. The Self-Help Association for a Regional Economy (SHARE) was a simple micro-loan collateralisation program to finance new production by local residents in partnership with a local bank. The organisation enabled 25 loans, creating new businesses that employed local people. SHARE depositors knew 'what their money was doing tonight'. They supported these businesses, told their friends, built a market for locally made products – and the result was a 100% repayment of the loans. Our little experiment inspired local banks to make more small, productive loans on their own. SHARE linked citizens directly with producers, and in this way the risk in building the local economy was shared. We gained a lot of skills during this period. We learned that what might look like a risky loan to a distant financial institution, when informed by local knowledge and supported by local action, turned out not to be risky at all, but a good step in shaping the kind of economy we wanted to see.

The next formative experience along the road to BerkShares was 'Deli Dollars'. Frank Tortoriello was the owner of a popular deli on Main Street in the Berkshire town of Great Barrington. A bank refused to give him a loan to help move his restaurant to a new location, so he turned to SHARE. Susan explains:

> We were focused on start-ups. Frank had his own base of loyal customers. We suggested he borrow from them by issuing his own scrip. Printed scrip currencies were widely used in America in the early 1930s Depression Era. So, with our help, Frank printed Deli Dollars to finance renovation of the new location. Customers could use the scrip to buy their favourite sandwiches once the new shop was opened. The notes were marked 'redeemable for meals up to a value of ten dollars' and sold for eight dollars. Frank raised $5,000 in thirty days and won lots of community support. Customers stashed notes away for future meals, gave them away as presents, and even traded them for goods at local stores. Repayments were staggered over a year by placing a 'valid after' date on each note. Frank signed every note individually like a check to discourage counterfeiting. He repaid the loan from his community in cheese-on-rye sandwiches, rather than hard-to-come-by federal dollars.

Great ideas are infectious. A local farm family wondered if they could use the same idea to raise funds to pay for the high cost of heating their greenhouses through the winter. Customers would buy notes in the late autumn for redemption in plants and vegetables in the spring and summer. Another farm was damaged by fire and needed help.

> In 1989, with help from SHARE, the two farms got together and issued Berkshire Farm Preserve Notes with a head of cabbage at the center instead of the head of a president. The notes read 'In Farms We Trust' and sold for nine dollars each.

The popularity of these printed scrip currencies inspired the next experiment. By then Susan Witt and her colleagues had coined the name 'BerkShares' for a future currency for the region. The Southern Berkshire Chamber of Commerce agreed with the Schumacher Society to issue BerkShares as an experimental summer promotion. Customers were given one BerkShare for every ten dollars spent in a participating business over a six-week period. During a three-day redemption period customers could spend their BerkShares just like dollars in any of the 70 participating stores. In its first year of operation, 75,000 of the notes were given away, representing three quarters of a million in trade. During the three-day redemption period, 28,000 were returned and spent – a great success for a give-away programme.

One of the strengths of the Berkshire County in Western Massachusetts is its tradition of small, independent local banks. The initial success of the scrip program persuaded five local bank managers to get involved with the BerkShares committee in planning a year-round currency to support the local economy.

> Small locally owned banks give their branch managers significant flexibility over how they do business. Local managers realised that BerkShares would help them expand their customer base and also help the small businesses they served. They judged this was worth the extra administration and training of tellers required to introduce a second currency. From BerkShares' perspective, our local banks have existing storefronts in user-friendly locations. They are trusted record keepers of our credits and debits with each other. They provide a valuable infrastructure for building and maintaining a local economy. We felt it essential to work with and be supportive of our local banks, handing them responsibility for record keeping of the flow of the currency, while BerkShares members searched for and developed viable import-replacement business for the region.

It would take another 15 years for their plans to come to fruition. BerkShares local currency launched in September 2006. Citizens can now walk into 13 branches of 5 local banks and exchange $95 Federal for 100 BerkShares (B$), which they can spend at one-to-one value in 400 businesses in the Southern Berkshire region, an area with a year-round population of only 19,000 people. Businesses that wish to redeem BerkShares back into dollars return 100 B$ to any of the thirteen branches and receive $95.

Those shouting loudest about the evils of centralised government money from the federal reserve were now faced with a question: did they have the conviction to use the positive alternative that was now in place – a democratically structured, place based, non-profit issued local currency? The bar was raised. It sorted out those who only talk about transformation from those willing to step into a new system and be players. It meant going to Main Street and having face-to-face relations with store keepers and professionals. Choices were limited. Prices were not always the lowest.

Some critical design choices were made.

We have been criticised by some for issuing a dollar backed currency rather than jumping to an independently valued currency. Quite simply, convertibility with federal dollars gives businesses in a small town the confidence to take part. And because we wanted to bring people back to Main Street, we decided to create a visible hand-to-hand currency rather than start with an electronic platform. We commissioned excellent designers to make the notes, which feature landscape paintings by Berkshire artists and important historical figures of the region. We print on high quality security paper. All the currency is kept secure until delivered to the banks from the printers; we unpack the notes and deliver them under the eyes of an independent accountant to witness and record everything. BerkShares, Inc. (the non-profit organisation that runs the currency) has no BerkShares; they are all held by the bank until exchanged for federal dollars by citizens coming to the banks. In our first six years of operation, we have had only one instance of counterfeiting – a single note – which we dealt with quickly by issuing small fluorescent lights to high BerkShares volume businesses for detecting our high quality paper. It actually led to heightened awareness and vigilance amongst bank staff and businesses.

Why not just use dollars and support local shops?

Money habits are as deeply ingrained as food habits and just as difficult to change.

People are promiscuous with their money. They jump from one credit card deal to another, always looking for the lowest price. They buy books on the internet rather than locally. But price savings does not reflect the value of having a local bookshop or wholesome food. Our BerkShares currency pins money down and makes it work harder before it leaves.

Early traffic in the currency was huge, with every fourth customer at the banks buying BerkShares out of curiosity. It has probably had more global media attention than any other local currency in the world.

Nothing here is done in a vacuum; we are on a very public stage. TV crews still come and go: Wow! The very fact of the currency makes people question who, how and why money is issued in a way that all the academic papers in the world couldn't do. Then they ask: how can we take the money issuance back and make it work to support our values?

BerkShares has become a symbol for many who want to reconnect economy and community. The website gets 10,000 hits a day. Such attention does not make Susan Witt complacent. Trade is quieter these days and she knows how far they still have to go to realise their vision.

> BerkShares is not yet an independent currency but rather a very sophisticated discount programme with features built in to evolve. We are at about step 30 of a 50-step strategy in becoming an independent currency. The first step was the SHARE programme 30 years ago. The long-term goal of BerkShares is to finance the creation of new import-replacement jobs in the region, not just to facilitate local exchange – although that is important, of course. The real genius of a currency is creating money from nothing to finance new production. Our vision will only be realised when we have developed a robust loan program in BerkShares. But it was always going to be impractical to jump straight to that. We have come through an age of extreme globalisation in which local businesses had to survive. Only since the finance crisis are more people waking up to alternative visions and the potential for localisation as a counterbalance.

> Local banks now know that there is not a run on the currency and the dollars stay there. Businesses and individuals have worked out how to use a second currency. People have stopped suspecting that someone must be making money on the 5% discount and they understand that it discourages people from trading out too quickly. The currency is still not totally convenient to use but, in these times, merchants are willing to stretch a bit.

> We are over many hurdles, over the negative chatter. And new allies have come on the scene: the Transition Town movement is raising support for local currencies and the Occupy Movement has helped build interest in a move out of big banks and back to cash. There is still capital for us in the romanticism people project onto a community which issues its own currency to show its independence and self-reliance but that is not quite enough for us.

BerkShares Inc. has worked out a plan with local banks based on the original SHARE model, using dollars as collateral for the banks to issue BerkShares loans. People are already pledging dollars to back the loans.

Susan Witt continues to pursue a high vision grounded in a long-term strategy for change:

> One of our most inspiring Schumacher Lectures was given by Gar Alperovitz, a historian, political economist and board member of the New Economics Institute. He was addressing those motivated by the Occupy Movement: "If you don't want capitalism, what do you want? I don't want to hear the 'no'. I want to understand the 'yes'. And I want to know if you are prepared to spend the next two decades of your life to bring about the change you seek. Because that is what it will take and then some." There are no instant solutions in bringing about a new economy. The first step is preparing for the long-term. We realise it will be at least another ten years until we begin to reach our goals with BerkShares.
>
> For many people the leap from thinking about home economics to community economics is a big one. The workings of our economic institutions seem abstract, distant, beyond our influence – though they have such a profound effect on our lives. Those who aspire to live consciously at this time have a responsibility to make sure that economic life reaches its highest and most idealistic potential, creating economic systems that connect us more deeply to each other and the health of the natural world.

CHIEMGAUER, GERMANY

Based on an interview with Christian Gelleri.

KEY FEATURES

TYPE: Circulating currency   **DATE FOUNDED:** 2003

REGION SERVED: Chiemsee, Bavaria, Germany

MAIN PURPOSE: Support local economy

BENEFITS: Mobilises spare business capacity; revitalises high street businesses; makes money go further

PARTICIPANTS: 600 businesses; 2,388 consumers; 220 voluntary organisations

CORE MECHANISMS: Local fiat backed by Euros; printed circulating currency designed by local artists with full security features; demurrage fee of 2% per quarter; electronic Regiocard; microcredit loans

NAME OF CURRENCY/STANDARD OF VALUE: One Chiemgauer = One Euro

TURNOVER: 6 million Chiemgauer in 2011

GOVERNANCE: Chiemgauer e.V (association) and Regios Co-operative

MANAGEMENT: 3 full-time managers plus 20 volunteers

COST RECOVERY: Membership fees; demurrage fees; exchange fees

WEBSITE: www.chiemgauer.info

Lake Chiemsee lies at the foot of the Bavarian Alps in the heart of one of Germany's most prosperous regions. Günther Juraschek runs a local drinks store in the small town of Stephanskirchen, where he has become well known for his friendly and efficient service over the last 30 years. Recently he started trading in Chiemgauer, the local currency. When you spend euros, you can go for a whole day without speaking to anyone but the local currency starts conversations.

> Chiemgauer suits our business perfectly. We are different from many drinks shops. We don't just sell a crate of lemonade. For us, it's more about personal contact and having some fun. We know our customers and our customers know us.

Günther's business buys locally produced apple juice, water and beer with local currency and the profits are spent in other local shops and businesses. Local voluntary organisations buy drinks from Günther's store with local currency received from donations by Chiemgauer members, thus closing an economic circle in the region.

The Chiemgauer started in 2002, when six students at the Waldorf school in Prien-am-Chiemsee decided to start a local currency as their school project. In the first year, only a handful of businesses and 130 individuals signed up, generating a turnover of just 75,000 euros. Even so, businesses were willing to pay a 5% fee on all transactions, 60% of which funded the building of a new sports hall for the school. Fast forward to 2011: 2,388 individuals traded with 600 businesses, generating a total turnover of 6 million euros worth of trade in local currency, equal to 0.2% of the region's gross product.

The Chiemgauer's success formula:

- Promotion of consumer loyalty to locally produced goods and services.

- Backed by euros to create business confidence.

- Small penalty for changing local currency back to euros creating automatic donations to local organisations and funding for administration.

- Circulation incentive to keep currency moving.

Participants can spend, lend, invest or make gifts with Chiemgauer within a closed regional network of businesses, consumers and voluntary organisations. This combination of features creates a chain reaction of buying, selling and giving that achieves economic and social goals at the same time.

How does the Chiemgauer work?

Individuals join the Chiemgauer Association and receive a free Regiocard for electronic payments. They can either buy Chiemgauer currency with euros (one Chiemgauer = one euro) or offer their goods and services to others already possessing Chiemgauer. They can use the Regiocard to make automatic payments in some of the local businesses or use the circulating notes. Each time consumers bring Chiemgauer into circulation, 3% of the amount is automatically transferred to a community group of their choice, which means they can support their own club or good cause through their purchases. They may not exchange Chiemgauer back into euros.

Shops and businesses pay a one-off registration fee of €100.

There are three types of business account:

1. Standard tariff: 10 euros a month and 5% fee on exchanges back to euros.

2. Active tariff: 5 euros a month and 10% fee on exchanges back to euros.

3. Free tariff: Minimum exchange of 1,200 euros to Chiemgauer per year and 10% fee on exchanges back to euros.

Businesses may exchange Chiemgauer for euros at any time. The 5% or 10% fee (depending on their tariff) covers part of the currency's administration expenses and is inclusive of the 3% donation to community groups.

Voluntary organisations are special beneficiaries in the Chiemgauer system. Individual Chiemgauer members converting euros into Chiemgauer choose which voluntary organisations they wish to receive their 3% automatic donation. In 2011, 2,388 individuals donated 50,000 Chiemgauer (worth 50,000 euros) to 220 organisations. These voluntary groups have a total membership of 100,000 people, which means that the donations of a couple of thousand individual participants directly help large numbers of people and the benefits of the currency ripple far out into the region, way beyond the directly registered members.

Chiemgauer works in active co-operation with 6 regional banks and 50 issuing offices around the region to manage the exchange of euros to Chiemgauer. They sell 100,000 Chiemgauer and get 98,000 back each month so the circulation increases by an average of 2,000 Chiemgauer per month. Electronic transactions via the 'eChiemgauer' system of bank accounts are increasing. Regiocard payments are transferred directly from the customer's euro account to the Chiemgauer account of the business. If the customer's euro account is registered in the eChiemgauer system, the 3% donation to a voluntary organisation is transferred according to the customer's instructions. If not, the donation is directed to the Chiemgauer association. For transactions from a Chiemgauer account to a euro account, the exchange fee is billed.

The circulating currency is available in several denominations: 1, 2, 5, 10, 20 and 50 Chiemgauer. Notes have 14 security features including ultra-violet colours, imprinting of the logo, watermark, copy-proof colours, and individual serial numbers. Each quarter the Chiemgauer lose 2% of their value, or 8% per year, which can be restored on payment of a euro fee. Notes can be renewed up to seven times before they expire after two years. Old notes can be exchanged for new ones. Its advocates estimate that the Chiemgauer circulates nearly 2.5 times faster than the euro and never leaves the region, so it does more economic good along the way.

Chiemgauer is not only backed by euros but also by powerful ideas and deep personal commitment. Christian Gelleri, the former Waldorf school teacher who inspired his students with the idea of starting a currency, was himself inspired by two great early 20th Century thinkers – Rudolf Steiner and Silvio Gesell – when he was still a teenager.

> Steiner emphasised the need for concrete, grassroots projects growing organically through the creativity of individuals and groups. They have to be useful for the participants and they have to be both idealistic and pragmatic.

Economist J. M. Keynes said that the future would learn more from the spirit of Silvio Gesell than from Karl Marx. Gesell taught Christian the idea of 'money with legs' or 'money that rusts'. This kind of money slowly loses it value over time and then expires, just as natural products, like grain, rot or metal rusts. Nobody wants to hold onto such money for long so they pass it on quickly. The increased circulation of money benefits everyone with higher trading levels and business turnover.

> Why should money expire? Because the economy is like a dynamic bloodstream. Money that doesn't flow damages the economy. People have told me I am crazy to consider the 'ancient' idea of a money tax, which keeps money flowing. Economists say that the money bubble and the following inflation is a more comfortable solution. This is not a must for regional currencies but the Chiemgauer community has decided to establish a money that never slows down in circulation. The advantage is that everybody keeps money moving.

Chiemgauer is showing the world that local money with a circulation incentive (also called demurrage) can work in practice in the 21st Century.

Christian Gelleri is no dewy-eyed idealist, however. He studied business administration before training as a school teacher so he practises a pragmatic idealism.

> The first aim was to bind the money and let it flow within the community. Binding purchasing power as marketing experts would say. Other objectives were to foster co-operation, strengthen the local economy, increase sponsorship for non-profits, reduce food transport, reduce money speculation and increase regional investments.

From the start he realised that you have to design your currency carefully:

I wrote down my first very rough ideas for a design in 1998, inspired by
modern Gesellian Dieter Suhr, the WIR Bank in Switzerland (p.34), the
Austrian Wörgl experiment of the 1930s (p.50) and the ideas of Steiner. It
took about three years from my first concept to implementation of a tiny
version of the original 'big dream'. If you want to start a local currency, you
have to be absolutely clear about the vision. You have to check the benefits
to participants. Then you have to define the region and choose a town or
municipality with optimal preconditions. It's important to offer solutions that
are based on creating a balance between globalisation and regionalisation
and a balance between economic, ecological and social necessities.

Christian and his colleagues analysed other local currency models for their
strengths and weaknesses. They decided that the mutual credit model created
too many inactive accounts and would not be the best to achieve their goal of
engaging businesses to support the regional economy. They opted instead for a
euro-backed currency with a monthly demurrage fee to encourage circulation.
The Chiemgauer is designed as a half-open system that acts like a membrane
for the region: you can buy into the system with euros but you pay a penalty to
convert back to euros. The costs of the exchange are defined by the community.

Christian left the school in 2005 to work full-time for the new organisation
running the Chiemgauer and, uniquely amongst local currency organisers, he
takes his whole salary in Chiemgauer. He leads a team of 3 full-time managers
and 20 volunteers, who are part-paid in euro and Chiemgauer to run regional
offices.

Chiemgauer has its critics. They say that a regional currency is like an economic
straitjacket because you withdraw from the free market with those outside the
region.

That's true. But we believe the pros outweigh the cons. It's like a fitness
studio where, because you've already paid for it, you go twice a week.
Regional money is an effort that keeps me healthy. I sign up to it because
if I take part and others do too, we are all in better shape. It's a matter of
awareness, but beware: not all individuals stay aware all of the time so we
have to introduce a rule, which reminds us regularly to be aware. Quarterly
stamps (a demurrage fee) are only uncomfortable for those who forget to be
aware. And they forget only once or twice; after some time nearly everybody
follows the rules and circulation increases.

Others say it can't work because people only care about themselves, but,
if you talk with people in the right way, there is a fair chance that their
sense of the common good develops more than only their self-interest. The
amazing thing is that individual consumers gain no personal advantage from

Chiemgauer but they want to support the region and they can decide which non-profit organisation receives a bonus. For many people those are enough reasons to use the local currency. They have a different view of money as a collective instrument.

Growing a regional currency brings many challenges to the organisers:

- Shall we grow fast or slow?

- Do we follow a business plan or go a more organic and idealistic route?

- What form of governance do we need? What happens about disputes?

Christian describes the governance of the Chiemgauer:

> It's important to understand that the community decides all rules of the Chiemgauer. It's a basic democratic institution. If a rule isn't good we change it. We started the Chiemgauer Regional Association in June 2003 to give us a forum for making decisions. By 2007 it was clear that we also needed a more robust form of governance to support further economic growth and we founded the Regios Co-operative (Regios eG), which now manages all transactions of the Chiemgauer and four other regional currency systems. Regios eG is also a certified Micro-Credit Institute, which offers loans in both regional and national currency to support the growth of young enterprises. Mediation mechanisms are built into the governance structure in case of disputes.

What are the most important lessons learned in organising the Chiemgauer?

> If I was starting again now I would begin with micro-credit and an electronic payment system as they give you the most flexibility, have lower costs, bring more income and they are easier for the users to understand. Many businesses did not join because the notes were too complicated to use.

> We keep trying to convince the mayors of local towns to use the currency and eight communities already advertise on the back of the notes. We hope that people will be able to pay their local taxes with Chiemgauer in the future. I would like to see 1,000 businesses and 10,000 individuals taking part before I feel we have secured the future of our system. Your main aim is to do yourself out of a job eventually by encouraging volunteers to take on key tasks to make the system sustainable. Overall, I am pleased that Silvio Gesell's century-old theory of demurrage, which I discovered at the age of sixteen, can work in practice – with lots of hard work.

SOL Violette, France

Based on an interview with Frédéric Bosqué,
translated by Etienne Zoupic Hayem.

KEY FEATURES

TYPE: Circulating currency   **DATE FOUNDED:** 2011

REGION SERVED: Toulouse, France

MAIN PURPOSE: Support local economy

BENEFITS: Mobilises spare business capacity; revitalises high street businesses; makes money go further

PARTICIPANTS: 80 businesses; 700 consumers

CORE MECHANISMS: Local fiat backed by Euros; printed circulating currency designed by local artists with full security features; sliding demurrage fee of 2% per quarter

NAME OF CURRENCY/STANDARD OF VALUE: One SOL Eco = One euro

TURNOVER: 40,000 SOL Ecos issued since 2011

GOVERNANCE: SOL Violette Association

MANAGEMENT: 20 volunteers, 3 internships and 3 full-time workers

COST RECOVERY: Membership fees; public funding

WEBSITE: http://www.sol-violette.fr

Liberté, egalité, fraternité: three powerful words that sparked the French Revolution and which are now driving a financial revolution of regional currencies called SOL in nine regions of France.[6] SOL is short for solidarity or *soleil* (sunshine) and this bright vision is shedding a few rays of light on how local economies could work.

SOL originated with the Collectif richesse, a group inspired by philosopher-activist Patrick Viveret.[7] He argues that we are going to the wall if we continue on the path of unsustainable production patterns, compounded by an increasingly authoritarian financial capitalism; but, in fact, the wall that we fear so much is more of a series of walls in our minds. If we change our perspective, use our imaginations and embrace our common humanity, we can find a way through the walls. He recommends seven principles for action to guide us towards the 'exit':

---

6 http://www.sol-reseau.org/

7 http://fr.wikipedia.org/wiki/Patrick_Viveret

- Articulate hope and responsibility.
- Organise a friendly atmosphere.
- Place the joy of living in the heart of alternative projects.
- Change our relationship to money to one of empowerment and life.
- Promote high quality democracy.
- Connect our creative potential.
- Impose on ourselves the principle of congruence.

SOL also means 'the ground' as well as sunshine and was the name of a currency backed by the church during the French Revolution. This double metaphor describes the two distinct phases SOL has gone through in its evolution so far: a 'revolutionary' pilot phase inspired by a 'heavenly' vision followed by crisis and coming down to earth.

The original three pilot projects were created with European funding in Paris, Brittany and Northern France as a kind of loyalty points system for ethical/ green consumption – it was not possible to convert euros into SOL points. It was a top-down project with large project partners that dominated the decision making: one partner was mainly interested in delivering loyalty cards at a profit and the original idea of a backed unit of account was corrupted. Technical problems on top of this led to a crisis of confidence which damaged the projects. Following the crisis with the SOL pilot projects, the movement regrouped and analysed its mistakes.

> We had an important four-day gathering, where we debugged everything and recreated the SOL Movement with a new technological basis. We studied the Chiemgauer model and paper money. We also wanted to get away from a top-down project and find a way to organise more democratically. So we metamorphosed into SOL Version 2: Association SOL, where consensus must be reached on all issues.

> Three large social enterprise partners from the pilot phase – Chèques déjeuner (dining loyalty points), MACIF (insurance) and Crédit Coopératif (bank) – formed a new co-operative organisation to provide technical support to SOL projects called ECO Sol.

Frédéric Bosqué is the co-ordinator of SOL Violette in Toulouse; he is an entrepreneur who had some very negative experiences with the financial system during the dot-com boom in the early 2000s: investors disappeared overnight, he had to lay people off and declare bankruptcy twice, and he lost all of his possessions.

> After this crisis I made two big decisions: to put my skills in the service
> of the social economy because there is too much destruction of value in
> the market and to spend part of my time studying financial mechanisms to
> understand better where they go wrong.

He reinvented himself as a social entrepreneur and runs a social enterprise that
employs 50 people to support people with disabilities. He is also involved in
three other enterprises: an organic food co-operative that buys food directly, a
campaign group for basic income, and SOL Violette.

Frédéric Bosqué found out about the original SOL pilots from an internet search
in 2005. He contacted SOL and proposed a fourth region in the south. They
created a proposal, which had some support from regional politicians, but it was
rejected because the regional government did not believe it was sound.

> This was before the finance crisis raised so much awareness about problems
> in the money system and also our own presentations were not coherent
> enough at that time. But we instinctively knew that the SOL idea, with its
> three dimensions of SOL Co-opération (marketplace), SOL Affecté (impact
> measurement) and SOL Engagement (rewarding participation), had the
> capacity to heal the sick patient of the economy. We continued with our
> research, and to network and run conferences on the subject at a local level.
> Eventually we attracted enough local partners to get funding and the support
> of the regional government.

The Mayor of Toulouse, Jean Paul Pla, gave the project his full backing with
9,000 euros of funding to plan the project in 2010, followed by grants of
120,000 euro in 2011 and 130,000 euro in 2012 for technical development
and staffing. One of the impressive things about SOL is its governance model,
which aims to involve as many people in decision making as possible, whilst
maintaining efficiency. SOL Violette began its first meetings in 2010 with 150
people representing 4 types of participant: citizens, co-operative companies,
funders and local government. They decided against the traditional model with
a president, secretary and treasurer. Instead, they divided themselves into 5
collèges (advisory groups), and each collège sends representatives to a main
decision making body, which consists of 17 vice presidents!

During the first year of working together, each collège was asked to address the
following questions about SOL:

- What is the currency for?

- How do people get currency?

- Which services should be prioritised for circulation of currency?

- What are the trading rules?

- What governance charter do we need?

- How to create more equality between different economic actors?

All big decisions are taken by consensus. with all objections registered. This means that everyone gets to have a say in the matter, even if they do not agree with the final decision. As a last resort, say in the case of a particularly important decision, there is the possibility of a two thirds majority decision.

SOL Violette launched in May 2011 and embodies the new SOL Version 2 that emerged from the original crisis: individuals invest euros, which back the issuance of 'SOL Ecos', a currency that is accepted for trade by local companies; the euros are kept in a bank account and the SOL currency is a *titre de dette* (title to debt) like in the financial markets. SOL currency can be redeemed for euros at a 5% penalty. There is also a sliding demurrage charge of 2% every three months, measured from when the note leaves the till of a particular shop.

By early 2012, 700 individuals and 80 businesses had generated 40,000 SOL of turnover with 30% of currency redeemed for euros (called 'network leak' by organisers).

> These indicators are really important; we call them the network growth rate. If the amount of euros pledged in remains greater than the leak of currency back into euros, it means we are converting the 'real' economy into a sustainable economy. If not, then the euro is winning.This is why we keep an eye on the stocks of SOL at businesses and help them to spend their SOL. We recommend they:
>
> 1. Pay themselves or wages in SOL.
>
> 2. Tell us who their suppliers are so we can integrate them into the network or put them in touch with businesses from SOL.
>
> 3. Become an exchange point, so we can convert the euros of our members into SOL.
>
> 4. Give SOL as gifts rather than normal discounts. This way, businesses keep more euros and control the purchasing power they distribute in SOL.

This strategy helped us reduce the leaks by half by the end of the year.

Since the 1950s, when the town of Lignières en Berry tried to issue its own currency, there has been a national monetary legal code specifying that a local currency may only be issued within a member based network of people who can be identified. So, people must register with SOL Violette before they can gain currency and trade. All notes issued have an encrypted, scannable tag for traceability, which also allows organisers to track circulation patterns. Mobile payments and automatic transfers will soon be possible. A parallel hour based currency called Sol Temps for social favours or community participation is planned for the future.

The city government of Toulouse used SOL creatively by investing 30,000 euros and giving 30 Sol per month to 90 families in poverty for them to buy food. These credits then go into circulation through the SOL network.

SOL Violette is run by 20 volunteers, 3 internships and 3 full-time workers, part paid in SOL. Of the operating costs, 80% are financed by the Toulouse local government, 15% by private foundations and the rest through companies & participants' fees. By 2017, they aim to achieve a more balanced funding mechanism: one third from local authorities, one third from private foundations and donations, one third from membership fees. SOL Violette has created a strong local partnership of leading organisations including the city government, ethical banks and foundations. Other regions are planning to copy the SOL Violette model in the coming years.

What are the most important lessons?

> We ask all participants both quantitative and qualitative questions and we find that our participative governance model has taught people so much about financial mechanisms: learning by doing.

> We are making the transition towards the civilisation that is coming: a civilisation where human emancipation can continue, respecting the common good and individual freedom. Even though our current efforts are relatively small, we believe that the SOL model can transform the financial system. What is powerful today was small yesterday and our ancestors made that possible. Today we have the same opportunity to make powerful what is still small, so even if it is small, get started!

Ithaca HOURS USA

Based on an interview with Paul Glover.

KEY FEATURES

TYPE: HOURS   **DATE FOUNDED:** 1991

REGION SERVED: Ithaca, New York, USA

MAIN PURPOSE: Support local economy

BENEFITS: Mobilises spare business capacity; revitalises high street businesses; makes money go further

PARTICIPANTS: Over 500 businesses (in 1999, since reduced); thousands of consumers; voluntary organisations

CORE MECHANISMS: Local fiat backed by promise to supply local goods and services; printed circulating currency

NAME OF CURRENCY/STANDARD OF VALUE: One HOUR = $10, based on a standard hourly wage in Ithaca in 1991

TURNOVER: 1991-1999: millions of dollars equivalent; $30,000 of interest-free HOUR loans

GOVERNANCE: Non-profit organisation

MANAGEMENT: Recent change. Not known at present

COST RECOVERY: Advertising in own newspaper HOUR Town; Donations of accommodation and food to support the organiser

WEBSITE: http://ithacahours.com/ or http://ithacahours.org/ or www.paulglover.org

---

As a young man, Paul Glover left the small city of Ithaca in New York State for a few years and returned in 1991 to begin a revolutionary experiment to transform the local economy:

> Our city needed more money and more control of what money does so we thought, 'Why not print our own?'

Armed with a degree in marketing, a natural talent for community organising and the ability to talk the language of both artists and businesses, he began waving photocopies of his new local currency notes at his friends.

> This is going to be money. We'll trade it with each other. Sign up here.

Ithaca HOURS was born. Each HOUR was worth $10, a generous hourly wage in Ithaca in 1991. Each note carries the words 'In Ithaca We Trust' to emphasise the primary purpose of the currency: to support the local community and its economy.

> Local cash strengthens trading between local residents, local businesses and local nonprofits. By printing our own money, we gain control over investments and interest rates. Whereas global currency markets lack human values, local currency markets are real places where people become friends, lovers, and political allies. National currencies control people; local currencies connect people. We've added millions of dollars worth of trading to the local economy – a kind of informal import replacement program – which has even increased local sales tax collection. We've facilitated many business start-ups and new friendships. We have enrolled thousands of individuals and over 500 businesses. We've made HOUR grants to over 100 community organisations and up to $30,000 of interest-free HOUR loans. Grants made to nonprofits get spent in local businesses and keep currency circulating.

Paul has summarised the main lessons he learned from eight years of full-time organising with Ithaca HOURS in his book *Hometown Money*[8]. Here is his own six-part recipe for success:

1. Hire a networker.

2. Design credible money.

3. Be everywhere.

4. Be easy to use.

5. Be honest and open.

6. Be proudly political.[9]

He loves **networking.** The streets are his office, the place he makes things happen.

> Playing Monopoly is easier than building anti-monopoly. Running a local currency is hard work. Your volunteer core group – your Municipal Reserve Board – may soon realise that they've created a labor-intensive local institution, like a food co-op or credit union. That's why every local currency needs at least one full-time networker to constantly promote, facilitate and troubleshoot circulation. Lots of talking and listening and that's labour intensive. National currencies have armies of brokers managing circulation.

---

8 http://www.paulglover.org/currencybook.html

9 http://localcurrencycouncil.org/index.php/component/content/article/29-a-recipe-for-successful-community-currency

Local currencies must each have at least one such networker. You have to help local businesses find ways to spend currency they've earned or you may offer them loans in local currency so they can employ people to do their plumbing or carpentry; you have to set up deals and trades.

You also have to create local alliances to support what you are doing. I attended many meetings and festivals. The Credit Union was an early and prominent backer. The Chamber of Commerce paid for our tourist brochure and has been grateful for millions of dollars worth of free publicity for the region. Reduce your need to pay the Networker with dollars, by finding someone to donate housing. Then find others to donate harvest, health care, entertainment.

Designing credible money creates interest, visibility, a user base and trust.

Design professionally – cash is an emblem of community pride. Make the currency look both majestic and cheerful, to reflect your community's best spirit. Feature the most widely respected monuments of nature, buildings, and people. One Ithaca note celebrates children; another displays its bioregional bug. The Beverly Martin commemorative HOUR is the first paper money in the U.S. to honour an African-American woman.[10] Use as many colors as you can afford, then add an anti-counterfeit device.

Hours are real money, based on the community labour standard. They might even revive the national funny money that is so mired in the debt standard. And hours could benefit macroeconomies, the stability of whose money depends ultimately upon the stability and vigour of village economies. We are a commodity currency, since our cash is backed by thousands of individuals and hundreds of businesses, especially including the produce of local farms. HOURS may become a separable unit of value if national currencies collapse, insulating us from hyperinflation. See my article 'Labor: the New Gold Standard'.[11]

Being everywhere means establishing a recognisable presence.

Prepare for everyone in the region to understand and embrace this money, such that it can purchase everything, whether listed in the directory or not. This means broadcasting an email newsletter, publishing a newspaper (at least quarterly), sending press releases, blogging, cartooning, gathering testimonials, writing songs, hosting events and contests, managing a booth at festivals, perhaps a cable or radio show. Do what you enjoy; do what you can.

By 1999, Ithaca HOURS became negotiable with thousands of individuals and over 500 businesses, including a bank, the medical center, the public

---

10 www.paulglover.org/hourcurrency.html

11 http://paulglover.org/1107.html

library, plenty of food, clothes, housing, healing, movies, restaurants, bowling. The directory contained more categories than the Yellow Pages. We even created our own local non-profit health insurance.

Imagine millions of dollars worth of currency circulating, to stimulate new enterprise, as dollars fade. Printing money is itself a powerful marketing tool. Without sending a press release, thousands of stories have been written about HOURS. Our currency has been reprinted, often in full color, in hundreds of newspapers and magazines. During 1996, for example, I handled 1–3 media interviews daily. Media attention helped us greatly: many local people began to take HOURS seriously when they saw it featured on their favorite national TV show. But most essential were stories in HOUR Town, the bimonthly directory, which clarified our purpose and benefits while displaying thousands of ways HOURS could be spent.[12]

Being easy to use means that local money should be at least as easy to use as national money, not harder. And you need to be proactive in keeping the currency moving.

Get ready to issue interest-free loans. The interest you earn is community interest – your greater capability to hire and help one another. Start with small loans to reliable businesses and individuals. Make grants to groups. I intervened with local businesses dozens of times to help them spend their HOURS. I offered them loans when I found people ready to do their plumbing, carpentry, painting, etc.

Being honest and open means that all records of currency issued are displayed upon request. Ithaca HOURS are issued by the central administration so issuance is carefully controlled.

Limit the quantity issued for administration (office, staff, etc.) to 5% of total, to restrain inflation. Currency users can attend twice-monthly potlucks at which anyone attending can propose policy and vote.

Being proudly political means using the local currency as a starter for important conversations about political issues.

Local folks from all political backgrounds find common ground using local cash. But local money is a great way to introduce new people to the practicality of green economics and solidarity. I enjoyed arguing with local conservatives, then shaking hands on the power we both gain trading our money. Hey, we're creating jobs without prisons, taxes and war!

Has anyone changed their mind about money or economics through using Ithaca HOURS?[13]

---

12 http://paulglover.org/hourarchives.html for the period 1991–1999

13 www.paulglover.org/hoursuccess.html

HOURS have been taught in many colleges and high schools. Their purpose, and critique of national money, has been featured in thousands of stories and broadcasts.

My favourite stories are of the Ithaca children who assume every city has its own money, and are surprised to find that many other places lack their own. Some children in Ithaca prefer to be given their weekly allowance in HOURS.

Best of all, HOURS were stolen during break-ins. And one street thug was so enthralled by HOURS that he ended a robbery to learn more!

Neal sells organic food at the Farmer's Market and has spent HOURS for movies, bread, his son's play group, a calendar, and his house's food fund.

I'm really excited about HOURS and feel good about taking them. I always carry some in my pocket. I visit friends elsewhere and show them Ithaca's barter newspaper. I show them our money that says 'In Ithaca We Trust.' That's the bottom line, right?

Deborah has earned HOURS selling insulating window shades. She campaigns for energy-efficient housing.

An awful lot of people aren't able to afford to insulate. They can't afford their heating bills either. A lot of folks keep their heat low. Energy conservation is good economic development: most insulating work uses local labor, the money recycles locally more times. Presently most fuel dollars go elsewhere. Utility companies don't yet take Ithaca HOURS, but I do.

Rabbi Eli offers Hebrew lessons and Bar/Bat Mitzvah lessons.

The barter list has been very useful. Recently I traded lessons for violin repair.

HOURS are a very creative social support network, a good model for preserving kindness and compassion in the economy. They avoid the mass business focus and remind us that we're serving other human beings.

Bill teaches jitterbug and swing dance for HOURS and spends them mainly on food and other small items.

HOURS make people think more about what money is. We're making a big cultural change with HOURS, back to the community meaning of money, and we should be patient as it develops.

In 1999, Paul moved on to new challenges and transferred the system to a volunteer board. Since then there have been far fewer participants and trading has greatly decreased. Across the USA, 80 other communities copied the Ithaca

HOURS model but only a few of them have survived and none have imitated the success of the original.[14]

Can Ithaca HOURS work without Paul Glover? It certainly seems like the first point of his success formula is true for a business focused currency: without a full-time networker it is just too difficult to maintain interest and participation, particularly when businesses are hard pressed enough to keep the ordinary dollars flowing through the till.

14 E. Collom, 'Community currency in the United States: the social environments in which it emerges and survives', *Environment and Planning A*, volume 37: 1565 –1587, (2005). Online at www.envplan.com/epa/editorials/a37172.pdf

ARGENTINE STORIES

If we want to know how local currencies might perform in a really acute crisis – what the challenges might be and how to overcome them – lessons from Argentina are crucial.[15] Peter North of Liverpool University has studied the global complementary currency movement for 20 years.

> In Argentina, the barter networks (*Redes de Trueque*) grew to a size where they helped literally millions of Argentines to get through an awful financial crisis from 2000–3, and became as normal a part of Argentine life as a Visa card. Nowhere else have alternative currencies grown to such a mass level of usage.[16]

The chapter on 'Argentina's Barter Networks' in his book *Local Money* tells a sobering story of idealism, too-rapid growth in crisis conditions, corruption and ultimate failure, although millions benefitted along the way.

Margrit Kennedy, co-author of this book, visited leaders of Argentina's local currencies. They had learned some important lessons that may help others in similar situations to avoid some of the more dangerous traps. The first 'barter market' – she was told – began in 1997 with a pumpkin plant that spread from one neighbour's garden to another. The two neighbors agreed to share their surplus food and 20 people in the industrial Bernal region of Buenos Aires followed suit. Soon a local non-governmental organisation called PAR (Programa de Autosuficiencia Regional – Regional Self-Reliance Programme) began to create a network of 'prosumers' (producing consumers). By the year 2000 around 15,000 people were a part of the network, which was based on the Ithaca HOURS model from New York. The idea began to spread even further as the economic crisis crept up on the country and escalated into fullscale disaster in December 2001, when the IMF refused any more help, and the peso lost 80% of its value overnight. Savings accounts were 'frozen' and nobody could get at their money: a familiar phenomenon in Argentina.

Exchange systems began to mushroom. Two competing national organisations promoted barter networks during the crisis:

- PAR's Global Barter Network (Red Global de Trueque – RGT), which developed a franchise system with start-up kits. Groups around the country started systems with these materials.

---

15 P. North, *Local Money: How to Make it Happen in Your Community,* (2010), Ch.8: 'Argentina's Barter Networks'.

16 *Ibid.*

- Solidarity Barter Network (Red de Trueque Solidario – RTS), a more localist and bottom-up network encouraging people to develop and run their own systems.

The currency in both cases was called 'creditos'; other local currencies were linked loosely to the national Peso, others were bought for Pesos at a discount, others could not be exchanged for Pesos. Usually markets were set up to help with the exchanges in the new currencies. Peter North comments on the results:

> By 2001, the organisers claimed 4,500 markets were used by half a million people spending 600 million creditos across Argentina. The real figure is unknowable.[17]

Margrit Kennedy was told – by the founders of the RGT – that, in their heyday, about 2 million people were members of their network. She actually saw the room filled with application forms right to the ceiling, and the safe, which the administrators had to open for the police, after they had been accused of fraud. The police took all the cash they had accrued from selling the creditos. Their belief was that the government was jealous about the success of the system and tried to eliminate it.

Both national organisations – the RGT and RTS – promoted creditos, and both had strengths and weaknesses. RGT argued that the scale of the crisis needed a strategic approach with rapid deployment rather than the slow organic community development promoted by RTS, but one of RGT's regional representatives began to print Creditos without backing and created runaway inflation. Eventually, the whole scene got politicised and the media stepped in.

> In November 2002, a prime-time television show exposed what it called the 'great barter scam'. Stolen goods were being sold, millions of credits were forgeries and the food on sale was poor quality. 'You are being taken advantage of', the programme claimed. Overnight it seemed that the whole concept of barter catastrophically lost credibility, and over the coming months node after node closed down. A year later no more than 10% of them survived.[18]

Carlos Louge, an Argentinian professor of economics, commercial lawyer and social activist with a group called New Paradigm, describes what has happened since:

> In Argentina, social money has almost died, since it was in 'combat' with the media and the government in 2002. Some internal and political struggles

---

17 *Ibid.*

18 *Ibid.*

inside the movement caused its total fall and lack of credibility. But, our country is finally growing faster, after five decades of crisis. We almost don't have any problems of unemployment today.

A group of local currency organisers from Argentina were brought together by Carlos Louge and Facundo Márquez for a phone conference in early 2012 to describe the lessons learned from the crisis a decade ago and how to apply these lessons today.

Marcelo Caldano runs a Community Hours Bank for the SOL Foundation in the town of Capilla del Monte in Córdoba Province.[19]

It was started in 1999 with the purpose of supporting a local preschool and primary school. Parents are paid for a range of activities: cleaning, administration, gardening, etc. Since then, it has grown to involve the municipality, social organisations, merchants and residents in general. The price of working hours is agreed by each participating institution; the SOL Foundation pays its own staff 15 soles (suns) per hour.

One of the biggest failures of the barter network movement in Argentina was mass over-issuance of unbacked currency. SOL learned an important lesson from this experience. All currency issued is now backed by goods and services contributed by local companies: if they have contributed 20,000 dollars in merchandise, they have the potential to issue 20,000 soles. Each note goes into circulation when it is paid to employees or is used to purchase goods and services by members. This provides working capital to implement projects and simultaneously improves the quality of life of members. The prices of the merchandise or services are equal to or less than the same merchandise in the local market because it is a non-profit activity.

They use specially designed software that counts the stock of goods, currency in circulation, the personal accounts of the partners and institutions, loans, fees paid and owed, and so on. If clots in circulation are detected, organisers persuade savers to start spending and get those in debit to commit themselves to future work. People can take loans: someone needing 400 soles to buy a bicycle is given the full 400 soles in exchange for signing 5 obligations to pay 80 soles by working for the community.

The local government offices use social currency to provide medicines, mattresses and building materials to families in poverty. For instance, they employ a plumber who is willing to accept local currency for installing new

---

19 http://habitat.aq.upm.es/bpal/onu02/bp599.html

pipes; the recipient provides their labour for other services to the community in return. The school has mobilised 40% of its resources through social currency, 80% of the budget of a tutoring centre for children with learning disabilities is powered by the currency and a Technological Support Center of a remote National University operated 90% of its budget for over 7 years in the currency.

The Community Hours Bank has won many awards at local, provincial, national and international levels. Judges were impressed by how the system can support community projects and, at the same time, improve the quality of life for families outside the formal economic circuit. The bank had a lot of media attention during the crisis of 2001–2003 and organiser Marcelo Caldano was nominated for an Ashoka Fellowship in 2003.[20]

Participants have learned that everyone has something to give, no matter what social class they belong to – they just need to agree on common projects. They have learned to make social capital visible and how to develop various financial tools to improve the community. The social currency system diversifies ways of mobilising resources at the community level without being tied to the central government and helps people to survive the global crisis.

Carlos Perez Lora used to run the Mar y Sierras (Sea and Mountains) Region Solidarity Barter Network in the Province of Southeast Buenos Aires.
From 2001, the initiative grew a network of 5 main nodes and 140 sub-nodes serving 56,000 members, with about 350,000 people benefitting from the system and an annual turnover of 1.5 million Creditos.

The main aim was 'reconstitution of the social fabric', destroyed during the dictatorship and governments that followed: its purpose was not just to create jobs but also a social movement leading towards cultural transformations based on solidarity and mutual assistance. The barter network was designed as a school of democracy, where members learn together through co-operative activities and become closely involved in the economic, social, cultural and political issues that affect their lives. The network supported social work, a school of medicine, blood banking, tourism and legal services.

Margrit visited one their markets, in one of the seven locations in the city of Mar el Plata in 2002. She was very impressed by the way in which all the accounts were publicised. In the entrance area one could see how many Creditos had been issued, and where and how they were spent. Everything was openly displayed for

20 http://argentina.ashoka.org/node/3968

the visitors of the market as well as the merchants. Thus both parties were able to see which goods and services were lacking and what was available in abundance. Since the region of Mar el Plata stretched for hundreds of kilometres between the sea and the mountains, all the different produce from the warmer to the cooler climate zones were available in the markets. In addition they had a system of allowing only those producers of goods and services into the network who had something to offer that was in demand in order to avoid over-capacity in one and under-capacity in another of the 21 areas defined as necessary. These included everything from food to building work, clothes, pharmaceutical products, artwork and hairdressing.

The governance structure was sophisticated with a network of nodes accountable to a general Prosumers Assembly. The Assembly appointed local coordinators and auditors and they were proud of their organisation and its transparency. This was not enough to buck the general trend of decline of barter networks in the country and the last nodes disappeared in 2005.

Daniel Ilari coordinates a system in the municipality of Venado Tuerto.[21]
This has the wonderful name of *El juego de DAR Y RECIBIR* (The game of giving and receiving). At the height of the 2001 crisis, 1,500 families took part and the local government accepted part payment of taxes with local creditos. Today, only a hundred families take part, using a printed paper currency called 'points', which loses 10% of its value every 6 months. Participants have a clear understanding that the currency is for buying and selling and cannot be used to save. On the other hand, there are always participants who accumulate credits and lose a lot of value when the demurrage fee is applied. They plan to start a kind of internal university where participants can learn and teach each other using 'points'. The local authority now supports the system with gifts of sunflower oil that can be traded. A local flour mill also contributes flour. These and other staples (milk, eggs) are maintained at a 2-to-1 equivalence with the national currency to combat inflation.

Javier Goglino is the organiser of Proyecto Mutuo (Project Mutual)[22] in Mar-tínez, a Buenos Aires suburb.[23]
This is a mutual credit system with 75 members who did $10,000 worth of trade in creditos in 2011. They use Cyclos software to track all exchanges and have

---

21 www.eljuegodedaryrecibir.blogspot.com/

22 www.proyectomutuo.org

23 www.globalpressinstitute.org/global-news/americas/argentina/social-currency-systems-emerge-supplement-money-argentina

the usual challenges of mutual credit systems with large negative and positive balances to manage. They try to recruit businesses looking to create loyalty amongst customers but the system is relatively dormant with low trade.

Gabriel Picardi runs Munitario.[24]

This is a mutual credit system based on a universal virtual currency called 'minutes', which currently has 60 individual members. Gabriel himself covers 13% of his daily needs with local currency. New members are sponsored by existing members and have a debit limit of 250 points. Once established, this is extended to 1,250 points. Participants get a virtual showcase for their offerings and their needs.

The most important lessons Margrit Kennedy learned from the Argentinian experience were, first, that the fast expansion of a system in a national crisis situation is a dangerous moment, which must be met with great care and sophistication. The systems that survived in Argentina were those in which the governance included transparency of the decisions towards the users.

Secondly, the credito was not considered to be money at first. Therefore, the Argentinian Government did not levy any taxes for transactions in credito. That may not have been too big a loss when the numbers of participants in the system were small - around a few hundred or even a few thousand members - in a relatively poor area of Buenos Aires. But, when the movement grew in a short time to encompass other regions and to serve possibly millions, this became another matter. Thus the tax issue should be taken seriously – as is the case in most regional currency projects today.

---

24 www.Munitario.com

Currencies that grow community

Some local currencies aim to strengthen community spirit, grow local networks, encourage neighbour-to-neighbour exchanges and volunteering for local projects. Participants may also gain new skills for the job market or develop new business ideas, which also strengthens the local economy. Such systems may eventually grow to serve a whole region or inspire the growth of inter-regional networks.

Systems whose primary focus is to grow community. Secondary effects may include economic benefits.

● **Blaengarw Time Centre, Wales**

○ **Community Exchange System, South Africa**

○ **Dane County Time Bank, USA**

Key:

○ **Main purpose:** grow community. **Core mechanism:** mutual credit.

● **Main purpose:** grow community. **Core mechanism:** local backed fiat.

Blaengarw Time Centre, Wales

Based on an interview with Geoff Thomas.

KEY FEATURES

TYPE: Time Centre   **DATE FOUNDED:** 2006

REGION SERVED: Blaengarw, South Wales

MAIN PURPOSE: Grow community

BENEFITS: Helps local non-profit organisation to get help for community projects; says thank you to community volunteers; makes money go further

PARTICIPANTS: 1,000 members; 30 community groups; 15 social enterprises

CORE MECHANISMS: Local fiat backed by rewards; printed circulating currency

NAME OF CURRENCY/STANDARD OF VALUE: One Time Credit = One hour of work

TURNOVER: 60,000 hours of service to the community per year

GOVERNANCE: Creation Development Trust, a non-profit organisation

MANAGEMENT: Two managers plus volunteers

COST RECOVERY: Sponsorship and funding

WEBSITE: http://www.creation.me.uk/projects.htm

Menus are important in Blaengarw, an ex-mining village at the top of the Garw Valley in South Wales – both food menus and event menus. People learn to cook in the community Food Studio, serve in the café and earn time credits for their efforts.

The community hall hosts events such as:

> Stand-up comedy
>
> Live music
>
> Theatre
>
> Films
>
> Showstoppers cabaret and tribute nights
>
> Bingo
>
> Tea Dances
>
> Under 11s discos

One hour of work in the cafe equates to one hour at an event in the community hall.

The Blaengarw Time Centre opened its doors in 2006. The centre is run by the Creation Development Trust, a community enterprise, and is based in the large old miners' welfare hall. Dawn Davies, Chief Executive of the Trust, has been inspirational in driving the project forward, giving constant support to coordinators David Pugh and Don Sage. A community that was plagued by the typical diseases of post-industrial areas – unemployment, loneliness and community breakdown – is telling itself a new story of hope and inclusion. What makes this new story possible is one powerful idea: a community can act as its own bank. It can create the credit it needs to get essential work done. So long as the credit is backed and people can get value in return, the bank is sound.

This idea was brought to Blaengarw by Geoff Thomas, Chief Executive of Time Banking Wales. A native of the South Wales Valleys, with a degree in anthropology and many years of experience as a community organiser, he has always been interested in how people construct their social reality together and has a strong sense of his own history.

> My grandfather learned to read and write in a Miners' Institute. He didn't have much money but he was socially wealthy. Each member of an Institute had something to contribute, people recognised the value of your work. Nobody was better than anybody else in these new social environments. They were founded on mutuality, on give and take: you learned something and you passed it on to someone else.

Blaengarw Workmen's Hall includes a 250-seater auditorium with a stage, childcare room, dance studio, dark room, training suite and general-purpose rooms. Activities include coffee mornings, arts classes, information technology classes, a youth club, dance and drama workshops, sugar craft and after-school clubs. The main hall hosts many live events and performances.

The hall is a great community asset that survived, thanks to the Development Trust, but it was still not working to capacity when organisers developed the simple idea of a Time Centre: for each hour of service you give to the community, you are thanked with an hour in return. In the first year, 150 people participated. Now there are over 1,000 members and 30 groups, 15 new social enterprises and many new learning opportunities. Participants contribute 60,000 hours of service per year to their community. On average 600 people visit the hall each week. Entry to events is charged in time or in cash: a two-hour bingo night is two time credits, and a three-hour theatre performance is three time credits.[25]

Geoff believes the key to its success is ownership.

> As a child growing up in the 1950s, I would look at a building like a Welfare Hall in the community and ask 'Who does this belong to?' and my uncle would say 'This belongs to us.' Later on, people said, 'That belongs to the Council or the Health Authority.' They stopped caring about it. There are two extremes: the state controls everything or you destroy monopolies and have a totally open market. We are saying that we need to put mutuality back into the conversation. We don't advocate either the state or the individual in control. We need to reinvent the 'us'; we are doing this together.

> Agencies of the state talk about beneficiaries of services, the market talks about clients and consumers, we talk about members. When people become a member of something, they feel a sense of ownership, like they had for the old Institutes. People need to become part of the process of change and renewal voluntarily. And time banking gives us a method to do that. It is based on core values that echo our Valleys culture: strong social support networks; the notion of membership; treating people as assets; active citizens. It speeds up change because it gives a structure to change. It helps us become part of a large collective of social solidarity in a community of place. Not far beneath the surface we still have a memory that this is how we used to do things in South Wales.

> Time banking changes peoples' hearts and minds and engages them because it has a neutral base. Would you like to become a member? Anyone can take part. It is open to all, non-judgmental, non-threatening. A time credit is just a tool to get people together; it creates new types of wealth in non-market settings based on equality of time.

Time banks usually focus on connecting neighbours and friends to each other through circles of exchange. The Time Centre has a different purpose and so a different approach: its primary aim is to engage individuals to help the whole community.

People are invited to get involved in a range of helping activities:

- Help in the Time Centre – assisting the after-school clubs, helping with social events, maintenance, administration, mentoring, delivering leaflets.

---

25 Time2Grow Evaluation,
   www.timebankingwales.org.uk/userfiles/Time2Grow%20-%20%20Evaluation.pdf

- Help in the Community – participating in community-based projects, summer play schemes, events, environmental and arts projects.

New members receive a simple introduction to the process:

Step 1 - Become a member of the Blaengarw Time Centre by signing up and collecting your welcome pack.

Step 2 - Have an informal chat with an organiser about what you can give to the Time Centre and what kind of events you would like to attend.

Step 3 - Begin to gain Time Credits by helping at the Centre or participating in a community project.

Individual members with similar interests connect through the centre and form new groups, such as festival groups, a card-making group, a 'knit and natter' group, etc. The time centre also helps new initiatives in the community to become more sustainable. The sculpture studio began with a professional sculptor running a drop-in studio in the village. Members of the community began to work with the sculptor to produce a large piece of public art and they now run the sculpture studio group themselves and earn time credits for teaching other members, who pay in time credits to attend classes.[26]

Members can earn time credits by making birthday and Christmas cards, by teaching members of the youth club to knit hats and scarves, or by telling their stories in the digital storytelling project. They use their credits to attend film evenings, attend the tea dance or go to the café for the meal of the day.

The project has created an active learning culture. People value the learning because they have to earn their place on the course and people complete courses more often than they used to. At the end of the course, participants from learning groups actively share their skills with the community. Members of the Welsh learners class now earn time credits by helping with Welsh classes in the local primary school.

The local Social Club is a business which now accepts time credits as well as cash for entry to its events programme. Attendance has increased and profits have risen dramatically through the secondary takings at the bar; participation in the time bank has helped it to remain a viable business in the area.

---

26 Case Study 3, 'Bottom-up community development – Blaengarw Workmen's Hall Time Centre in New Wealth of Time', *New Economics Foundation*. Online at http://www.scribd.com/doc/53064161/19/Community-development-and-regeneration

The 'Fix My Street' project alerts the authorities to problems like loose paving stones or faulty light bulbs. Street Ambassadors receive five time credits a month to attend meetings with police and council officials. Police say it makes their job much easier because it develops a collective intelligence about problems.

The Time Centre has also inspired several micro social enterprises like the 'Four to Six Club'; organisers pick up the children of working parents from school and bring them to the Centre for a couple of hours each day; the parents pay in cash or time.

The old community café has been transformed into a Food Studio: participants get qualifications in food, hygiene and nutrition and put their learning into practice on the production side. The Studio gets income from both pounds and time credits. In the traditional market economy, the straitjacket of one currency, this café struggled. Now, on this dual currency platform the café can survive.

The same principle can be applied to other businesses: they are all studios where people can learn a trade with a qualification and then earn time credits to practice their skills.

An empty shop over the street from the café has been reopened as the 'Real Food Box', sourcing local food from a 50 mile radius and building up a customer base through the internet, with a delivery service to local people at competitive prices. An ambitious Local Heritage Group has been inspired by the Food Studio to reopen an old Italian café just down the valley as a heritage café.

The community has also come together to do large projects. In Summer 2007 Blaengarw held its first festival for 21 years with over 7,000 time credits issued. It has now become an annual event in the calendar and a great symbol for the effects of the Time Centre on the community.

Time credits in a Time Centre are issued by fiat from the 'central bank' rather than by members when they trade. All credits issued must be backed and redeemable to maintain confidence. Organisers David Pugh and Don Sage explain:

> Time credits are no different from any other currency. You have to keep coming up with ideas for people to spend their time credits. Otherwise you risk the currency crashing. If there aren't enough things for people to spend them on, they lose interest and the whole thing fizzles out.[27]

27 It's About Time, www.recruit3.org.uk/1282.file.dld

Although the rewards menu at the Time Centre and other community activities provided by the central administration are the main backing for the currency, time credits also circulate as currency for exchanges between individuals before redemption. Time credits are transferable and can be given as gifts to friends and family.

Geoff Thomas and his colleagues Becky Booth, Dawn Davies and Ceri Green have been inspiring many other communities around South Wales to use similar methods.[28] Time Banking Wales researches new applications of time banking in communities. It learns from practical experiments, develops methodologies to improve practice and makes the benefits available to others. It supports public organisations to use time banking to increase active citizenship. A Time Centre has two great advantages over other community development techniques: it creates a big knowledge bank of local assets and needs and it provides the rewards to motivate people to connect those assets to those needs.

> We have done a lot of prototypes in various communities and we know it works. In the end it is not about particular programmes but how to get everyone to subscribe to a common vision of community engagement using a common currency that runs through the community landscape.

The results are clear in Blaengarw. Creation Development Trust won the BURA Award for Regeneration and the Big Society Award from the UK Government.

Former First Minister of the National Assembly for Wales, Rhodri Morgan, said the Blaengarw project was 'a classic example of the kind of innovative approach to volunteering that the voluntary sector is famous for. It would be difficult for a local authority, or for our departments of Government, to come up with such a scheme. However, that is exactly what voluntary sector bodies can do and what we cannot do. They can come up with bright ideas'.

---

28 Time Banking Wales, www.timebankingwales.org.uk/ and Spice, http://justaddspice.org/

COMMUNITY EXCHANGE SYSTEM, SOUTH AFRICA

Based on an interview with Tim Jenkin.

KEY FEATURES

TYPE: Local Exchange Trading System   **DATE FOUNDED:** 2003

REGION SERVED: Based in South Africa, hub of global network

MAIN PURPOSE: Grow community

BENEFITS: Enables exchanges between individuals; makes money go further

PARTICIPANTS: 395 local systems in 43 countries; 22,500 individual accounts; 1,690 family accounts; 720 community organisation accounts and 1,020 company accounts

CORE MECHANISMS: Membership based; mutual credit 'currency' created by clearing positive and negative balances between members when they trade; backed by promise to supply local goods and services; all transactions recorded; active brokering of trades; web based software system – both a trade 'bank' and a marketplace; no printed circulating currency

NAME OF CURRENCY/ STANDARD OF VALUE: Varies in each country; CES publishes exchange rates between participating currencies based on recommended minimum wage in each country

TURNOVER: Not available.

GOVERNANCE: Non-profit company

MANAGEMENT: Manager plus volunteers

COST RECOVERY: National currency donations; local currency fee = 1% of local turnover

WEBSITE: www.ces.org.za

December, 1979. Tim Jenkin bursts through the 15th door of the notorious Pretoria Prison, apartheid South Africa's maximum security jail, and runs free.

Tim grew up in a wealthy, white family, totally ignorant of the sufferings of the black majority population around him. After an epic political transformation, he became a secret operative for the African National Congress (ANC), keeping up appearances with a daytime job whilst preparing leaflet bombs with ANC propaganda by night. His luck ran out when the police discovered his activities and he was sentenced to 12 years in prison. After his escape he went to England where he continued to work underground. In 1987, he published his story under the title *Escape from Pretoria*.[29]

When Nelson Mandela finished his long walk to freedom and apartheid finally collapsed, Tim had great hopes for a fundamental transformation of society. But not much changed.

> Apartheid ended in a legal sense but we realised that the real power was economic power. The basic structures of economic apartheid didn't change. With increasing prosperity there was some movement of people from the black community into the middle classes but that was all.

One day he read an article about the Local Exchange Trading System (LETS) in Australia. He immediately saw its potential to help the 25% unemployed in Johannesburg. A local LETS was set up and trading was done with homemade printed cheque books. Monthly statements were issued and a quarterly directory was printed, all very clumsy by today's standards. This first system only lasted about a year but Tim was bitten by the local currency bug. His years as an underground ANC activist had prepared him for the gruelling work of local organising, working long hours for little return and learning from mistakes in the hope of contributing towards change.

In 1994, the ANC asked Tim to set up a website, one of the first in South Africa. At that time you could list all of the websites in the country on one page. He developed the skills to create databases and dynamic websites and started experimenting. The idea of local currency would not leave him alone: he joined the South African New Economics (SANE) Network[30] and had many discussions about community currencies.

> My next attempt was sparked off by someone in my hiking club saying it would be a really good idea to list our skills in a database so we knew what each person could do. I built in a primitive transaction interface for members to do their own self-administration, which was an innovation at the time. I demonstrated it to members of the hiking club and suggested that we could trade amongst ourselves without money. People thought it was a great idea, but there was not enough interest in the club to sustain it.

James Taris, an Australian LETS evangelist, ignited huge interest on his visit to South Africa in 2002. People were ringing up asking how to join but nothing existed at that point. Tim and others formed a committee, gathered ideas and did research while Tim demonstrated his software. Cape Town Talent Exchange

---

29 T. Jenkin, *Escape from Pretoria*, (1987).

30 www.sane.org.za

launched in February 2003. Growth was slow with only 5 trades per month to begin with.

> We decided to hold a monthly market to stimulate trade. I had the computer there to record exchanges. People were fascinated. We said, 'Join up and you can get X,Y or Z.' People walked off with a box of vegetables feeling like they had stolen it. Most felt obliged to give something back.

By the end of 2003, there were six local exchange systems around South Africa and in May 2004 Tim started linking them together on the same web server. They called it the Community Exchange System (CES). Demand for trade between systems grew rapidly and they needed a technical solution. First they experimented with a cumbersome system of multiple virtual members, and finally created a single virtual member in each system that keeps a record of remote trades.

At this point in the story, something remarkable happens – a kind of evolutionary leap. In January 2005, a member of the Cape Town Exchange visited Logan LETS in Australia and told them about their internet based software. The Australians realised they could abolish their time-consuming central administration overnight by getting members to manage their own accounts in real time. As word spread, more and more Australian and New Zealand LETS began to join the CES, trusting the administration of their local systems to a remote server in South Africa.

> The local administrators found it amazing. It doesn't matter how many members you have, one click of a button can service a single member or hundreds. They had more time to deal with other things like advertising their system and organising local events. No more burnout.

By April 2012, the Community Exchange System had expanded to host the administration of 395 local systems in 43 countries, consisting of more than 22,500 individual accounts, 1690 family accounts, 720 community organisation accounts and 1020 company accounts. It is the world's only international clearing system for local currencies.

> We could never have predicted such growth but it has become popular because it is a user-friendly sign-up-and-go model with a working account available in a few minutes, just like Facebook. It has the experience and suggestions of hundreds of users built into it, so in a sense it is designed by its users. A local system has no hosting or server costs or need for programmers.

CES is a registered non-profit company, with an elected board and subject to annual audit. It has a standard set of rules for users and a Charter setting out the expectations for exchanges to follow.

CES makes sure that people applying to set up a local system are serious. They make it clear that, even though individual users will do a lot of their own administration, the local administrators have to create the framework for the local system to flourish. The CES web site contains a sophisticated system of administration levels:

Super Admin (CES): full privileges.

Local Admin: local management functions from address lists to newsletters.

Local Member Admin: setting up members to creating accounts.

Coordinator: ordinary members who do account functions for others.

User: self-administration of own account.

Local administrators have access to a range of functions for managing their local system. For instance, they can create semi-autonomous sub-areas within their local system and can check the balance of trade between those areas. The administrators (395 in 43 countries) are a global learning community, supporting and helping each other with new ideas. There is also a mobile phone interface using a cut-down version of the user interface with no buttons and all text.

In the CES system, the seller always enters the data for the transaction. Some systems activate optional credit/debit limits. Many systems remove them. The accounts in each local system theoretically balance to zero, on the classic mutual credit model.

CES had to intervene once when the balance of trade between two neighbouring systems reached an imbalance of 100 to 1. They stopped trade in one direction until a better balance was reached. The whole CES now has a built-in balancing mechanism with maximum ratios and automatic blocking of remote trades that go over these limits.

CES recommends that local systems use a transaction fee of 4% to derive revenue for their own administration time. Some systems have abandoned member fees in the national currency because they no longer need the income. CES also charges each participating system a global levy of 1% of turnover to cover its own time and this will be reduced in future as CES grows. They also receive very helpful national currency donations from happy customers worldwide who want to put something back.

Tim designed his first system using Microsoft technologies because there was not much choice at the time.

> I used what was there and got stuck in that. It was never really designed from scratch, it just grew and we patched as we went. It's a terribly complex mess but it works. Some people don't like it because it's not Open Source but we couldn't abandon Microsoft overnight. We are working towards Open Source applications but, as users are constantly asking for new features to the current software, the downloadable version never keeps up with the 'real thing'.

Another weakness is the centralised nature of a system running on one server.

> We plan to decentralise CES through what we call Clearing Central. It is a central clearing house that will permit trades between different servers and systems. This will allow separate CES servers in different regions and countries; each server can host any number of local exchanges and the separate servers can talk to each other. To enable users to see what is available from other places, there will also be a requirement for a single global marketplace, something like eBay or Gumtree.

Has CES helped the unemployed and the poor in South Africa?

> We tried to introduce CES to the townships. It was all done manually because people didn't have computers or internet cafés. People had to stand in a queue and wait for a printed list of phone numbers. The system worked quite well for a while but then the funding stopped and the system collapsed. The city authority in Cape Town is obliged to provide services to poor areas but they never get anything back. Theoretically, they could spend CES credits in the community by paying their workers and allow the workers to pay local taxes in local currency.

Participation in CES has transformed the lives of some people.

> Some people get frustrated with the system because they don't get what they want and just ignore it. Others glow about it – like Dawn Pilatowicz, in Cape Town Talent Exchange, who is wheelchair bound. She used to find it difficult to get help. Now she has an army of helpers. And there are many like that. They all realise it is about a strong, social network.

In recognition of his untiring efforts, Tim Jenkin was elected to a Fellowship by the Ashoka Foundation in 2007.[31] CES was featured in a *Time Magazine* article in 2008.[32]

Tim is still running for freedom, not just for himself, but for all those who are losers in the game of capitalist economics. He has designed CES so that as many as possible can participate.

> We wanted it to be like national currency in that you are there by default as a user for life. It's a different way of doing money without any barriers. My reward is seeing it grow and be used.

---

31 www.ashoka.org/fellow/timothy-jenkin
32 'Alternative Currencies Grow in Popularity', *Time Business*, (2008).
   Online at www.time.com/time/business/article/0,8599,1865467,00.html

DANE COUNTY TIME BANK, USA

Based on an interview with Stephanie Rearick.

KEY FEATURES

TYPE: Time Bank   **DATE FOUNDED:** 2006

REGION SERVED: Dane County, Wisconsin, USA

MAIN PURPOSE: Grow community

BENEFITS: Enables exchanges between individuals; says thank you to volunteers; makes money go further

PARTICIPANTS: 1,900 members

CORE MECHANISMS: Membership based; mutual credit 'currency' created by clearing positive and negative balances between members when they trade; backed by promise to supply local goods and services; all transactions recorded; active brokering of trades; web based software system – both a trade 'bank' and a marketplace; no printed circulating currency

NAME OF CURRENCY/STANDARD OF VALUE: One Time Credit = One hour of service

TURNOVER: 60,000 hours since 2006

GOVERNANCE: Dane County Time Bank non-profit organisation with local 'Kitchen Cabinet' neighborhood steering teams

MANAGEMENT: Three paid staff

COST RECOVERY: Funding

WEBSITE: www.danecountytimebank.org

Wisconsin was the first state in the United States to provide collective bargaining rights to public employees in 1959. In Febrary 2011, after years of tax cuts, the administration of Governor Walker introduced a Budget Repair Bill that required unions to give up their collective bargaining rights in order to save on benefits and pensions. It sparked the biggest public protests in Wisconsin's history, with hundreds of thousands of participants occupying the State Capitol and city centre.

Artist-activist, Stephanie Rearick, was on the barricades inspiring the crowds protesting the bill:

> We have plenty of money for war and prisons and tax cuts but not for
> schools and public employees. What's our problem here, that we don't have
> enough teachers or students or factories? Aren't there people who know
> how to make stuff, like less polluting cars? Why do we take for granted that

people have to work two or three crappy jobs producing junk that's wasteful and no one needs?

It's not the economy stupid, it's the stupid economy! (CROWD CHEERS)

What kind of world can we create that's worth living in? Why do we accept that banks can create money and loan it to us at interest? Why do we accept this system?

I don't accept those rules, we can change the rules and play to win and our game is way more fun![33]

Stephanie is director of the Dane County Time Bank in Wisconsin, joint owner of Mother Fools local coffee house and a singer-songwriter with seven recorded albums.

She has been politically active about many different issues for 20 years and always knew that the way we do money is at the root of many social and economic problems that bothered her. In the early 90s she heard about Paul Glover's Ithaca HOURS system in New York and was intrigued by the idea of money that stays in the community. In 1996, she was part of a 15-member group that launched Madison HOURS, closely modelled on the Ithaca system. HOURS is still going but did not have the social impact Stephanie had hoped for.

We weren't connecting with disadvantaged communities as we'd hoped. When I came across timebanking, I thought it was simple and elegant and solved problems we had grappled with through Madison HOURS. I am convinced that the equal value of time exchange is critical to help marginalised people and that time banks can play a crucial role alongside other mutual credit systems.

They convened meetings with local leaders in the mayor's office to persuade them to start a time bank.

Officials sponsored a feasibility study but it was two conferences in particular that gave us the real inspiration: the Bard College conference on local currencies, organised by the Schumacher Society, and the Time Banks USA conference. At the Bard College conference, Bernard Lietaer told us that we all needed to experiment to find out what works best. At the Time Banks conference, Edgar Cahn's vision of co-production inspired us and we learned a lot from local time bank organisers too.

We went home and started planning the time bank without official support. It was a blessing that the time bank was not funded at the start so we could make it more robust and get people involved in shaping it. People from Time

---

33 www.youtube.com/watch?v=ykT4msyg3G4

Banks USA trained us and we then made a strategic decision to start in one neighbourhood with diverse needs, not a stereotypically activist one.

They launched in October 2005 with 20 people and now have 1,900 members spread across Dane County, a region of about 1200 square miles with a population of 500,000 people that includes the City of Madison, capital of Wisconsin. Members have exchanged 60,000 hours of service in 6 years of operation.

Einstein discovered that time is money

Their main aims were to connect different sectors and to promote collaboration and resource sharing. The 2010 annual report[34] shows the results:

- Members exchanged 12,100 hours of service, meaning that people save money to spend on essentials and generate more wealth for themselves by tapping into their skills.

- 125 community organisations got work done which they could not otherwise afford.

- The Time Bank Youth Court, inspired by Edgar Cahn's experiments in Washington DC and formally recognised by Madison's police department, is based in a school and pays the staff helpers in hours. Some of them donate their hours to the school, which buys in yoga teaching, art workers and mentors for kids in trouble. There is a measurable reduction in fighting.

---

34 www.danecountytimebank.org/uploads/3/9/5/6/3956131/2010_annual_report.pdf

- Madison Gas and Electric Company partnered with them to train their members to do home energy surveys and managed to reduce participants' average consumption by 10%.

- Maxine's Time Bank Store allowed members to exchange goods with each other and also partnered with four other community health associations to create a new Wellness Cooperative.

What's the secret?

I'd been involved in lots of different campaigns and I noticed how people with similar goals were fighting each other for resources to survive. I've never seen anything that gets so many people involved across all boundaries, connecting people based on what makes us all human: our need for each other. As an antidote to fighting for crumbs, we make pie together.

Money is permission, people are looking for permission to make things better; the time currency gives people that permission. Time banking is the one thing I have found that gets to the roots of many of our social problems, instead of just fire fighting the effects. I love seeing people having permission to solve their own problems in their own community using this tool and seeing what they come up with.

People start feeling like an extended family you can call in time of need. I've also noticed levels of compassion and patience rise. Some people are less difficult to deal with because they feel that people care about them. People with mental health problems have transformed their situation in some cases. People become more generous because they feel wealthy, giving stuff away as gifts.

Like many local currency systems, they struggle to find the best way of making decisions...

> The ideal structure for a time bank hasn't been invented yet. We base all our decisions on our core values – we treat each person as an asset to the community; we practice give and take; we value and reward each person's contribution as real work; we weave a web of mutual support and we respect each other – and then try to make sure that members are actively engaged in putting these decisions into practice. We're constantly learning. We've had good people but also struggled with how to be inclusive and get people into roles that are right for them. At one point, by trying to include all groups, the board got too big so we had to downsize it a bit. We have an 80% decision making process, which is close to consensus. The co-operative model is closer to our ideal and we are exploring it for the future. The most important thing is that the time bank is never an end in itself. We've always viewed it as a resource base from which to develop projects.

... and organising themselves.

> Time banking has to be easy to use, it should be part of everyday life for people.

> One good thing about the internet and modern software is that people can do their own administration so less work needs to be done centrally. At the same time, we have to be aware that there are still many people who are not computer savvy. So, we have developed a system of online buddies for offline members to help them with their accounts.

They have developed local neighbourhood-based steering teams, called Kitchen Cabinets, that are chosen by local people. They are responsible for outreach and other member contact in order to keep Time Bank exchanges flowing and healthy in their neighbourhood. This may involve: identifying people and organisations who can bring more diversity to the Time Bank; organising events to maintain a sense of community and neighbourhood feel; staying in contact with members to help in making matches and checking on quality of exchanges.

They also have specialist Action Teams for the whole Time Bank: Special Events; Fundraising/Resource Development; Outreach and Community Relations; Membership – Policy, Procedure, Functionality.

Three paid organisers ensure that it all works.

Stephanie and her colleagues have been so inspired by time banking that they have begun a new initiative called Time for the World,[35] which aims to share what they have learned around the world and inspire others to get involved.

---

35 www.timeftw.org

Enough of us have seen a kernel of something really great; we think we are onto something big. Somewhere within the economic and social crises that surround us are the seeds of a different world. As all those seeds are discovered they should be cast widely so that anyone can experiment and grow things from them. We need to recognise what we don't know yet and develop a very broad view of where our efforts need to go and how to get there.

Time for the World has five components:

- BuildFTW is about open community organising experiments.

- CodeFTW is about engaging programmers, coders and hackers to link different communities of practice through systems of incentive, recognition and reward.

- ShareFTW invites people to share documents, templates, marketing materials, media, data, code, designs, teaching materials, anything.

- TeachFTW is a way to draw attention to opportunities to learn.

- BankFTW is more like a river bank. It holds records and helps guide efforts; it helps everyone show what they've contributed and to remember that every contribution matters.

What are the most important lessons to be shared?

Time banking is very practical. People come to it to meet their needs, not with thoughts of economics. Then their experiences open their minds to what an economy really is and what it could be. We have whole new audiences coming to discuss these issues. We have all learned so much about community, about economics at the grassroots. I think we need to see local community economies as ecosystems needing enough variety for them to flourish. It has shifted things for me in ways I did not realise I had that much room to shift!

Governor Walker pushed his Budget Repair Bill through in late 2011. Unions lost their negotiating rights and hundreds of teachers were axed. Dane County Time Bank is more needed than ever to help people to help themselves. But maybe some lyrics from Stephanie's song, *Up The Wall*, should have the last word:

Fasten all your safety belts and hold on for a freaky freaky fall.
But first this roller coaster's gonna slow down to a creepy creepy crawl.
Write down all your wishes and submit them to the gently weeping wall.
And when I make that leap I'll have to trust that you'll be there
to break my fall.[36]

---

36 http://stephanierearick.com/?id=lyrics#wall

Other regional models

Community Way, Canada

Community Way[37] was developed on Vancouver Island in Canada by one of the pioneers of community currencies. Following an economic recession in 1983, Michael Linton designed and started the world's first Local Exchange Trading System (LETS) and has continued to promote community currency systems ever since. Community Way is an innovation in the mutual credit model, where the currency issue is limited to a group of responsible businesses and is then convertible into conventional funding to benefit community causes. Local businesses donate Community Way Dollars (cw$) to non-profit organisations whose supporters exchange Canadian $ for cw$, giving them funds to operate, and cw$ can be used to purchase goods and services at participating businesses, who spend them with other businesses, donate them back to another non-profit organisation, or top up staff bonuses. Community Way is currently being piloted in Vancouver and several other sites in Western Canada. Michael Linton intends to spread this and other open money ideas even more widely via mobile phone apps at the 2012 London Olympics – a kind of 'guerilla marketing' for sane economics that may spark communities both in London and around the world to play too.

Liquidity Network, Ireland and UK

The *Liquidity Network*[38] is a set of principles for a designed currency that originated in Ireland from the work of the economist Richard Douthwaite at the Foundation for the Economics of Sustainability (FEASTA).[39] It focuses on the need to create and maintain liquidity within trading networks, and to do this quickly, cheaply and safely using mobile and web technologies. Its key characteristic is that new currency is spent or given into circulation rather than created via debt. The money supply is monitored and can shrink or grow to meet demand. A mixture of fees and bonuses is used to reward those using the network and to encourage trading among those who are not. Variations include: rewarding pro-local or pro-environmental behaviours; it can be local authority-led/commercially-led/community-led; it can be scaled to national implementations. In 2012, a separate Community of Practice – the Feasta Currency Group – was established on Facebook to facilitate professional dialogue between currency advocates.

---

37 www.communityway.ca/

38 http://theliquiditynetwork.org/

39 www.feasta.org

NEWT, Wales

The *NEWT (New Energy Wealth Tokens)*[40] is an adaptive framework to support and develop a wide variety of currency models, its flexible structure accommodating, and drawing inspiration from, a very wide variety of tested currency models. Currently in the very early stages of development in Mid Wales, the NEWT began with the more modest objective of creating an energy-backed exchange currency to amplify the value of a community-supportive surplus generated by a locally-owned and -controlled renewable energy installation, with the addition of an energy-backed store-of-value currency following almost immediately.

The NEWT design will progressively add new application-specific currencies, along with metasystemic elements to assist in the planning of long-term survival and stability of economic units (whether primary productive operations such as businesses or support elements such as community banking partners), and is intended to interoperate flexibly with other systems.

Dual Currency, USA

DualCurrency Systems[41] is a Minnesota company founded by US entrepreneur Joel Hodroff and a group of socially responsible investors. The company is relaunching in 2012 as *newincentives4change* to help employers, large and small, to improve employee engagement and reach social responsibility benchmarks. Employees (and community members) will earn spendable rewards for community volunteerism, meeting wellness and eco-sustainability goals and more. These part-cash and part-noncash transactions turn underutilised capacity (empty restaurant tables, airline seats, college desks, etc.) into new community wealth. Businesses increase sales and cash profits, while community members save money by spending Corporate & Community Social Responsibility Dollars (CSR$).

Regional Economic Communities, Germany

This concept was developed by Anna-Lisa Schmalz and Tim Reeves in Germany (Regionale Wirtschaftsgemeinschaften) and is described in detail on the Web in English and German under a CCBY licence.[42] The concept can be instantiated in any democratic and participative legal form, e.g. a public company based on shares. The authors favour a co-operative, which is then

---

40 www.esrad.org.uk/NEWT

41 www.dualcurrency.com/

42 http://regional-economic-communities.info/ and http://rewig-muenchen.de/

called a ReeComm (German: ReWiG). It is about engaging and empowering local citizens to become joint owners of regional businesses that strive for sustainability; and inviting local citizens and businesses to trade on a virtual marketplace using a mutual credit-type currency called the Grok. The Grok is issued by its users, but only to the extent of deposited securities that have *already* added value to the ReeComm, making it a particularly trustworthy and stable currency. Besides the economic and sustainability aspects, the authors place much importance on social sustainability, i.e. active community building. The first ReWiG was incorporated in Munich, January 2011, the second in Southern Bavaria in February 2012. Development continues rapidly.

Sectoral currencies

Regional currencies aim to serve people in a geographically defined area. Another class of complementary currencies narrows the focus to specific social issues or groups of users and are sometimes called sectoral currencies. This section provides short descriptions of the most important ones.

Young people

Time banks are particularly good at engaging young people to get involved in community life. Examples of these are *Time Banks USA* and its *Time Dollar Tutoring* and *Youth Courts* projects; *Time Banking Wales* and *SPICE* with their *Time for Young People* projects.

Pensions

Fureai Kippu in Japan and *Talente Tauschkreis Vorarlberg in Austria* have programmes for people to care for others and save credits to receive household help and care when they are older. The city of Sankt Gallen in Switzerland is the first formal implementation in Europe of the Fureai Kippu system. These embryonic projects could pave the way for future schemes on a larger scale.

Education

Bernard Lietaer made a proposal for a new currency called *Saber*[43] to solve the funding crisis in the Brazilian education system in 2004. One version of it has been implemented by Professor Gilson Schwartz in Brazil; and another version is operational on a pilot level in two secondary schools in the city of Ghent, Belgium. The same principles could easily be adapted for use elsewhere.

Le Ropi[44] is a euro-backed currency initiated in Belgium in October 2011 by a group of active citizens and businesses called *FINANC'éthique Mons.* Supported by the provincial government of Hainaux and inspired by the *Saber* model, the project started in a local school with a design competition for the notes. Students earn currency for project work and it is spent in local businesses. Fair Trade Week gave the currency a big boost. Features by French, Russian and Ukrainian TV stations, as well as Al Jazeera, caused them to accelerate their plans. The currency takes its name from a mythical local boy called Le Ropieur, who is a kind of trickster figure.

---

43 www.complementarycurrency.org/ccLibrary/brazil_education_currency_system_Lietaer.pdf
44 http://financethiquemons.agora.eu.org

L Currency[45] is a project of The Holistic Education Foundation Co. Ltd. (T.H.E. Foundation) on Merseyside. Members use a software package called 'tgl' – 'teaching, giving, learning' to pursue their innate talents and interests, and are then rewarded in L currency (L = local, loyalty, learning, liquidity and leisure; L1=£1). The website includes secure member areas, a search engine, trading bays, skills exchange, projects, a social networking platform and interactive community TV channels – 'like a local Ebay, Tesco-online, MySpace and Youtube rolled into one for the benefit of human beings'. Membership is free, with fees payable only when members choose to trade goods and services in the shopping village or skills exchange. 'Civic Universities', where students develop their own internships to collaborate with local people and businesses, are being considered. Students would learn-and-earn L currency, while gaining hands-on experience within local and virtual communities. A full EPOS system has been developed with L Bank cards, card readers and mobile phone application, enhanced with a text service and in-house printers for on-line orders. Following pilots in 2011, tgl has developed a Town Team across a broad range of social landlords, community trusts and local organisations. Communities anywhere are invited to use and evolve the software and systems, in collaboration with T.H.E. Foundation.

Social, cultural and civic activities

Civics[46] is a proposal by Bernard Lietaer to fund the labour component of communal programmes and strengthen the co-operative economy. Citizens earn *Civics* (one *Civic* = one hour of work) by working in environmental and arts projects, organised and monitored by local non-profits. All local citizens have the option to pay a local tax, – e.g. 10 *Civics* per family per year – which the local government uses to pay the workers in the programmes, or to opt out and pay the normal local tax in national currency. Community members would also nominate *Civics*-earning activities. Local governments can generate and measure those civic activities with widespread participation more precisely, with minimal financial cost and so improve this very important aspect of civil society. Non-profit organisations can motivate and organise more volunteers, whilst gaining an income stream in conventional currency from the sale of excess *Civics* to those preferring to purchase rather than earn them. Citizens would enjoy a flourishing community and a higher quality of life and those with time and/or interest in civic activities could earn additional income from others needing *Civics* or preferring to purchase them.

---

45 www.tgl.tv/users/login and http://www.youtube.com/watch?v=BVrwM5Gkl_Y

46 www.lietaer.com

Environment

Eco-Pesa, Kenya[47] was a local currency pilot project led by Will Ruddick. Mobile Money (M-PESA) is incorporated into all mobile phones in Kenya and a very popular way of transferring funds. It raised the awareness of millions of people about the idea of a 'second currency'. Will wanted to increase the effectiveness of aid money in community development and environmental programs by encouraging increased local circulation of those funds. The pilot project involving 3 informal settlements and 75 small businesses, ran for a year from May 2010 to May 2011. An awareness of community action and local purchasing was raised: people collected 20 tons of rubbish and planted 1,000 trees; one new business selling tree seedlings was created. Will Ruddick aims to apply the lessons learned to community development and forest resource management in defined bio-regions.

Maia Maia project[48] in Perth, Western Australia is an 'emission reduction currency system' (ERCS),[49] a new kind of locally issued currency that can be derived and spent globally. It is based on the value to society of reducing greenhouse gas emissions and other environmentally destructive activities. One hundred Boyas – a currency named after the local Nyungar people's word for traditional rock trading tokens – equals a reduction of 1 metric tonne of greenhouse gases by the local community, in accordance with an average Social Cost of Carbon cited in reports of the International Panel on Climate Change. Positive stories of climate change action, embedded on each counterfeit-proof note and accessible on the internet via QRCode technology, also create the value of a Boya. This association of economic value with storytelling is also inspired by the exchange of 'song lines' by aboriginal peoples. Communities that achieve a 10- 50- or 100-tonne carbon reduction plan from alternative energy, waste composting, and tree planting can issue 1000, 5000, or 10,000 boyas to award to members and volunteers. Boyas have been issued by schools (Coolbinia Primary, where the idea was developed by a parent group), neighbourhood associations, environmental conferences, landcare groups, and overseas aid associations. A small number of local businesses currently accept them in trade. Although a local initiative, carbon for projects has been

---

47 W. Ruddick,'Eco-Pesa: An Evaluation of a Complementary Currency Programme in Kenya's Informal Settlements' *International Journal of Community Currency Research* 15 (A) 1–12, (2011). Online at
http://www.ijccr.net/IJCCR/2011_%2815%29_files/IJCCR%202011%20Ruddick.pdf

48 www.maiamaia.org/

49 http://en.wikipedia.org/wiki/Emissions_Reduction_Currency_System

sourced from development projects in Ghana and Uganda, and the University of Vermont is undertaking a pilot project.

Energy

Reconomy[50] aims to pay thousands with *SunMoney* local currency to generate electricity using pedal power, and then discount the energy when purchased with *SunMoney* to produce a demand for the currency that will build local marketplaces. The pilot project is a People Power Station at Vigyan Ashram science school in Pabal, Maharashtra, India, – globally renowned for innovative work. The generator design has won national awards. Kevin Parcell, the project designer and adviser, is also working in Massachusetts, USA, to enable people to pay for 'Net Energy Metering Credits' with SunMoney.

Renewable Energy Dollars , a currency using kilowatt hours as the basic unit of value, were first proposed by Shann Turnbull in a 1983 book, *Handbook of tools for community economic change*. The idea has inspired several people to try out experiments in this direction and still holds out promise for the future.

Community Banking

The *Common Good Finance[51]* plan for a new democratic economy features RCredits™. Starting in Greenfield, Massachusetts, USA and managed from the start, it ensures businesses and consumers have plenty of places to spend their community-created money. New members are given RCredits, plus more every time they buy or sell within the system. RCredits uses computerised bookkeeping, simple mobile phone texting or internet, electronic photo identification, and user-customised security procedures. Participating communities discuss and decide what businesses to fund, using innovative direct democratic methods. Partnering with local banks and credit unions, CGF will offer Common Good Accounts, using dual currencies of US dollars and RCredits.

Real Money. Real Democracy. Real Power.

---

50 http://reconomy.net

51 http://commongoodfinance.com/

Ethical and Sustainable Business

Lewes Pound,[52] with its notes picturing the revolutionary Thomas Paine, attracted TV crews from Russia at its launch in 2008. Organisers of this Transition Town currency in the South East English coast town are now rethinking their strategy as interest has waned.

Bremer Roland[53] was Germany's first modern regional currency in 2001, serving the Bremen-Bremerhaven region of northern Germany. Its main emphasis is the support of organic agricultural businesses through local supply chains.

Sterntaler[54] is one of Germany's leading regional currency systems, based in the Berchtesgaden area on the Austrian border. Franz Galler, an ex-finance manager, started the system in 2004 to support regional exchange. They have developed an innovative 'three shell model', consisting of a euro-backed circulating currency, an exchange ring and a time bank operating in parallel.

Coinstatt[55] has served ethical and fair trade businesses in the industrial Ruhr region of Germany since 2007. Business director Peter Krause-Keusemann has now diversified the operation into educational activities for regional and ethical economics through the Coinstatt Akademie, which arranges online learning and large educational events.

VBSR Marketplace[56] provides a mutual credit clearing system for ethical and sustainable businesses in the Vermont region of the USA. Business director Amy Kirschner integrated the system into an existing social network called Vermont Business for Social Responsibility (VBSR).

Tláloc[57] currency was started by activists in Mexico City in 1995 and continues to serve a network that is involved with the World Wildlife Fund and the World Social Forum. They issue a special ECOSOL currency for use at annual fairs.

LOAVES[58] (Local Original Ashhurst Voluntary Exchange System) is launching in the Ashhurst and Pohangina Valley area of New Zealand in 2012. Target for startup: 50 businesses. The currency will be in the form of vouchers: $1, $5,

---

52 http://thelewespound.org/
53 www.roland-regional.de/
54 www.regiostar.com/3.0.html
55 www.coinstatt.org/
56 http://vbsrmarket.com/
57 http://redtlaloc.blogspot.com
58 www.youtube.com/watch?v=JdNWxl6D6J4

$10 and $20, all designed by a local artist, backed by New Zealand Dollars and accepted by participating businesses. Phil and Sharon Stevens lead a group called RECAP, which has been planning the currency for two years. Palmerston North City Council gave the group a local initiative grant to get the scheme off the ground and the Living Economies Educational Trust also supports it.

Disaster relief

Lyttleton Time Bank[59] is a key part of Project Lyttleton in a small New Zealand harbour town. The Time Bank started as a community building tool in 2004 and met its greatest challenge during the earthquakes of 2010/2011. The local medical centre was a member of the Time Bank, which was able to mobilise its members to provide essential relief to victims.

Intentional community

The Eko Community Currency[60] is a project of the Ekopia Resource Exchange at the Findhorn community in Scotland, a spiritual and ecological community established in the 1960s. The currency supports exchanges amongst community members and its thousands of annual visitors, particularly through the Phoenix community shop. It is launching a special issue of notes for the 50th birthday of the community in 2012.

---

59 www.lyttelton.net.nz/timebank

60 www.ekopia-findhorn.org/eko.shtml

Chapter 8
Research, develop, support – the role of agencies

We have seen what a complex task it is to design and sustain a viable regional currency system. A few of the world's leading examples, like WIR Bank, Ithaca HOURS, Community Exchange System, Equal Dollars, BerkShares or Brixton Pound, have succeeded through a combination of creativity, leadership and perseverance. Other systems have sought guidance from agencies set up for the purpose.

Agencies arise when there is a need for information and support. In this chapter we profile five of them:

The *International Reciprocal Trade Association (IRTA)* is a classic industrial trade body set up by members of the business exchange industry to promote standards and provide information.

STRO evolved from an environmental campaigning organisation into a research and development outfit specialising in local currencies and the Open Source Cyclos software to support them.

QOIN was set up by former employees of STRO and specialises in electronic payment systems for local currencies.

The *Regiogeld e.V* arose from the early regional currencies in Germany that needed an umbrella to promote standards and networking.

CommunityForge offers new economic tools to enable real-world and virtual communities to declare their own localised currencies, and to trade in them using Open Source software. It is based in Geneva, Switzerland.

Other organisations and resources include:

LETSLink UK is a volunteer group providing advice to Local Exchange Trading Systems in the UK.

Timebanking UK, Timebanking Wales, SPICE and TimeBanks USA are all funded agencies providing specialist help to time banks.

The *International Journal of Community Currencies Research* (IJCCR) was started by Colin Williams and Mark Jackson in 1996, when Colin was at Leeds Metropolitan University. It is now co-edited by Gill Seyfang and Colin Williams at the University of East Anglia. It is the only specialist academic publication focused on local currency theory and practice.

The *Complementary Currency Resource Center* is an online, collaborative resource centre coordinated by Stephen de Meulenaere, a former employee of STRO in Indonesia.

The *Community Currency Magazine* is run by self-organised volunteers and is currently edited by Matthew Slater of CommunityForge.

There are other more generic think tanks and agencies that promote local currencies as part of a wider brief to promote new economic thinking. These include *New Economics Foundation (nef)* in London, which has now partnered with the *New Economics Institute* in the USA (formerly EF Schumacher Society); *South African New Economics Network; Living Economies Network* in New Zealand.

There is a constant cross-fertilisation of ideas and models. Knowledge gained from practice is shared with the global community of practice and agencies play a unique dissemination role in this process.

Collaboration and adaptation are particularly important in the area of software. STRO's Open Source Cyclos software is in widespread use in European and South American systems; QOIN has further adapted Cyclos to enable mobile payments, used by currencies such as the Brixton and Bristol Pound; CommunityForge has developed another Open Source application running on Drupal.

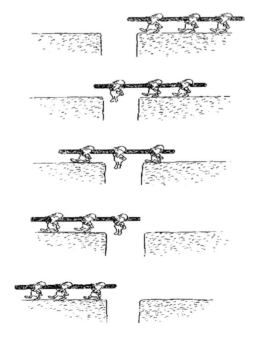

International Reciprocal Trade Association (IRTA)

Based on an interview with Ron Whitney.

www.irta.com

IRTA is a non-profit organisation that promotes high standards of practice amongst business exchange systems through education, self regulation, ethics and government relations. Started by leaders of US business exchanges in 1979 to represent their interests, IRTA is the oldest barter trade association in the world and has been active in promoting and improving the industry ever since. As stated in Chapter 5, IRTA estimates that over 400,000 companies worldwide use trade exchanges to share their excess business capacities and underperforming assets and to earn an estimated $12 billion dollars in previously lost and wasted revenues.[1]

Ron Whitney, IRTA's Executive Director, started a business exchange in the Philadelphia area in 1993 after working in the legal, real estate and insurance fields. He immediately grasped the potential of trade and barter as a bona fide business model and has become one of its most passionate advocates. After serving in several positions on the IRTA board, he became Executive Director in 2007.

> I believe in this industry to the bottom of my toes. I have seen first-hand benefits at every level, from individual traders to Fortune 500 companies. Our core mission at IRTA is to spread a good word about the benefits of organised trade without money. We advocate the importance of having a barter strategy that provides an alternative marketplace for participants to increase their revenues, preserve cash flow and maximise underused assets. These powerful benefits are available in good or bad economic climates.

> There is a very important bottom line fiduciary responsibility for those managing business exchanges: you are creating an economic system, which brings with it the responsibility and duty to run the exchange in a professional and prudent manner.

Prior to 1979, the business 'barter' industry was an unregulated free-for-all in the USA. People were setting up multiple exchanges and disappearing after helping themselves to goods and services from members. IRTA set out to raise the bar to entry and establish enforceable professional codes of conduct. The first battle was with the authorities: the Internal Revenue Service (IRS) was carrying out random audits of exchanges and had no clear guidance on how to treat non-cash transactions. Members feared the industry would be outlawed.

---

1 http://www.irta.com/modern-trade-a-barter.html

IRTA lobbied the government and played a key role in framing the Tax Equity Fiscal Responsibility Act (TEFRA) of 1982, which recognises 'trade dollars' as US dollars for tax reporting. Business exchanges are now required to report 'proceeds from barter exchange and brokerage transactions' of all members to the IRS, so it is treated just like cash revenue. This obligation legitimised the barter industry and weeded out the cowboys.

In the 1980s and 1990s, IRTA created a members library containing advice and information about all aspects of setting up and running effective exchange systems. In 2012, it wrote an advisory memo on how to deal with exchange deficits,[2] which is just as critical an issue to local exchange systems as it is to nations. Here is an extract:

> The barter exchange must have the authority to assure adequate liquidity exists in the barter system by regulating the supply of trade dollars (money supply) needed to finance the smooth turnover of products and services being offered in the exchange. Simply put, there needs to be enough trade dollars in the system for members to be able to buy goods and services they wish to purchase...

> Excessive deficit spending by a barter exchange will cause serious liquidity problems that threaten the financial stability of the entire exchange. However, properly managed exchange deficits, which fall within the recommended IRTA guideline of 2.5 to 3.0 times the annualised average monthly trade volume (calculated only on one side), can increase trade volume and revenue by providing the right level of money supply sufficient to allow members to buy and sell freely within the system.

Ron Whitney and his board take IRTA's role as guardian of standards very seriously. Its Code of Ethics and Conduct is regularly updated.

> We think through every aspect of running an exchange. What are the obligations of a franchisee? What about exchanges that try to poach others' members? What kind of advertising is ethical? We have a 'three strikes and you're out' disciplinary process for IRTA members who breach our code, culminating in termination of membership. What IRTA does is critical, we as an industry have to self-police.

The new frontier is the internet, which opens up great possibilities and challenges at the same time. Anyone with good programming and marketing skills can set up a website, launch an exchange system and persuade people to use it without having any real knowledge of how to run an effective exchange. An IRS study of internet based barter exchanges found that the percentage

---

2   Irta advisory memo, Guidelines & recommendations for barter exchange deficits, March 28, 2012 revision. Online at http://www.irta.com/resources.html

of non-compliance for tax reporting was much higher for pure internet based exchanges than with the traditional regional non-internet-based barter exchange sector. The proliferation of on-line barter systems has made IRTA's role of maintaining industry standards even tougher.

On the other hand, the internet also brings opportunities for innovation and growth on an international level. In 1997, IRTA created The Universal Currency Clearinghouse[3] (UC) to provide an on-line seamless international trading platform for its members. UC is an added benefit for IRTA members who traded 6 million 'trade credits' (6m US dollar equivalent) in 2011. About 80% of UC business is travel related and transaction fees are kept to a very low 0.25% to cover costs. Things have clearly come a long way since the early days of the industry when people were recording exchanges in a ledger book with a pencil.

IRTA's role extends way beyond insisting its members conduct their businesses in an ethical and professional manner. IRTA also advocates to protect and preserve the industry against governmental regulations that could negatively impact the industry, as Ron Whitney explains:

> Recently, an IRTA member exchange in North Carolina told us that the NC Bar Association was ready to prevent attorneys from participating in barter exchanges, based on an argument that to do so violated their State based Code of Conduct for attorneys. IRTA immediately appeared before the NC Bar Association to point out the importance of organised trade, that it was totally legal and widely accepted as an alternative payment system. It was not, therefore, a violation of their legal code. It completely turned the situation around: the Bar Association passed a resolution supporting attorneys participation in NC barter exchanges and the NC Bar Association opinion is now used as the model for the other States in the USA to permit the participation of lawyers in barter and trade systems.

Ron has also served on an advisory group to the IRS in Washington, helping to inform government officials about the potential economic benefits of reciprocal exchange. At least fifteen States are considering launching different types of currencies. IRTA members are involved in discussions with the Chinese government and the City of London too (p.222).

> This is a very exciting time of huge activity as cities and counties running deficits see how can they use mutual credit clearing house systems to maximise their capacity. We are also seeing the first signs of consolidation and convergence of all sectors in mutually owned systems that benefit every level of society. Management, risk and profit are shared collectively

---

3 www.ucci.biz/

between participants in quasi public-private partnerships that operate in the best interests of the whole. The future is limitless. We are going to see an explosion in the next few years as businesses, government and consumers learn of the powerful benefits that barter and trade systems can offer in solving many of the economic ills of today's world.

STRO, Netherlands

Based on an interview with Henk van Arkel.
www.socialtrade.org

STRO (Social Trade Organisation) is the world's leading research and development agency for local currencies. A group of volunteers started STRO, an environmental campaigning organisation and publisher, on Earth Day in 1970. Its early actions were focused on issues like deforestation, climate change and species loss. It also developed far-sighted eco-tax and CO_2 emission proposals. Since the 1990s, STRO has specialised in local currency technology. Managing director Henk van Arkel explains why:

> We target the steering mechanisms in society. In the 1970s, we identified money and taxes as key mechanisms that steer society and effect environmental and social relations. Since we did not know how to get around the monopoly of central banks, we first focused on eco-taxes that steer economic activities in a more ecologically sustainable way. Then, as computing power increased in the 1980s, we understood that the nature of money as information would change. It would allow more people to exchange information about ownership titles to assets and resources. The monopoly on money would dwindle at some point and this would open up new opportunities for alternatives, so we decided to pick up the challenge.

STRO focused its resources on researching and developing new money systems to demonstrate that alternatives are not only possible but workable in real economies.

Henk van Arkel was a teenager when he ran his first environmental campaign in 1965. This was when he first learnt about the far-reaching negative effects of the money system and the alternatives to it.

> An old man explained to me that, however many campaigns we fight to save the whales or the rainforests, there is a hidden foot on the accelerator of environmental destruction: compound interest. The need to repay interest fuels the pressure for constant economic growth, which creates a built-in self-destruct mechanism. But he also told me stories about alternatives: how the mayor of Wörgl, Austria organised an interest-free local currency in 1932 (p.50),[4] which created jobs and public works in the depths of the economic depression; how, in 1956, the French town of Lignières-en-Berry issued its

---

4 www.reinventingmoney.com/documents/worgl.html

own currency[5] that was popular with both employers and employees; how other towns wanted to imitate these successful local experiments and how the central banks closed them down.

The old man's stories inspired me because these currencies were initiatives that could beat the dominant money *within the market*. This insight directed our search at STRO for alternative monies or different ways to facilitate exchange and release the potential of real wealth. We eventually understood the difference between the market economy and capitalism: markets are an open and competitive way to optimise the capacities of the people involved under certain conditions, whereas capitalism is a restricted economy with monopolies concentrating wealth and creating imbalances in economy, society and nature. We realised the opportunities to beat the capitalist monopoly money, the national legal tender money, using the market.

In the 1990s, the Local Exchange Trading System (LETS) model developed by Michael Linton in Canada was becoming very popular in Europe. STRO helped to give it a big push in Holland and Belgium, as well as in Germany and France, and this gave them very valuable and practical lessons in the challenges of implementing exchange systems. It became clear that alternative money in itself does not guarantee the kind of breakthrough that is needed.

STRO believes that there is no single right way to organise and that differences are important because they provide opportunities to learn.

Research and development comes from a global community of practice: we stimulate others to do 'something like' rather than copying directly. We want people to look to themselves and their own creativity rather than have one centre to tell them what to do. They may have specific local circumstances that lead to new innovations.

Around the year 2000, STRO started working in Argentina and Brazil, beginning a strong bond with South and Central America that continues to this day. In 2002, STRO developed the Fomento project, combining micro credits and local currencies for Banco Palmas in Brazil (p.24). In the court case brought by the Central Bank the judge agreed with Banco Palmas and STRO that the Central Bank could not ban alternatives for neighbourhoods that were outside the formal economy.

STRO has tested a wide variety of organising and issuing local currencies for different social and economic purposes:

---

5   www.barataria.org/i/5/i.5.4.htm

- Currencies that are backed by the production of locally produced biofuels – the nuts are pressed and processed locally and used locally rather than exported.

- Currencies that are backed by the capital of a large co-operative.

- Currencies that are backed by international aid money to build a school – local builders accepted the new local currency for their labour; they then spend the currency in the local businesses.

The benefits of STRO's projects to the poor, its willingness to innovate and learn from practice, are impressive. But this was not enough for Henk van Arkel.

> Our aim is to change the money system, not just in poorer areas. We kept on looking for a stronger model to create acceptance on a large scale. We went right back to the example of Lignières-en-Berry in 1956. They harnessed the power of consumers to pressure local businesses into accepting the local currency for purchases. They used the simple psychology of rewards and punishments: if you are loyal to the local, you get rewards; if you don't keep currency circulating, you get penalised.

> The introduction of such an innovative system needs to be self explanatory. Alternatives cannot afford huge training or marketing budgets. Parents, schools and shops teach us how to use national money from an early age. If you burn a banknote, you get very little profit from the heat but reality teaches you how to use it. You cannot compete with this training system. You need to find ways to embed new personal habits, which are better for the whole society, into daily life.

At this point they developed their most innovative model yet: Commercial Credit Circuit (C3). The purpose of C3 is to provide cheap credit to small companies. The liquidity that is used to facilitate trade is based on claims on future national currency. Credit in a C3 network, therefore, does not require money – only guaranteed/secured claims that money will be available in the future. C3 is a tool that can support government economic stimulation programs to facilitate cheap credit to small and medium-sized enterprises. In Uruguay, where the government supports the C3, the aim is to create a complete alternative trade circuit.

Henk and his team continue to research and develop even more effective alternatives that focus on systemic causes and effective solutions for social and economic problems.

> The concept of money in society is still dominated by the physical thing. You withdraw paper money anonymously from a cash machine. You know nothing about who created it or what transactions it has enabled along the way. It cannot be regulated. The new reality is that of digital money. This is basically information that can be processed in many ways but our management methods still treat money as if it were a commodity. STRO realised that computers could transfer information about money/value claims that allow us to set rules which, for example, push for a minimum circulation in a certain group of businesses in the community. In the future, a government will be able to determine whether the money they spend through an IT based exchange system will bring them the same amount of value in tax, which guarantees a balanced budget.

STRO decided to develop their own software for local currencies. A German adviser told them that banks who develop their own software expect costs of around 150 million euros. Twelve years later, STRO has created software with the full functionality for processes ranging from LETS and Time Banks to the newest banking technologies. The Cyclos 3.6 software[6] is published Open Source, which allows local currency systems to use it for free. It is in use by all STRO projects in South and Central America as well as community currency systems in Austria (Talente Tauschkreis Vorarlberg), Germany (ReWig, Munich) and England (the Brixton Pound and Bristol Pounds).

Cyclos 4 will include a patented platform for running currencies with functions to keep track of the age and circulation rate of currency. This helps to guarantee that the purchasing power will circulate sufficiently before it leaves an economic subgroup.

Henk van Arkel is now the same age as the 'old man' who sowed the idea of local currency in his teenage mind. With the help of his colleagues at STRO, Henk has grown a 'tree of knowledge' from that seed and it continues to bear fruit and scatter further seeds around the world.

Stephen de Meulenaere, former organiser for STRO in Indonesia, went on to develop the Complementary Currency Resource Center[7], a treasurehouse of resources for local currencies.

Rob van Hilten and Edgar Kampers worked for STRO in the 90s and now run a group of associates called QOIN. They work with local currency groups across Europe.

---

6 http://project.cyclos.org/

7 http://complementarycurrency.org/

QOIN, Netherlands

Based on an interview with Rob van Hilten.
http://qoin.org/

Rob van Hilten is an entrepreneur who, at the age of 16, started one of the first IT companies in Holland. Edgar Kampers has a degree in political science. They both fell in love with the idea of alternative money in the early 1990s, when they went to work for Stro (p.201). Together they created Noppes, a LETS-type system in Amsterdam which attracted 1,400 members, and Amstelnet, a business barter company that employed 9 people.

Rob and Edgar left Stro in the late 1990s and founded Barataria, a company that creates public-private partnerships to engage citizens in actions for sustainability, including the use of local currency. By 2002, they were employing 40 people. One of their most important achievements was NU-Spaarpas,[8] a major pilot project for the city of Rotterdam that used local currency to encourage consumer loyalty to 'green' products and behaviours.

After the dot-com crash in 2002, they faced bankruptcy. Edgar Kampers went to work for a large lobby organisation. Rob van Hilten became a management consultant for an international firm for the next four years.

> I wore a blue suit, drove a blue car and wrote blue reports. At this time, I learned a lot about the challenges facing local government; I saw many chances for local currencies in a maturing market, where national social welfare laws were handing over responsibility to local municipalities.

In 2007, they regrouped and rebranded themselves under the name of QOIN (Quality Coin), working mainly in northwest Europe. QOIN's mission is to achieve resilient communities and create positive social outcomes by supporting local partnerships to develop local currency technologies. Its network of 12 self-employed associates can respond with targetted local currency knowledge and expertise in a range of topics: local government, civil society, regional economy, employment strategies, SME finance, sustainability, and the cultural sector.

QOIN has a four-pronged approach:

1. Professional action research programmes in partnership with international institutions and funded by the European Union.

2. Consultancy and establishing local partnerships.

---

8 www.nuspaarpas.nl/www_en/html/info.htm

3. Project management.

4. Operational solutions for implementing local currencies: adapted Cyclos software; legal affairs team; administrative organisation; internal accounting solutions; preconfigured off-the-shelf local currencies in coloured domains:

> *Red* = Hybrid time banking model for social outcomes.
>
> *Blue* = Regional economic development model to create jobs and retain SMEs, e.g. Brixton and Bristol Pounds.
>
> *Green* = Sustainable consumption, e.g. Nu-Spaarpas.
>
> *Purple* = Cultural sector model developing earned income strategy, cheaper theatre tickets, shared costs of work, e.g. Exhibition Bank[9] and arts festivals.

QOIN has decided not to work with initiatives that are not serious or professional enough in their ambitions. They have, therefore, created several small barriers to working with them, e.g. by requesting payment for the assessment of the starting situation. Associates take clients through a '360 degrees approach': they take all local factors into account, narrow possibilities down and, if people are still enthusiastic, a small group is appointed to carry through the design process and decision making. All programmes have evaluation and quality assessments built in. In this way, QOIN aims to create a kind of 'quality stamp' for local currencies with a high chance of success built in from the start.

Rob van Hilten always carries local currency notes in his wallet to show to clients.

> It's the old principle of 'Show, don't tell'. The wallet tells the story. If they like the story behind the notes, I can then send them papers for them to get the full background and theory. The development process begins with an inspiring story, that this really happened.

---

9 http://www.exhibitionbank.com/

Regiogeld e.V, Germany

Based on an interview with Frank Jansky.
www.regiogeld.de

The emerging German regional currencies held their first Congress, hosted by
the Chiemgauer (p.144), in 2004. Frank Jansky, a lawyer and social activist with
20 years campaigning experience, heard about the congress on the radio and felt
an instant attraction to the regional currency idea. At the second congress, a year
later, the demand for information from the public was overwhelming and they
agreed to form an association to promote common standards: the Regiogeld
e.V (regional money association). Frank Jansky became its first chairman. It is
a largely voluntary role and he divides his time between dealing with external
enquiries from the media and internal problems within and between local
systems. Members meet once or twice a year at the national level and there are
also regional meetings at least twice a year. Board members or coordinators of
established systems give advice to new ones.

A website provides information to members and the media, with resources and
guidance for coordinators and developers. The most popular part of the site is
the map of Germany, which shows all the established and emergent systems.

> It reminds me of the map of Germany in Luther's time, with new Money
> Reformation groups sprouting up all over the place. Just as in the
> Reformation period, people have to decide not only what they are against
> but also what they are for. Regional currency practitioners need to form
> a positive movement towards a better society out of a protest movement
> against globalisation and corrupt finance. Then they will get accepted by the
> mainstream.

From his own early experiences developing local work vouchers in an area of
Sachsen-Anhalt, Frank learned that local systems need to: analyse their local
conditions carefully before starting; gain a range of allies to support their work
and integrate into existing networks and themes, such as regional marketing;
spell out the economic, social and educational benefits of local currency and
make it present everywhere like money; combine community development and
currency design knowledge; make sure cost recovery is done from day one;
remain party politically neutral at all costs; implement good governance – a
critical component for success.

> People are usually very motivated at first but if they do not get recognition
> from outside they can turn inward-looking, which often destroys the group.
> Organisers need to think of the currency like a new bank in the marketplace

– it needs a good image and to offer solutions to particular problems. You gain respect if you pose an alternative to mainstream banks and you can get invited to public discussions to make your case.

Regiogeld e.V faces its own particular challenges as an umbrella organisation with no funding. It has no hierarchy. Frank Jansky sees himself and other local coordinators as 'network nodes' representing values, standards and ideas, a resource to be drawn upon through a vibrant network of inter-connections. However, new initiatives needing a lot of support can be very demanding and although the association makes it clear that the common standards are recommendations to be followed, there is sometimes tension with newer members who perceive them as rules imposed from above. There is also some competition between members who run service-backed and euro-backed currencies.

The Regional Money Association has also been called upon to advise government ministers and civil servants. They advise officials not to place unnecessary hurdles in the way of local systems and not to write them off as alternative, but to recognise that citizens are doing something positive. Public officials should see these initiatives as emergent solutions to deep-seated social and economic problems of society and accept them as part of a dialogue with citizens instead of the usual government monologue.

One small but significant victory for the idea was won in 2008. Duden – the Oxford Dictionary of Germany – accepted *regionalwährung* (regional currency) as an official word.

CommunityForge, Switzerland

Based on an interview with Tim Anderson and Matthew Slater.
www.communityforge.net

CommunityForge describes itself as 'a non-profit association that designs, develops and distributes free, Open Source software for building communities with currencies'.

Tim Anderson is an American who moved to Switzerland in 1980 to work with the Montreux jazz festival. He has a Masters in International Development and has also worked as an English teacher in private banks.

> When I started asking questions about how banking works, people could not give me a straight answer. They are all trained to keep up appearances and build confidence in the public. Later, I built up a successful bike distribution business but got turned down by 20 banks for a loan when I hit cash-flow problems. That led to various personal problems and I now live in subsidised housing. I also found out the limits of social services. So all of these experiences have given me a passion to help communities to help themselves with local currency.

Tim became a co-founder and co-president of *SEL du Lac* (Geneva LETS) in 2006.

Matthew Slater is a computer programmer from the UK who went to Geneva to work for a charitable organisation. He wants to enable communities to reduce their dependence on money. He bumped into Tim Anderson at a *SEL du Lac* meeting.They shared similar beliefs and had an instant rapport.

> I think the current money paradigm, which is so damaging to our souls, our communities, and our biosphere, cannot be overcome by further profit seeking. By insisting on voluntarism, we are tapping into a deep well of human energy which is invisible to the capitalist economy, and which is quintessential to Transition. Using software licensing to create artificial scarcity ignores the needs of everyone but the licence holder.

It was clear to them that Open Source code needed to be at the heart of local currency software. Open Source code is the work of a global developer community of over ten thousand people, who contribute their time to develop software for the common good. Matthew started to develop modules using Drupal code and Tim invited him to deploy the first implementation of the software with *SEL du Lac*.

This experience taught them the need for better accounting and management tools for local currencies and the challenges of scaling up LETS to be a more important social actor. They started CommunityForge to give people the tools they need to run and replicate local money systems. Tim does the 'human interfacing' – training, lobbying, negotiating – and Matthew develops the software. Both Matthew's accounting 'module' and the CommunityForge package have been picked up by unrelated projects all around the world. Publishing the code gives communities the confidence that they won't be driven by someone else's agenda.

They learn things firsthand by absorbing and analysing what users are saying; then they try to improve the solutions. They aim to enable grassroots systems and eventually scale them up. It has taken them thousands of hours of unpaid work and they have also trained over a hundred people at workshops in Brussels, Paris, Marseille and Geneva.

> Training is hands on: you learn the tools and you can adjust the settings to see all kinds of data – volume and velocity of trade, members' offers and wants, etc. Good practices are built into the software:
>
> - Transparency – everyone sees what was traded for what amount.
>
> - Community building – you realise the potential of yourself and others.
>
> - Credit and debit limits – when you trade more, the limits are extended.
>
> - Self-management – all members manage their own accounts.
>
> - Helping others to take part – volunteers become Linkers for others, which also encourages others to become computer literate, a skills exchange between generations.
>
> - Governance – users define their rules.

Other features can also be built in on request, e.g. lending – putting goods into a common pool and hiring them out – and gifting – making donations to other individuals or groups.

Matthew and Tim have learned to test people requesting help to avoid the danger of wasting time on building websites that nobody will use. Existing systems make up 80% of their clients, 15% are startups who know they want to use mutual credit, and 5% are people who are experimenting. 300 LETS from the French speaking world are using the software. Many local organisers using this free solution show their gratitude by helping CommunityForge to develop: out of 300 members, 50 have co-developed the current toolset. Tim and Matthew are keen to let go of some of their tasks and CommunityForge is developing its internal governance and management structure to encourage more people to share the load.

Financing essential development costs is always a challenge. They considered a subscription model but opted for donations instead and in the first year got more income than from the subscriptions they had intended to charge. They call this 'building their confidence capital'.

Supported by the Chamber of Commerce for the Social and Solidarity Economy, CommunityForge is currently developing a local currency system to support exchanges between social enterprises and NGOs in Geneva. They work on the principle of 'predictive barter': they ask each member to estimate what they may be willing to earn or spend in the system and ask people to pledge these amounts. Initial estimates show the potential for one million francs a year in turnover just between 7 key members of this economy, and up to 10% of the total economy of Geneva.

Other projects include a new server for intertrading between local systems, active support for LETS in Belgium and a high profile presentation of their work with local currencies by advisor Professor Jem Bendell at the World Economic Forum and TED lectures.[10]

10 The money myth: Jem Bendell@TEDxTransmedia 2011
   http://tedxtalks.ted.com/video/TEDxTransmedia-2011-Jem-Bendell

Chapter 9
Learning from practice – the power of regional currencies

We know from the practice of local currencies that they have particular powers:

- A community can act as its own bank to provide credit to get essential work done.

- People are motivated to give service and to trade through this complementary medium of exchange.

- Local currency makes scarce national currency go further.

- Local currencies can act as an interface and semi-permeable membrane with the wider national currencies market to protect regions from the worst effects of negative globalisation.

Regional currency is the Harry Potter of currencies: a wizard with hidden powers.

These powers expand the field of monetary magic, which in turn expands the field of human possibility. Some local currencies show off one or another power best and a few systems can combine all of these powers together.

Power of problem solving

People set up community currencies in response to a number of social and economic problems, including the concentration of global economic power and wealth in ever fewer hands, a dysfunctional and socially unjust monetary and banking system, a lack of local purchasing power and the breakdown of local community.

Community currencies have proved that they can:

- Rebuild communities and strengthen local economies.

- Increase currency circulation, keep wealth local and increase the number of local trades.

- Improve the quality of life, help people to make new friendships, keep old skills alive, learn new skills, increase employability, get help in times of need, remain healthy, have fun and stay sane.

- Help protect local environments, local crafts and local identity.

- Be an effective vehicle to deliver policies for local economic development, poverty alleviation, social inclusion, community capacity building and sustainable development.

They achieve such a wide range of effects by adopting different designs that are tailored to local circumstances and goals.

Power of acting locally

Community currencies are focused on a geographical area or community of interest.

National currencies are kept systematically scarce in order to maintain conventional economies and some regions suck the life out of others by systematic transfers of wealth. Local currencies are always sufficient for local exchange needs, whatever the state of the national economy, and cannot be used outside that community.

The size of systems varies from as few as 10 members of a tenants and residents' group on a public housing estate through to hundreds of businesses and thousands of individual participants.

Power of valuing and sharing our gifts

Many people feel useless or surplus to requirements in the market economy. So many people have talents, ideas and skills that are going to waste. Community currencies encourage people to discover and share their gifts with each other. People can turn their time and energies into currency. They can either use the currency themselves or give their currency away to other family or community members, who spend it and let it circulate to bring benefit to others.

Power of mobilising under-capacity

The world is also full of underused resources that could be shared around better: spare business inventory, second hand goods that go to landfill, publicly owned leisure and arts centres that are not used to capacity, voluntary organisations with rooms and vehicles.

What is often lacking is the money (an information system) for matching up spare capacity (supply) with those who could benefit from it (demand). Various local currency designs provide that information system.

Power of harnessing volunteers

Another way for people to share their gifts is to offer a service that benefits the whole community. Voluntary and charitable organisations often rely on volunteers to deliver their services and yet struggle to find enough people to get involved. Local currencies offer a 'carrot' for involvement by offering something in return. They make reciprocity a core value of organisations whose mission is to serve. Those who wish to remain strictly volunteers have the option of simply giving their credits away to others.

Power of themes

Some of the most innovative and effective community currency designs are focused on solving one problem or benefiting a particular group. This may include:

- Incentives for community participation by *young people.*

- Support to *elderly people* for daily tasks.

- *Environmental projects* such as community gardens, litter collecting, cleanups, tree planting.

- *Healthy living* activities such as health support groups, exercise, walks, garden gangs.

- *Lifelong learning* activities such as learning support groups, adult learning classes, peer tutoring and mentoring.

- *Local business* growth and development.

People have set up successful currencies in schools, youth centres, doctors' surgeries, senior care settings, environmental programmes, chambers of commerce. This monetary variety is part of its strength, just as species diversity is to the biosphere.

Power of a network

Local currencies provide an instant network for people locally, whether they are born and bred in the area or moving there for the first time. They allow people to make new friendships and connections quickly, which can help people to build up confidence, learn new skills or try out ideas for new businesses. Networks remind people of ancient bonds of mutuality, which tied people together throughout history.

Power of integration into social economy

Local currencies have the potential to bring together the key elements of local society – local businesses, local citizens, local public agencies, local voluntary organisations – for the benefit of everyone. .

They can also be integrated into other methods of local economic development in the social economy, such as Credit Unions, Co-operatives, Micro-credit, Development Trusts.

Power of control

At this scale people feel a sense of belonging, trust and control over the local currency, something they don't feel with national currency. There are three key ways to achieving this:

- Careful system management.

- Democratic governance with written agreements.

- Self-management and self-control of participants.

The development of all three elements builds up confidence and accountability.

Thousands of experiments with community currencies worldwide have repeatedly shown the potential and significance of these small, local systems to give people improved quality of life and hope for the future in a more human scale, localised, convivial world.

Power of circulation

National currency often comes into a community and flows straight out again in the form of taxes to government, profits to distant shareholders or wages that are spent elsewhere. Local currency aims to stay and circulate because it cannot be spent outside that community. How many times does a unit of currency need to circulate to build a local economy or make it sustainable? Nobody knows, but it is clear that the more times currency changes hands the more work it is doing. The only problem might be if the work it is doing damages the local community or the environment, in which case other trading rules can be built in to exclude certain categories of goods and services from trading and to encourage trades that contribute to sustainability.

Power of time

The aims of most local currency developers are some form of sustainability: local wealth, local community, local environment, etc. Time is an important element. Sustainability does not necessarily mean that a currency will remain in existence forever. The point is whether the system achieves what it sets out to achieve, *not* the sustainability of the system for its own sake. Unfortunately, it is easy to get sucked into organisational maintenance as an end in itself and lose sight of the original goals.

How long is sustainable? Five, ten, twenty, a hundred, a thousand years? Forever?

What if we could create time limited currencies to achieve particular short-term objectives that serve long-term sustainability?

Here are some options:

Time Limited System – the currency *system* is dissolved after an agreed time period. Some systems may have very focused time-bound goals, which require a quick mobilisation of energies, such as the construction of a community building, garden or other resource. A currency can be constructed to motivate people to get involved then retired again.

Periodic Retirement – currency that has been issued is periodically retired in order to allow new issuance. Notes or vouchers with clear expiry dates are issued.

Currency that loses value over time – currency can lose value or purchasing power through inflation, lack of confidence in the system, lack of goods and services to spend on, or through a deliberate mechanism known as negative interest or demurrage, in which currency slowly loses its value over an agreed time period (theorists such as Silvio Gesell argued that money should reflect the deterioration of natural goods such as grain, etc.). Demurrage encourages faster circulation of currency and so favours the medium of exchange function of currency over the savings function.

Long-term system – some community currencies have remained in existence for many years, adapting their goals and system design to deal with changing circumstances. With good management and governance they can become an important tool for local sustainability and community building.

Powerful combination

An effective regional currency integrates these various magical powers into one powerful spell – for positive local and global transformation.

Chapter 10
Future positive

The best way to predict the future is to create it.
Abraham Lincoln

The chorus of critics over the failure of economists to predict the present financial crisis swells ever louder. Faith in governments, banks and corporations is being challenged like never before – Wikileaks has exposed government lies about wars and 'too big to fail' banks have collapsed or been rescued with taxpayers' money. Politicians seem impotent in the face of corporate and financial power. We are living through a kind of apocalypse. As the veil is lifted on hidden truths and deception on a global scale, long established institutions collapse in slow motion. The sheer size and complexity of their organisational structures seem to defy responsible management. Even the Dallas Fed, a branch of the US Federal Reserve system, is calling for the immediate breakup of large banks.[1]

We know that unprecedented rapid changes will be required in our civilisation if our species wants to survive on this planet. This means massive learning on all levels of society – all of us need to question our consumer habits, businesses needs to reduce waste and maximise their capacity to support sustainable consumption, community organisations need to use local monetary tools to mobilise people to protect and enhance their local environment, local governments should be supporting monetary innovations to improve the quality and sustainability of their services.

Too many of us have sacrificed our real values at the altar of profit and, in the process, stripped the economies of whole countries bare. We have reneged on the promises made to the elderly and have squashed the job hopes for millions of young people. How will we justify to our children and grand-children that we couldn't imagine using the information technologies available in our times to solve our monetary problems and that we opted, instead, to stick with our monopolistic monetary system?

It is as though a giant sun of possibility shines back at us from the future, casting long shadows over all our existing ways of being. By this light, we

---

1   Joe Weisenthal,
    http://www.businessinsider.com/dallas-fed-calls-for-breakup-of-big-banks-2012-3 - ixzz1q7tXrGtk

can see clearly that putting band aids on the complex interconnected crises of our time – financial instability, community breakdown, ecological degradation and climate change – will not save the patient. Human greed and weakness are not the only reasons for humanity's self-inflicted wounds. Our increasing knowledge of systems teaches us that sytemic factors, the rules of the game of money, drive many destructive behaviours. Change the rules, change the results.

Many new economic theories that take a more systemic view include regional currencies as a given, both for preventing the repeated kinds of failures we have seen and creating more long-term stability. More people are questioning whether the profit motive is the best measure of success or of progress and are now experimenting with new forms of sharing and community.[2] A new kind of 'glocalised' consciousness is emerging that prompts people to respond to global challenges by growing food, sharing transport, saving energy and creating community in our own villages, cities and regions. Strong local structures create a kind of immune system to protect local communities against destructive forces, such as money with no conscience breezing in and out again looking for the highest return. Instead of a single global currency monoculture of bank-debt money, we need a monetary ecology, where a variety of media, created by a variety of institutions, are flowing in parallel to each other.

Nature teaches us the need to maintain a necessary balance between efficiency and resilience and we can apply this knowledge to the design of new monetary systems that mimic complex living systems[3] Like the distribution of nutrients through complex root systems and the interplay of soil, sun, air and moisture in a forest, a local currency creates a circulation system for the assets and gifts of a community. A multitude of different currency systems provides a much stronger support for people in times of crisis and gives us the tools for transition towards stable currencies and the sustainable communities of tomorrow.

This book has shown the wide range of designs which serve different social and economic purposes. Only our imaginations limit the potential uses of complementary currencies. The main principle is to design a mechanism that matches underused assets with unmet needs.

---

2 Let's Share: The Growth of Peer-to-Peer Product-Service Systems,
   http://www.worldchanging.com/archives/011171.html

3 Bernard Lietaer, Is Our Monetary Structure a Systemic Cause for Financial
   Instability?Evidence and Remedies from Nature
   http://www.lietaer.com/2010/05/is-our-monetarystructure-a-systemic-cause-for-financial-
   instability-evidence-and-remedies-from-natureapril-2010/

The challenges facing organisers at each stage of the 'ORDER' process (Chapter 6) are: creating Ownership, Researching, Designing, Engaging and Reviewing to ensure viability. Successful initiatives may grow from the bottom up or from the top down, and they can be started by citizens, businesses or local government. The best predictor of success for a local currency is the quality of its leadership team and its daily habits (see Chapter 7). They need to motivate others and create a local network to support the idea.

"Ok, as soon as I give the signal, we start thinking post-industrially!"

Local currency organisers act as a bridge between the idealists who want to change the world overnight and the realists who say nothing will ever change. They constantly learn from practice and adapt their system to meet current needs. A viable system is like a flock of birds where a lively collective intelligence about direction and flow develops from every member.

Each system has different legal conditions that effect the operation of local currencies. Every organising team has to work within these conditions, get its cost recovery model, governance and management structure right and then market the currency to a wide public of individuals, businesses, voluntary organisations and government bodies.

We have seen too many systems fail because the organisers did not design it well, or did not learn from experience, or key people moved on. This makes it very difficult for other people in the same area to try again for a number of years, although some groups deliberately go dormant while they regroup. The purpose of this book is to help new developers avoid a pattern of rapid growth followed by a crash, and to manage a system with incremental growth and resilience.

The creative drive behind local currencies has always been business and social entrepreneuers who spot gaps in the economic and social fabric and patch them. They will continue to provide the ideas, energy and inventiveness needed to create real People Money systems. Now they are slowly being joined by regional governments facing a devil's brew of 'wicked' problems – a semi-permanent financial crisis, mushrooming social and environmental problems and ageing populations. Local authorities from Aberdeen to London are researching or planning regional currencies. The Brixton Pound has support from the chief executive of the local council. The City of London Corporation has commissioned research[4] into the potential of business exchange networks in the UK at local, national and international scale.

Several agencies work on researching, developing and supporting the implementation of local currencies. These invaluable resources are outlined in Chapter 8.

Practitioners from around the world share the fruits of their practice in the interviews featured in this book and there are many channels of communication for networking and dissemination.[5] They tell us what works and what needs improving. We learn much from both success and failure. There are also many paradoxes in practice, such as members who support the values of alternative, non-national money but who never trade in the currency, or popular businesses unable to spend what they earn, or a successful local currency attracting larger corporations to an area because it becomes trendy.

Compared to other movements within the social economy, like co-operatives or credit unions, modern local currencies are relatively young. The first successful co-operatives were created in Rochdale in the mid 19th Century and co-ops now operate all over the world.[6] They have a track record of a hundred and fifty years of development behind them. They too began as volunteer-led systems serving small communities and have now grown into sophisticated multi-million pound operations, like the Mondragon Corporation of Basque Co-operatives[7] and the Co-op supermarket in the UK. As we saw in Chapter 3, the development of local currencies was interrupted for reasons of power and control. Now they are playing historical catch-up.

---

4   Capacity Trade and Credit: Emerging Architectures for Commerce and Money. Online at www.cityoflondon.gov.uk/researchpublications

5   Rogers, J. 'On The Money, Getting the Message Out', *International Journal of Community Currencies Research*. Online at http://ijccr.net/IJCCR/2011_(15)_files/03 Rogers.pdf

6   International Co-operative Alliance, www.ica.coop/al-ica

7   http://en.wikipedia.org/wiki/Mondragon_cooperative

Small community currency systems like time banks and local exchange systems will continue to serve a limited membership in a small area; business exchanges will continue to operate in the commercial sector; other systems will begin to partner with neighbouring currencies or areas through trading agreements or through platforms like Community Exchange System (CES); and some will begin to serve whole regions more effectively.

Recommendations for action

People Money has not yet been applied on a larger scale. But the examples described in this book are varied and wide-ranging enough to show its potential for helping with a broad range of financial, social and environmental problems that, for the first time in human history, are brewing on a planetary scale. Although the socio-economic impacts of local currencies remain comparatively small, there is enough evidence of their benefits from practice to make them worthy of further study and support. The world's oldest successful regional currency – WIR Bank (p.34) – has reached a scale where it has macroeconomic impact. Germany's leading regional currency – Chiemgauer (p.144) – generates about 0.2% of Bavaria's regional product. And if there were further breakdowns in the official monetary and banking system, these systems could play a critical role in social and economic stability in the future. A spare tyre may sound superfluous until you have a blowout at midnight on the motorway way and an empty mobile phone battery.

Regional currencies transform a central aspect of today's economic difficulties into a central part of their solution for tomorrow. It is time to provide these new instruments with the start-up support they need to enable them to unfold their potential for good. This support must come not only from enthusiastic initiators, farsighted politicians and willing participants in the regions, but also from central banks giving protection and support, as they do in Brazil and Uruguay.

We make the following recommendations for action:

To developers

- Development processes – follow the 'ORDER' process (p.80) or something like it to make sure you cover all the bases.

- Training – offer training to participants and administrators; it will pay for itself.

- Network – use the contacts in this book as a starting point.

- Software – evaluate the various solutions on offer to make sure you find the application that fits your needs.

To policy makers

- Share this book with your colleagues and put it on the agenda for discussion.

- Get your staff trained in this social technology.

To researchers

- Share this book with your colleagues and put regional currencies on your research agenda.

People Money – the time is now

A new Bristol Pound has been developed by citizens with the full support of Bristol City Council, which has committed significant officer time to the project. It will be the first city-wide local currency in the UK and is due to launch in May 2012. Bristol Pound 'is a secure local currency designed to support Bristol's independent businesses, strengthen the local economy, keep our high streets diverse and distinct, helping build a strong community.'[8] It is a not-for-profit partnership between Bristol Pound Community Interest Company (CIC) and Bristol Credit Union. A media launch announcing a design competition for the notes was covered by journalists from as far afield as Spain, Italy, India and America.

As a partial solution to monetary scarcity, the citizens of the Greek port city of Volos have introduced the VEM[9] currency to help them during the euro debt crisis. A more radical approach would be for the local government to introduce the *Civics* currency, proposed on p.190, which would require the authority to accept local taxes in local currency and to pay for essential social and environmental projects with this rather than euros.

The Belgium city of Gent has mobilised the immigrants' community of the poorest neighbourhood of Flanders through the *Torekes*[10] currency, which can be spent on food, rent, transport, cinema and music events.

There are many other exciting initiatives in regional and sectoral currencies in development, as we profiled on pages 188-193.

---

8 www.bristolpound.org

9 http://www.guardian.co.uk/world/2012/mar/16/greece-on-breadline-cashless-currency

10 http://www.torekes.be/

The city of Nantes in France has announced the launch of its own currency in 2013.[11] The idea was included in the city's Agenda 21 plan in 2006 but it was not then a priority. Now the euro crisis has turned up the heat and prompted local officials to get cooking with local currency. The main priorities are to provide increased liquidity to local businesses, accelerate regional trade, help businesses save scarce euros and to create jobs.

The 'Nanto' is modelled on the Swiss WIR Bank, using a similar mutual credit clearing system without a circulating currency. But it will go much further than WIR because individuals, voluntary organisations and the local government itself will all be players too, and this takes the project into unknown and exciting territory. The city authority will bring public transport, car parks and leisure centres into the system and pay some salaries and social benefits in local currency. The inititiative is fully backed by the Chamber of Trade and responds primarily to the needs of small and medium-sized service and construction companies. The system will be managed by a regional co-operative bank, Crédit Municipal de Nantes, which has 28 million euros in assets.

Nantes is the first city authority in the EU to propose the launch of a regional currency as an economic safety valve to keep its economy alive, a wise precaution in the face of growing disillusionment/dissatisfaction in the dollar and euro economies. Regions issuing their own currencies strengthen their social and economic infrastructure just as local production of energy and food grow resilience.

Whether or not a national economy revives to prepare for yet another crisis and all the suffering it brings, regional currencies are here to stay for all the reasons we and the pioneer practitioners of these currencies have shown. The chorus of positive futures full of sustainable abundance is also growing ever louder.

---

11 www.lesechos.fr/journal20120306/lec1_collectivites_locales/0201923860599-nantes-se-donne-un-an-pour-lancer-sa-monnaie-locale-298556.php

APPENDIX ONE
Resources for developing regional currencies

Consulting, training and speaking

Margrit Kennedy	/www.margritkennedy.de/index.php?lang=EN
	www.monneta.org/index.php?lang=EN
Bernard Lietaer	www.lietaer.com
John Rogers	http://valueforpeople.co.uk
Thomas Greco	http://reinventingmoney.com/
Annette Riggs	www.communityconnecttrade.com
Richard Logie	www.tbex.com

Research, development and support

Complementary Currency Resource Center	http://www.complementarycurrency.org
International Journal of CC Research	www.ijccr.net/
Bibliography of Community Currencies Research	www.cc-literature.de/1.introduction
IRTA	http://www.irta.com
Stro	www.socialtrade.org
New Economics Foundation	http://www.neweconomics.org
New Economics Institute	http://neweconomicsinstitute.org
QOIN	http://qoin.org
CommunityForge	http://communityforge.net
Regiogeld e.V	http://www.regiogeld.de
SPICE	http://justaddspice.org
Timebanking UK	http://timebanking.org
Timebanking Wales	www.timebankingwales.org.uk
Timebanking USA	http://timebanks.org
LETSLink UK	www.letslinkuk.net

APPENDIX TWO
The business case for complementary currencies

From a purely economic viewpoint, the key point is to ensure that the value to the business is larger than the marginal cost of an additional customer. In the case of airlines, this marginal cost is the out-of-pocket costs of adding one passenger to this flight (basically the meals served on board), as all the other costs are "fixed". These other costs are called fixed, because they would be incurred regardless of whether someone sits in that seat or not.

The businesses that are the most logical participants in complementary currency systems are those with comparatively low marginal costs. Some businesses have virtually no marginal cost at all. For example, if a cinema isn't otherwise full, the marginal cost of an additional viewer is zero because all costs are fixed (the cost of renting the movie, air conditioning the room, paying the projectionists are all the same whether there is one viewer or 300). Therefore, a cinema could theoretically accept a new customer who pays up to 90% in complementary currency, and still be better off than if it wasn't participating in the system. Even if the cinema threw the complementary currency away after receiving it, it would still make more profit in conventional currency by bringing in this customer than would otherwise be the case. Of course, the cinema, its employees or its owner could also use the complementary currency themselves in one way or another, thereby further increasing the benefits of participating in the system. Another example: a restaurant typically has marginal costs of about one third. That is the part of what you pay that covers what you actually receive on your plate. There is usually another third that goes to the fixed costs: renting the location, heating the room, paying the staff, etc. And the final third is profit. Therefore, as long as a restaurant wouldn't be full anyway, it makes economic sense to bring in additional customers who pay half in conventional money, and the other half in complementary currency.

The conventional way for a business owner to reach full capacity would be to offer a general discount, but the disadvantage of that conventional approach is that it cannibalises the income generated by customers that would normally be there anyway. In contrast, accepting complementary currencies enables the business to differentiate between customers, without reducing the income from normal customers. Moreover, the business can decide itself that it only accepts complementary currency clients on weekdays, for instance, because it is usually fully booked on weekends. This is why airlines use frequent flyer mile programs to fill their seats, rather than general discounts, and have restrictions such as "frequent flyer seating not available around key holiday dates".

This is how complementary currencies can help businesses gain access to otherwise "unused resources" and mobilise these resources to realise unmet needs. Businesses can also use this additional payment medium for whatever purposes they wish. There are also "indirect advantages" for businesses in taking part. They are seen by their regional customers as active citizens supporting social and environmental quality of life without having to raise taxes.

About the Authors

Prof. Dr. Margrit Kennedy is an architect with a Masters Degree in Urban and Regional Planning and a Ph.D. in Public and International Affairs, who worked for UNESCO and OECD and was a professor for Ecological Building Technologies in the Department of Architecture at the University of Hanover. Projects in ecological architecture for the International Building Exhibition Berlin in 1987 led her to the discovery that it is virtually impossible to carry out sound ecological concepts on the scale required today without fundamentally altering the present money system or creating new complementary currencies. In her two books *Interest and Inflation Free Money* (1987 – translated into 23 languages since) and *Occupy Money* (2012) she explores the systemic problems of the present system and the advantages of using new complementary monetary designs. Her work in this field has been instrumental for the start of more than 60 regional currency initiatives in the German speaking parts of Europe. *www.margritkennedy.de, www.monneta.org, www.kennedy-library.info*

Bernard LIETAER has been active in money systems for 35 years in an unusual variety of functions. While at the Central Bank in Belgium he co-designed and implemented the convergence mechanism (ECU) to the single European currency system and served as President of Belgium's Electronic Payment System. He was General Manager and Currency Trader for the Gaia Hedge Funds, when *Business Week* identified him in 1990 as the world's top trader. He is currently Research Fellow at the University of California, Berkeley, and Visiting Professor at the Finance University in Moscow. He is the author of fifteen books relating to monetary and financial issues. *www.lietaer.com*

John Rogers cut his teeth with local currencies by running a local exchange system in Wales for 10 years. He co-founded the Wales Institute for Community Currencies at the University of Newport, which he directed with Geoff Thomas from 2003-2007. They coordinated research into the effects of time banking in ex-mining communities, which was published by the Joseph Rowntree Foundation in 'Hidden Work'. He now offers training and consulting for local currencies through Value for People and has spoken and led workshops at many international conferences.

http://valueforpeople.co.uk

Index

F

internal dynamics 80
Internal Revenue Service (IRS) 197
international aid money 203
International Journal of Community Currencies Research (ijccr) 195
International Reciprocal Trade Association (IRTA) 197
inter-regional commerce 44
inter-regional networks 167
investment 29, 133, 147
investment capital 57
Irving Fisher 46, 51
ISO 9002 international standard 104
issuance 49, 153, 158, 217
ITEX 108
Ithaca HOURS 55, 58, 63, 76, 79, **155**, 181, 195

J

Jane Jacobs 52
Japan 9, 189
JM Keynes 46, 147
Joaquim Melo, Banco Palmas 24, 28, 29
jobs 7, 8, 9, 20, 22, 26, 27, 50, 181, 201, 206, 225
Joel Hodroff, Dual Currency Systems, USA 187
John Rogers, Value for People 2, 226
joining fees 66
Josh Ryan-Collins, New Economics Foundation 122
Josiah Warren 47

K

Karl Marx 147
Kevin Parcell, Sun Money 192
Kitchen Cabinets, Dane County Time Bank 184
Koen de Beer, puntoTRANSacciones, El Salvador 117

L

Labor: the New Gold Standard 157
labour note 47
Labour theory of value 47
Lambeth Council 125
Langenegger Talente 128
launch **91**
L Currency for learning, Merseyside 190
leadership teams for local currencies 93
learning community 72, 177

M

Also available from Triarchy Press:

Money and Sustainability: The Missing Link

Bernard Lietaer, Christain Arnsperger, Sally Goerner, Stefan Brunnhuber

A REPORT FROM THE CLUB OF ROME – EU CHAPTER

In Money and Sustainability, Bernard Lietaer and his co-authors step back from the solutions offered here in People Money and explore the history and current conduct of the money system.

In the first section of the book they show how this system threatens not just economic stability but social and environmental sustainability as well. They start by making explicit the – often unspoken –paradigms that underpin our economic thinking and the three-layered collective blind spot that these paradigms induce.

Next they explain the mechanics of present-day monetary and banking instability in detail, supporting their argument about the unsustainability of the existing system by drawing on major new research into the physics of complex flow networks.

They highlight five core mechanisms of the present system that are directly incompatible with environmental and social sustainability. It amplifies boom and bust cycles; promotes and rewards short-term thinking; makes exponential growth compulsory throught the process of compound interest; concentrates wealth; devalues social capital (collaborative action based on trust and a sense of community rather than profit).

Finally in this section they examine the 'official story' about governments and the banking system, showing that governments are not helpless and explaining how the 'Fiat Currency Paradigm' allows central and local governments to establish alternative currencies to serve immediate social and environmental needs.

In the second part of the book, the authors set out nine detailed examples of private sector and government initiatives that can help install a flexible and resilient monetary ecosystem alongside our present, deeply flawed money system.

"We will never create sustainability while immersed in the present financial system... I used not to think this. Indeed, I did not think about the money system at all. I took it for granted as a neutral and inevitable aspect of human society. But ...I now understand, as proven clearly in this text, that the prevailing financial system is incompatible with sustainability."

Dennis Meadows – co-author of The Limits to Growth

About Triarchy Press

Good books and bright ideas about organisations and society

Triarchy Press is a small, independent publisher of the best new thinking about organisations and society – and practical applications of that thinking.

Our authors bridge the gap between academic research and practical experience and write about praxis: ideas in action. Those authors include:

Thought leaders in Design and Systems Thinking like Russ Ackoff and John Seddon

Experts in Cultural Theory and Complexity like Don Michael and Michael Thompson

Forward thinkers like Gerard Fairtlough, Bernard Lietaer, Jay Ogilvy and International Future Forum's Graham Leicester.

Visit **www.triarchypress.com** to find out more about their books and explore the Idioticon for examples of their thinking and ideas.

www.triarchypress.com

CPSIA information can be obtained at www.ICGtesting.com
Printed in the USA
BVOW061649130712

295186BV00004B/1/P